Treasures from the Royal Tombs *of* Ur

Treasures from the Royal Tombs *of* Ur

EDITED BY

Richard L. Zettler and Lee Horne

WITH ESSAYS BY

Richard L. Zettler

Donald P. Hansen

Holly Pittman

with

Kevin Danti

Steve Tinney

Jill A. Weber

Paul Zimmerman

University of Pennsylvania Museum
of Archaeology and Anthropology

Produced by Marquand Books, Inc., Seattle
Designed by Susan E. Kelly
Typeset by Christina Gimlin
Copyedited by Jennifer Harris
Proofread by Laura Iwasaki
Printed and bound by C & C Offset Printing Co.,
    Inc., Hong Kong
Photography by H. Fred Schoch

Library of Congress Cataloging-in-Publication Data

    Treasures from the royal tombs of Ur /
Richard L. Zettler and Lee Horne, editors ; with
contributions by Donald P. Hansen, Holly
Pittman, Richard L. Zettler, and others.
        p.   cm.
    Includes bibliographical references.
    ISBN 0-92-417154-5 (cloth : acid-free paper)
    ISBN 0-92-417155-3 (pbk. : acid-free paper)
    1. Ur (Extinct city) I. Zettler, Richard L., 1949–
II. Horne, Lee III. Hansen, Donald P.
DS70.5.U7 T7   1998
935—ddc21   98-9086

TREASURES FROM THE ROYAL TOMBS OF UR
Traveling Exhibition Venues

October 9, 1998–January 3, 1999
The Bowers Museum of Cultural Art
Santa Ana, Calif.

February 5, 1999–May 9, 1999
Frank H. McClung Museum
Knoxville, Tenn.

May 30, 1999–September 5, 1999
Dallas Museum of Art
Dallas, Tex.

October 17, 1999–January 17, 2000
Arthur M. Sackler Gallery
Washington, D.C.

February 20, 2000–April 23, 2000
Cleveland Museum of Art
Cleveland, Ohio

May 2000–September 2000
Pierpont Morgan Library
New York, N.Y.

October 2000–January 2001
The Oriental Institute Museum
Chicago, Ill.

February 2001–May 2001
Detroit Institute of Art
Detroit, Mich.

Contents

To Mary Virginia Harris in honor of her singular contributions to the University of Pennsylvania Museum's Near East Section and the Museum's Public Education Program

Figures

Preface

Since its founding more than 110 years ago, the University of Pennsylvania Museum of Archaeology and Anthropology has sent out over 350 expeditions to all parts of the globe. The Museum's celebrated collections now number more than one million objects, the majority of which derive from the Museum's own field research. A number of the Museum's objects are known to scholars throughout the world, and their utility is enhanced by the fact that many of them are supported by documentation, including field notes, photographs, maps, and drawings, that provides valuable cultural contexts for these objects.

One of the most famous and spectacular parts of this great collection is the material from the Royal Cemetery of Ur, excavated by Sir Leonard Woolley for the joint University of Pennsylvania Museum and British Museum expedition to Ur in the late 1920s. The "Ram Caught in a Thicket," the bull-headed lyre from the "King's Grave," and Queen Puabi's golden headdress are just a few of the best-known pieces that came to the University of Pennsylvania Museum as a result of this expedition. The "Ram," for instance, is featured in H. W. Janson's standard introductory text, *History of Art*, as an early example of complex art. Thus, the value of the Ur collection lies in its well-recorded archaeological context (Woolley's work was a model of its time) as well as in its fabulous art historical significance.

To my knowledge, the objects from the Royal Cemetery, as a collection, have not traveled since the formal division of the collection among the two museums and the government in Baghdad in the late 1920s. As plans for the renovation of our Mesopotamian galleries moved forward, the Museum realized that it had a unique opportunity to prepare a traveling exhibition so that people throughout the United States would have the chance to see some of the treasures of Ur. Furthermore, the preparation of the traveling exhibition offered the Museum's staff an opportunity to restudy, reconserve, and newly photograph the Ur materials. Most of the objects in this catalogue are being published for the first time in full color, and the accompanying text contains important new insights and scholarly rethinking about these important objects. The reader is invited to enjoy and appreciate the wonderful accomplishments of the ancient artisans of Ur and gain new understandings of the early civilization that produced the objects that still fascinate us today.

Jeremy A. Sabloff

The Charles K. Williams II Director
UNIVERSITY OF PENNSYLVANIA MUSEUM
OF ARCHAEOLOGY AND ANTHROPOLOGY

Acknowledgments

The University of Pennsylvania Museum of Archaeology and Anthropology's small staff is extremely dedicated and works hard to make its many and varied activities possible. The staff has worked particularly hard on *Treasures from the Royal Tombs of Ur* and deserves a full measure of the credit for both the traveling exhibit and the catalogue. While it is impossible to name them all here, we would like to acknowledge Pamela Jardine, Assistant Director for Museum Services, who guided the exhibit process. She steps down after this exhibit to pursue her own research, and we wish her all the best. Gillian Wakely, Assistant Director for Education, provided valuable advice. Virginia Greene and Lynn Grant in Conservation, as well as Leslie Guy and Brenda Smith, performed their usual miracles. We owe a special debt of gratitude to Tamsen Fuller, who undertook the conservation of the "Ram Caught in a Thicket," as well as other artifacts from the Royal Cemetery. John Murray, Museum Exhibits Designer, worked with Sparks Exhibits on the overall layout of the exhibit and individual cases.

We owe additional thanks to Michael D. Danti, Kevin Danti, Jana Fisher, Carole Linderman, Yelena Z. Rakic, Jill A. Weber, Shannon White (Fowler/Van Santvoord Keeper), and Paul Zimmerman in the Museum's Near East Section; Chrisso Boulis, Sylvia Duggan, and Jenny Wilson in the Registrar's Office; Alessandro Pezzati in Museum Archives; and Charles S. Kline, Photo Archivist. We would also like to thank Professor Marjorie Venit (University of Maryland) and Sydney Babcock (J. Pierpont Morgan Library) for their gracious assistance.

Karen Vellucci, Assistant Director for Publications, encouraged us to produce a catalogue. She herself worked on various parts of the catalogue and kept it on schedule. Lee Horne, Research Associate at the Museum and former Editor of *Expedition Magazine*, took on the tasks of editing the catalogue and writing text for the exhibit. She may have gotten more than she bargained for, but we

will always be in her debt. We would also like to thank Jennifer
Quick, Helen Schenck, and Amy Zoll for their contributions
to the catalogue. Various denizens of the Babylonian Section,
including Åke Sjöberg, Steve Tinney, and Phillip Jones, aided
us with Sumerian and Akkadian. Finally, we especially want to
acknowledge Fred Schoch, who, with the assistance of Francine
Sarin, brought the artifacts in the exhibit and catalogue to life
with his photographs.

Richard L. Zettler

Associate Curator-in-Charge,
Near East Section

Southern Mesopotamian Chronology

DATE BC		
	300	Greek conquest of Babylonia (330)
	500	Persian conquest of Babylonia (538)

NEO-BABLYONIAN DYNASTY
   Nabonidus (555–539)
   Nebuchadnezzar (604–562)

1000

End of KASSITE DYNASTY

KASSITE DYNASTY
1500
Fall of OLD BABYLONIAN DYNASTY

OLD BABYLONIAN DYNASTY
   Hammurabi (1792–1750)

2000   ISIN-LARSA DYNASTIES

THIRD DYNASTY OF UR
   Construction of the ziggurat at Ur
   Ur-Namma (2112–2095), Shulgi (2094–2047)

DYNASTY OF AKKAD
   Sargon (2334–2279)

2500   EARLY DYNASTIC IIIB
   Eannatum (Lagash), Mesannepada (Ur), A'annepada (Ur)

EARLY DYNASTIC IIIA
   Urnanshe (Lagash)
   Royal Tombs of Ur

(EARLY DYNASTIC II)

EARLY DYNASTIC I
3000
JAMDAT NASR PERIOD

4000   URUK PERIOD

6000   UBAID PERIOD
   Earliest known occupation of southern Mesopotamia

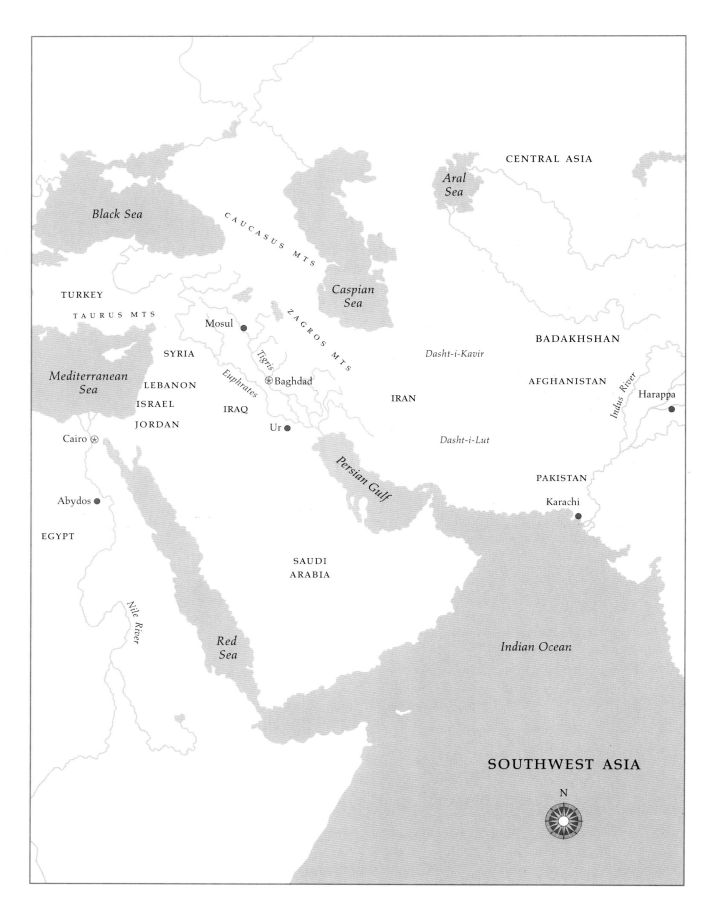

Black Sea

CAUCASUS MTS

Aral
Sea

CENTRAL ASIA

Caspian
Sea

TURKEY

TAURUS MTS

ZAGROS MTS

BADAKHSHAN

Mosul

SYRIA

Tigris

Dasht-i-Kavir

AFGHANISTAN

Indus River

Euphrates

Baghdad

Mediterranean
Sea

LEBANON

IRAQ

IRAN

Harappa

ISRAEL

JORDAN

Cairo

Ur

Dasht-i-Lut

PAKISTAN

Abydos

Persian Gulf

Karachi

EGYPT

SAUDI
ARABIA

Nile River

Red
Sea

Indian Ocean

SOUTHWEST ASIA

N

Tigris

Diyala

Tell Asmar

Euphrates

Khafajah

Baghdad

Tell Agrab

AKKAD

Jamdat Nasr

Kish

Babylon

Abu Salabikh

Nippur

Adab

ELAM

Shuruppak

Umma

Susa

SUMER

Girsu

Lagash

Karkeh

Karun

Uruk

Larsa

Shatt al-Arab

Ubaid

Ur

Nasiriyah

Eridu

Basra

EARLY MESOPOTAMIAN
CITY-STATES

Persian Gulf

N

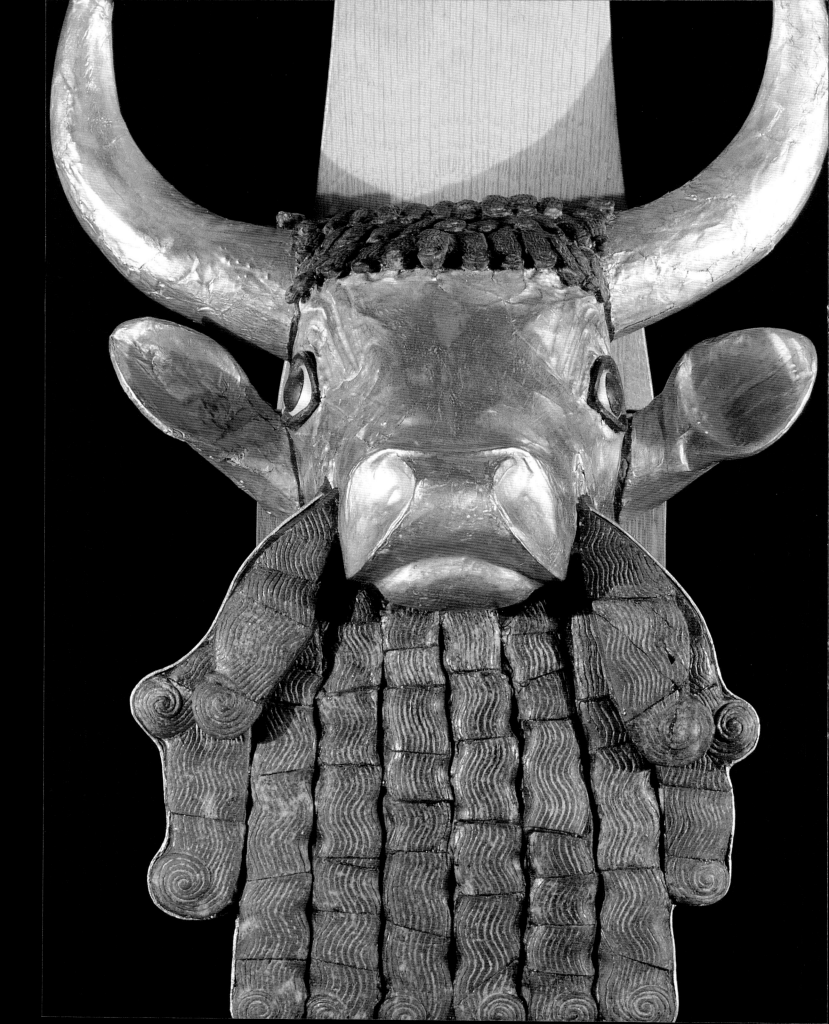

CHAPTER ONE

Early Dynastic Mesopotamia

Richard L. Zettler

Southern Mesopotamia has long been recognized as the "cradle of civilization." Cities dominated by temples and states ruled by kings had emerged there by the late fourth millennium BC; writing was "invented," perhaps at Uruk, at roughly the same time. Ancient Mesopotamia was indeed the earliest of the world's primary civilizations and provided, along with ancient Egypt, the foundations of western civilization.

As the word "Mesopotamia" (Greek for "between the rivers") implies, the Tigris and the Euphrates are the region's dominant features. Rising in the mountains of Turkey and fed chiefly by melt from winter snowfalls, the two rivers thread through the Turkish Mountains, cross the Syrian and Kurdish uplands, and emerge onto the floodplain north of modern-day Baghdad; they unite at Qurna to form the Shatt al-Arab, which flows on to the Persian Gulf.

Traditional site of the Garden of Eden (Gen. 2:10–15) and homeland of early Mesopotamian civilization, the southern floodplain lies between the Arabian Desert plateau on the south and west and the Zagros Mountains on the east; it gives out to the southeast, where the rivers lose much of their water into marshes. The area's inadequate and unreliable rainfall makes agriculture possible only with irrigation. Although irrigated land, riverine thickets, and steppe vegetation provide important natural resources for the traditional subsistence economy of farming and herding, southern Mesopotamia is otherwise resource poor. Commodities such as hardwoods, stones other than locally available limestones, and metallic ores must all be imported.[1]

This seemingly unpromising land had been settled since at least the seventh millennium BC. By the third millennium's Early Dynastic period, the area was divided into competing city-states and alliances of city-states, among the most important of which was Ur, on the southwestern margins of the floodplain. It was during this same period that the kings and queens of Ur were being laid to rest in a royal cemetery just outside the temple

Detail of the Great Lyre from the "King's Grave," cat. no. 3.

1

complex dedicated to the city's tutelary deity, Nanna, the moon god.

THE EVIDENCE

Archaeology is our major source for the earliest phases of human occupation on the southern Mesopotamian floodplain, at least until the Dynasty of Akkad (ca. 2350–2150 BC). Beginning with the seventh millennium BC, sites such as Tell Abu Shahrain (ancient Eridu) and Tell Ouelli have provided a material culture sequence for the Ubaid period.[2] Warka (ancient Uruk), Nippur, Khafajah, Tell Asmar, Jamdat Nasr, and Tell al-Muqayyar (ancient Ur) have yielded the most significant remains of the succeeding Uruk and Jamdat Nasr periods.

On the basis of the stratified sequences of temples at Khafajah, Tell Asmar, and Nippur, archaeologists have posited a division of the succeeding Early Dynastic period into three phases: a lengthy Early Dynastic I; a short and at best transitional (and possibly only regionally significant) Early Dynastic II; and a lengthy Early Dynastic III, commonly subdivided into earlier (A) and later (B) phases.[3]

The most important archaeological remains from Early Dynastic III come from Khafajah, Tell Asmar, Tell Agrab, Kish, Abu Salabikh, Nippur, Bismayah (ancient Adab), Fara (ancient Shuruppak), Tello (ancient Girsu), al-Hiba (ancient Lagash), Tell al-Ubaid, and Ur. The cemetery at Ur, with its graves of the city's kings and queens, yielded what are perhaps the most spectacular remains of the period (and arguably one of the most significant archaeological finds to date).

The development of writing in the Late Uruk period brought southern Mesopotamia into a protohistoric period. The early corpora are apparently the administrative records of temples or other large organizations; they provide tantalizing data, but they remain too few and too difficult to understand to fill out our archaeologically

derived reconstructions. Although the language of some of the earliest texts has yet to be identified, later texts are written in Sumerian, an agglutinative language with no known relatives, living or dead.[4]

For the history of these early periods, we can also turn to the later Sumerian King List (see the sidebar "The Sumerian King List"), with its successions of dynasties and lists of their kings, including the semilegendary kings of Uruk: Enmerkar, Lugalbanda, and Gilgamesh. Gilgamesh and the others are commonly thought to have existed in Early Dynastic I. Indeed, the term "early dynastic" was applied to this archaeological period precisely because some of the early dynasties recorded in compositions such as the Sumerian King List were thought to have fallen in that period of time.

Initially used to record economic activities, writing quickly expanded its domain to encompass legal records, historical writings, and literary compositions,[5] and Early Dynastic III represents a more fully historic age. For the first time, royal inscriptions flesh out and enliven the Sumerian King List's dry succession of kings and dynasties. Royal inscriptions occur on a variety of artifacts: building materials such as bricks and door sockets; votive objects such as statues, relief-carved plaques, and bowls; cylinder seals; freestanding relief-carved stelae; and clay objects such as cones and vessels.[6]

Excavated royal inscriptions derive from many sites. Some of the earliest royal inscriptions are those of Mesalim, king of Kish. Two found at Bismayah and Tello also mention local rulers. For example, the inscription on the stone macehead from Tello reads, "Mesalim, king of Kish, temple builder for Ningirsu, set this up for Ningirsu. Lugalsha'engur is the ruler of Lagash."[7] Later inscriptions from Tello indicate that Mesalim acted to settle a border dispute between Lagash and its northern neighbor Umma.[8] Whether Mesalim

The Sumerian King List

The Sumerian King List is a composition that purports to list the dynasties and kings that ruled southern Mesopotamia from antediluvian times to the early second millennium BC. Known from multiple copies, it was probably compiled from the written traditions of some half-dozen cities, as well as from epic-historical texts. Its final redaction dates to the end of the first dynasty of Isin, as is proved by the king with whom it ends, Sin-magir (1827–1817 BC). Thorkild Jacobsen's *The Sumerian Kinglist*, published in 1939, remains the definitive edition.

The King List begins with kingship lowered from heaven to the city of Eridu. It then lists the kings associated with that city's ruling dynasty in the format *Royal Name (RN)*$_1$ reigned so many years, *RN*$_2$ reigned so many years, and so on. If *RN*$_2$ was the son of *RN*$_1$, it notes that fact and occasionally provides a short note or detail for which a particular king was famed. With the end of each dynasty, the King List tallies the number of kings and number of years reigned and segues to the succeeding dynasty using the formula "*Geographical Name (GN)*$_1$ was smitten with arms and the kingship was taken to *GN*$_2$." The King List then proceeds to name the kings of that city's dynasty using the same regular and uniform format as it used for Eridu.

The first part of the King List includes eight kings, all with fantastic reigns, ruling in five cities (Eridu, Badtibira, Larak, Sippar, and Shuruppak) for a length of 241,200 years. The King List is then interrupted by a flood that swept over the earth, but continues after the flood, when kingship was again lowered from heaven, this time to Kish. The last two kings of Kish, Enmebaragesi and his son, Agga, are arguably historical figures, although both are given fantastic reigns of 900 and 625 years, respectively. With the collapse of the Kish dynasty, kingship fell to Uruk, whose dynasts include some of the best-known figures of Sumerian literature: Enmerkar, Lugalbanda, and Gilgamesh. The King List gives all three fantastic reigns but ascribes divine status to both Lugalbanda and Gilgamesh. Ur's first dynasty follows the Uruk dynasty, with Mesannepada, A'annepada, Meskiagnanna, Elulu, and Balulu, all of whom have credible reign lengths. The list does not include the Royal Cemetery kings Meskalamdug and Akalamdug, who are thought to have preceded Mesannepada as Ur's rulers (see p. 22).

In all, the Sumerian King List enumerates sixteen dynasties following the flood, a period of rule by Guti tribesmen from the Zagros Mountains, and then dynasties at Uruk, Ur (the so-called Third Dynasty of Ur founded by Ur-Namma), and Isin. While at least in part a credible historical source, the Sumerian King List is not without its limitations. First, it makes the assumptions that southern Mesopotamia was a unity composed of a number of prime city-states and that only one at a time ruled over the others. Royal inscriptions, however, indicate that some of the dynasties given as consecutive were in fact contemporary. Second, the list does not include some apparently important cities and rulers known from independent archaeological and epigraphic evidence. These include the Early Dynastic kings of Lagash, at least one of whom (Eannatum) had claimed the title king of Kish (Cooper 1986: 41–42).

was in fact from Kish or some other southern city, his inscriptions and activities suggest a superordinate tier of kingship in southern Mesopotamia by Early Dynastic III, with the title king of Kish taken by those rulers claiming hegemony over Kish (and probably the northern floodplain) or over all of southern Mesopotamia.[9] Royal inscriptions, however, seldom provide sufficient information to reconstruct political history. The major exception is a corpus from Tello and al-Hiba, which details an ongoing boundary dispute between Lagash and its northern neighbor Umma.[10]

Corpora of tablets from Fara, Abu Salabikh, and Tello and smaller numbers of tablets from other sites add to the information in royal inscriptions. The Fara and Abu Salabikh tablets date to the beginning of Early Dynastic IIIA, ca. 2600 BC.[11] The Fara texts consist of hundreds of published and unpublished tablets found in the early-twentieth-century German excavations, as well as in the University of Pennsylvania Museum's 1931 excavations.[12] Between one-third and one-half of them come from a building that the excavators dubbed the "Tablet House."[13] Although the nature and identity of the Tablet House is uncertain, it was likely associated with a large organization.[14] In addition to lexical texts, the tablets include records of fields and plow teams allocated to individuals and records of the distribution of grain. Excavations at Fara also recovered a substantial number of ostensibly private sale contracts. The contract tablets were found in small scattered groups distributed at random across the mound, suggesting that they had been kept in the houses of individual purchasers.[15]

The Abu Salabikh texts consist of more than five hundred tablets found in the 1963 and 1965 excavations.[16] With one exception, the tablets were found in pits cutting into a building or buildings in Area E. This corpus consists largely of scribal exercises and lexical and literary fragments.

The Lagash corpus consists of approximately 1,600 tablets that stem from illicit excavations at Tello in 1902.[17] The documents date to Early Dynastic IIIB, more specifically to a fifteen-year period that included the reigns of the last three rulers of Lagash (Enentarzi, Lugalbanda, and UruKAgina) in the mid-twenty-fourth century BC. The documents were part of the administrative archive of the household of the city ruler's wife.[18] The Lagash texts include records of the distribution of rations to various categories of personnel.[19]

This brief summary of the evidence demonstrates the breadth of sources available to the student of Mesopotamian history. Although still subject to discussion and interpretation, the relative wealth of Early Dynastic III archaeological and written material provides us with a richer picture of early Mesopotamia than can be drawn for any of the previous periods.

EARLY DYNASTIC MESOPOTAMIA
By Early Dynastic III (and likely earlier), southern Mesopotamia was divided into twenty or thirty city-states, each consisting of a principal center (or centers), with smaller towns and villages dispersed across its countryside. While data on the southern city-states' population at large are meager, two important characteristics stand out. First, the population was decidedly urban and southern Mesopotamia has recently been dubbed the "heartland of cities."[20] Surface surveys designed to document all archaeological sites of the period provide rough demographic data. These surveys suggest that 80 percent of the population lived in cities of more than 40 hectares (about 100 acres), while a mere 10 percent lived in settlements smaller than 4 hectares. Adams describes this distribution as hypertrophic, an "unnatural" condition for an agricultural civilization with pre-industrial transport technology.[21]

Second, the population was a linguistic mix (or perhaps a linguistic and ethnic mix, if the latter concept applies to early

Mesopotamia). While Sumerian was perhaps the dominant written (and presumably spoken) language, a significant Semitic-speaking population existed, particularly in the northern part of the floodplain. Semitic personal names are known from Kish, and the overwhelming majority of the scribes who copied the Abu Salabikh literary and lexical texts have Semitic names[22] and used some Semitic words in administrative documents.[23] Semitic names also occur in texts from Fara, Adab, and Ur. Indeed, Puabi, one of the queens buried in the Royal Cemetery of Ur, has a Semitic name.[24] Some scholars suggest that the southern floodplain was divided between a predominantly Sumerian-speaking south and a predominantly Semitic-speaking north, each with distinctive cultural traditions.[25] Others, taking an arguably more cautious approach, acknowledge the linguistic mix while emphasizing southern Mesopotamia's effective cultural unity.[26]

Available written documentation provides considerable evidence for both peaceful interaction and military conflict among the southern city-states. A long-known group of Fara texts, for example, attest to the mustering of considerable numbers of men from Uruk, Adab, Nippur, Lagash, Shuruppak, and Umma, perhaps for a common undertaking, although whether this was for work-related or military purposes remains an open question.[27] Administrative texts from Lagash document peaceful commerce among the city-states as well as with more distant lands such as Elam (in Iran) and Dilmun (probably modern Bahrain and its vicinity).[28] The rich finds of exotic materials from the somewhat earlier Royal Cemetery of Ur confirm southern Mesopotamia's involvement in far-flung trade networks (and indeed reflect a sort of early Mesopotamian worldview). These materials include semiprecious stone such as lapis lazuli, probably from Badakhshan in northern Afghanistan;[29] carnelian, perhaps from Iran or the Indus Valley;[30] calcite and

calcite stone vessels, probably from eastern Iran, northern Afghanistan, or southern Turkmenistan;[31] obsidian from Anatolia;[32] copper and/or bronze and gold, probably from a variety of sources such as Anatolia, Egypt or Nubia, Iran, and Afghanistan;[33] and silver, probably from Anatolia.[34] Finished products include the calcite vessels mentioned above; metallic-ware pottery vessels, whose contents are unknown but which had to have been imported from the area of the Upper Euphrates in Syria;[35] and Iranian painted pottery.[36]

Each of these city-states had a principal guardian deity. Enlil, the air god who headed the southern Mesopotamian pantheon, was chief deity at Nippur. Given the hierarchical nature of the pantheon, Nippur consequently served as the religious (and strategic political) center of early Mesopotamia. Inanna, goddess of love and war, was chief deity at Uruk, where An, the sky god, also had his major temple. The list continues: Enki, god of freshwater, at Eridu; Utu, the sun god at Larsa and Sippar; Nanna, the moon god at Ur; and so on.

In official ideology, the city was the property of its principal deity. The deities nurtured and chose the city's ruler, variously called *lugal* (literally "big man" or king) or *ensi* or *en* ("governor," the form depending on the city).[37] The inscription on the Stele of the Vultures (fig. 1), erected by Eannatum of Lagash to commemorate his

Fig. 2. Limestone plaque depicting Urnanshe, first king of Lagash, Early Dynastic IIIA. White limestone, H. 40 cm. Louvre Museum, Paris. © Photo RMN—P. Bernard.

of bricks on his head (fig. 2). The inscription reinforces the image: "Urnanshe, king of Lagash, son of Gunidu, son of Gursar, built the temple of Ningirsu, built the temple of Nanshe, built the temple of Abzubanda."[39]

The city ruler acted on the deity's behalf in other contexts, even on the battlefield, as we see on another of Eannatum's inscriptions:

> For Ningirsu, warrior of Enlil, Eannatum, ruler of Lagash, chose in her heart by Nanshe the powerful mistress, who subjugates the foreign lands for Ningirsu, son of Akurgal, ruler of Lagash. . . .
>
> When he destroyed the ruler of Umma, who had marched on the Gu'edena, he restored to Ningirsu's control his beloved field, the Gu'edena. The territory in the region of Girsu, which he restored to Ningirsu's control and named Lumagirnunta-shakugepadda for him . . . he dedicated to him.[40]

Military conflicts and shifting alliances among and between city-states comprise the bulk of our written documentation. The ongoing boundary dispute is the best documented of such intrastate conflict, but wide-ranging conquests are covered as well. Eannatum, for example, claims victories not just over southern city-states such as Umma, Uruk, Ur, and Akshak, but also over regions beyond the southern floodplain—Subartu in the north and Elam in what is today southwestern Iran.[41] Artifacts from the Royal Cemetery of Ur such as the "royal standard" and monuments such as Eannatum's Stele of the Vultures provide us with graphic depictions of battles and their aftermaths.

Toward the end of the Early Dynastic period, Lugalzagesi, originally of Umma, claimed wider dominion than apparently any other king up to his time. His inscription on stone vessels dedicated to Enlil at Nippur reads in part:

victory over Umma, witnesses the relationship between city, ruler, and deity:

> Lord Ningirsu, warrior of Enlil . . . Ningirsu implanted the semen of Enlil for Eannatum in the womb . . . , rejoiced over [Eannatum]. Inanna accompanied him, named him Eanna-Inanna-Ibgalakakatum [Eannatum's full name, meaning "Worthy in the (temple) Eanna of Inanna of Ibgal"], and set him on the special lap of Ninhursag. Ninhursag offered him her special breast. Ningirsu rejoiced over Eannatum, semen implanted in the womb by Ningirsu. Ningirsu laid his span upon him, for (a length of) five forearms (cubits) he set his forearm upon him: (he measured) five forearms, one span. Ningirsu, with great joy, gave him the kingship of Lagash.[38]

One of the city ruler's most important duties was to build and maintain the principal deity's temple (along with the temples of the city's other gods and goddesses). A well-known relief-carved stone plaque of Urnanshe, first king of Lagash, depicts him in the act of temple building, with a basket

When Enlil, king of all lands, gave to Lugalzagesi the kingship of the nation, directed all eyes of the land (obediently) toward him, put all the lands at his feet, and from east to west made them subject to him; then, from the Lower Sea, (along) the Tigris and Euphrates to the Upper Sea, he (Enlil) put their routes in good order for him. From east to west, Enlil permitted him no rival.[42]

Lugalzagesi had defeated UruKAgina, the last king of Lagash, in the course of his rise to the top, and UruKAgina's inscription recording his depredations ends with a curse:

The leader of Umma, hav[ing] sacked Lagash, has committed a sin against Ningirsu. The hand which he has raised against him will be cut off! It is not a sin of UruKAgina, king of Girsu. May Nisaba, the god of Lugalzagesi, ruler of Umma, make him (Lugalzagesi) bear the sin.[43]

The curse was both ominous and prophetic. Lugalzagesi, in his turn, was defeated by another essentially Early Dynastic ruler, Sargon, who had established his capital, Akkad, in the northern part of the floodplain. An Old Babylonian copy of Sargon's inscriptions records that he captured Lugalzagesi and led him in a neck stock to the gate of Enlil's temple in Nippur. With Sargon and his Dynasty of Akkad, the Early Dynastic period came to an end and a new chapter of unification and empire began.

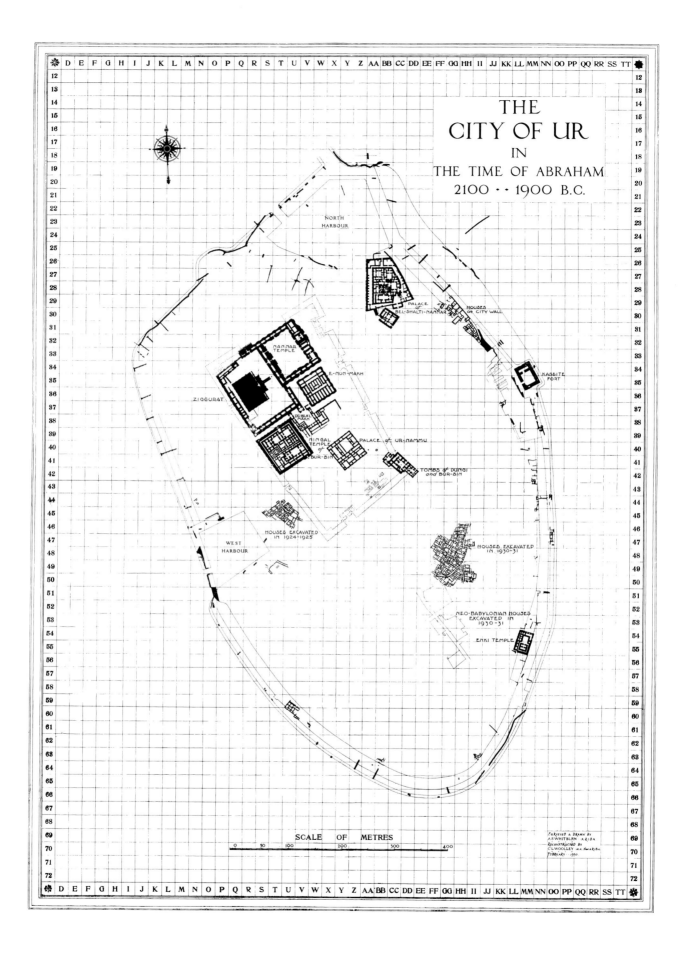

THE
CITY OF UR
IN
THE TIME OF ABRAHAM
2100 · · 1900 B.C.

NORTH
HARBOUR

PALACE of
BEL-SHALTI-NANNAR

HOUSES
ON CITY WALL

NANNAR
TEMPLE

E-NUN-MAKH

KASSITE
FORT

ZIGGURAT

DUBLAL-MAKH

NINGAL
TEMPLE
of
BUR-SIN

PALACE of UR-NAMMU

TOMBS of DUNGI
and BUR-SIN

WEST
HARBOUR

HOUSES EXCAVATED
IN 1924-1925

HOUSES EXCAVATED
IN 1930-31

NEO-BABYLONIAN HOUSES
EXCAVATED IN
1930-31

ENKI TEMPLE

SCALE OF METRES

0   50   100   200   300   400

SURVEYED & DRAWN BY
A.S.WHITBURN A.R.I.B.A
RECONSTRUCTED BY
C.L.WOOLLEY M.A HWM.A.R.I.B.A.
FEBRUARY 1930

CHAPTER TWO

Ur of the Chaldees

Richard L. Zettler

ROYAL TOMBS OF UR RICH IN TREASURE

Crowns and Cloak of Queen Shub-ad Marvels of Artistic Work.

KING'S GRAVE A SHAMBLES

Fifty Persons Sacrificed to His Spirit—Wife's Piety Led to — Tomb's Desecration.

Copyright, 1928, by The New York Times Company. Special Cable to THE NEW YORK TIMES.

LONDON, Feb. 22.—More complete details of the discoveries at Ur that have rewarded the joint expedition

Fig. 4. Headline from the *New York Times* (Feb. 26, 1928) announcing the discovery of the tomb of Queen Shub-ad, now known as Puabi. Photo: University of Pennsylvania Museum Archives.

OPPOSITE Fig. 3. Woolley's plan of the excavated remains of Ur, dated February 1930. At the top left of the mound, Nebuchadnezzar's later rectangular *temenos* wall is shown in relationship to the earlier Nanna temple complex and ziggurat (see fig. 9). Reprinted from Woolley 1931: pl. XXVIII.

Perhaps no excavation in the more than 150 years of archaeological work in Mesopotamia has excited as much public attention as C. Leonard Woolley's work at ancient Ur in the 1920s and early 1930s (fig. 3). Ur was fabled as the city of the Sumerian moon god Nanna and the traditional home of the biblical patriarch Abraham (Gen. 12:4–5). In the thirteen years of excavations, newspapers around the world printed countless articles. *The Illustrated London News,* England's "window on the world,"[1] reported the results of Woolley's discoveries at Ur in some thirty features, at least two with color illustrations.

Of all Woolley's discoveries, the mid-third-millennium BC tombs of the Royal Cemetery of Ur, with their rich inventories of gold and evidence of human sacrifice, received more intense coverage than any other (fig. 4). Woolley's excavations competed only with Howard Carter's discovery of the intact tomb of the boy pharaoh Tutankhamen for public attention. As a result of the extensive publicity, Iraqis and tourists from all parts of the globe, including European royalty and even the author Agatha Christie, flocked to the inaccessible site in the Iraqi desert. Christie later married Woolley's young assistant, M. E. L. Mallowan, and set her 1936 mystery *Murder in Mesopotamia* amid an excavation in Iraq. She attributed Ur's prominence in the popular media not only to the intrinsic interest of Woolley's discoveries but also to Woolley himself. As she wrote in her autobiography:

> Leonard Woolley saw with the eye of imagination: the place was as real to him as it had been in 1500 B.C., or a few thousand years earlier. Wherever he happened to be, he could make it come alive. While he was speaking I felt in my mind no doubt whatever that the house on the corner had been Abraham's. It was his reconstruction of the past and he believed in it, and anyone who listened to him believed in it also.[2]

TELL AL-MUQAYYAR

Tell al-Muqayyar (ancient Ur) lies near the city of Nasiriyah in the southwestern floodplain of the Tigris and Euphrates Rivers. The mounded ruins, roughly oval in shape, measure approximately 1,200 meters northwest to southeast and 800 meters northeast to southwest. They rise to a height of approximately 20 meters above the surrounding plain, with the ruin of the ziggurat, or temple tower, on the northwest end of the site rising even higher. A long, broken line of smaller mounds extends more than 1,500 meters to the north-northeast. Today the Euphrates runs to the east of the site, but in antiquity it probably curved to the southwest (fig. 5).

The Italian nobleman Pietro della Valle was probably the first westerner to visit the ruins, in the mid-seventeenth century. He noted their local name and commented on the fragments of baked brick and stone with cuneiform signs that he found littering the site.

> June the nineteenth, . . . I went in the forenoon to take a more diligent view of the ruins of the above-said ancient building. What it had been I could not understand; but I found it to have been built with very good Bricks, most of which were stamped in the midst with certain unknown letters which appear'd very ancient. I observed that they had been cemented together in the Fabrick, not with lime, but with bitumen or pitch, which, as I said is generated in these Desarts: whence the Hill upon which these ruins are, is call'd by the Arabians, Muqeijer, that is, Pitchy. . . .
>
> June, the twentieth, Surveying the above-said ruins again I found on the ground some pieces of black Marble, hard and fine, engraven with the same Letters as the Bricks, which seem'd to me to be a kind of Seal like what the Orientals use at this day: for their Seals are only letters or written words containing the name of him whose Seal it is, together with some Epithet of humility or devotion, Titles of Honor, or some words according as every one pleases; not being perpetual to the family, as ours are. Amongst other letters which I discovered in that short time, two I found in many places, one of which was like a jacent Pyramid thus, $\triangleright$, and the other resembled a Star of eight points in this form $*$.[3]

The British explorer J. B. Fraser examined the ziggurat when he passed by in 1834; he described it as "one of the most interesting relics of antiquity I have seen in this country."[4] William Kennett Loftus, a member of the Turko-Persian Frontier Commission and a pioneer excavator of southern Mesopotamian ruin mounds, visited Tell al-Muqayyar more than fifteen years later and published a measured description and early illustration of the ziggurat (fig. 6).[5] However, it was J. E. Taylor, British vice-consul at Basra, who, in 1853–54, first undertook excavations at Tell al-Muqayyar.[6] He did so at the urging of H. C. Rawlinson, British resident in Baghdad and an early decipherer of cuneiform, and with the support of the British Museum. Although Taylor excavated at various points across the mound, he concentrated his efforts on the ziggurat. With

Fig. 5. Aerial view of Tell al-Muqayyar (ancient Ur) taken in November 1922. Photo: University of Pennsylvania Museum Archives.

extraordinary good luck, he discovered intact inscribed clay cylinders (fig. 7) from "capsules" at the corners of the second stage of what we now know was the neo-Babylonian version of that structure. The cylinders recorded the ziggurat's rebuilding by Nebuchadnezzar's successor, Nabonidus (555–539 BC); they permitted Rawlinson to correctly identify Ur of the Chaldees as Tell al-Muqayyar.[7] Taylor also excavated part of a well-preserved baked brick structure with narrow arched doorways, which we now know to have been part of a Kassite reconstruction of a building called É-dub-lal-mah (see pp. 14–15).

With the end of Taylor's excavations, Tell al-Muqayyar lay undisturbed until the end of World War I, while other expeditions undertook excavations elsewhere in the south. Prominent among them was an American expedition associated with the University of Pennsylvania that excavated at Nuffar (ancient Nippur) from 1889 to 1900. The British Museum returned to Mesopotamia only after the area fell into British hands in World War I. The British Museum then quickly applied to the military authorities to attach an archaeologist to the army in the field, with a view to protecting antiquities and, if possible, undertaking excavations. The museum commissioned R. Campbell-Thompson, an Assyriologist and a former assistant in the museum who happened to be serving in Mesopotamia, to begin the work.[8]

Campbell-Thompson excavated Ur for a week in 1918 but was more interested in a nearby mound named Tell Abu Shahrain, already identified then as ancient Eridu.[9] Campbell-Thompson's decision to work in the area of Ur was due more to military circumstance than to choice. The British had not yet taken Mosul, so continuing at sites in the north such as Nineveh where Austen Henry Layard had worked[10] was out of the question. Many southern sites such as Warka, where Loftus had worked, were

outside the army's protected zone. Ur was close to the military center of Nasiriyah and readily accessible by train from Basra.[11]

In late 1918, the British Museum sent H. R. Hall, then a captain in the Intelligence Corps, to continue Campbell-Thompson's work at Ur.[12] Allotted seventy Turkish prisoners of war as laborers, Hall worked continuously for three and a half months, from mid-February to the end of May 1919. Basically, Hall followed Taylor's

Fig. 6. The ziggurat at Ur. Reprinted from Loftus 1857: facing p. 129.

Fig. 7. H. C. Rawlinson's copy of the inscriptions on clay cylinders recovered during excavations of the ziggurat at Ur in 1854. The inscriptions permitted him to identify Tell al-Muqayyar as the ancient city of Ur. Reprinted from Rawlinson 1861: pl. 68.

earlier excavation strategy. He put in trenches at various points around the mound of Ur, but he confessed an interest in "finding buildings, which could be planned by an . . . architect."[13] He therefore focused his efforts on clearing the southeast face of the ziggurat and uncovering the southwestern part of a building, which he termed "Building B." We now know this to have been a palace attributed to Ur-Namma and Shulgi, first kings of the Third Dynasty of Ur, that lay to the southeast of the ziggurat. Hall also exposed a stretch of the enclosure (temenos) wall of the Nanna temple complex built by Nebuchadnezzar (604–562 BC).

While at Ur, Hall simultaneously continued Campbell-Thompson's work at Tell Abu Shahrain. In the last two months of his field season, he began excavations at the smaller site in the desert called Tell al-Ubaid. There he made the spectacular discovery of architectural elements and sculptures that had once decorated the temple of Ninhursag, a mother goddess, built by a king named A'annepada; we now know that A'annepada was second king of the First Dynasty of Ur and a descendant of the kings and queens whose tombs Woolley would later uncover.

THE JOINT EXPEDITION
The end of World War I entailed the settlement of a number of political and military questions, including the assignment of the mandate for Iraq, the suppression of tribal insurrections in southern Iraq, and the determination of the permanent form of the government of Iraq. These political issues delayed the resumption of excavations for nearly three years after Hall's return to England in mid-1919. By then, the University of Pennsylvania Museum had become involved in the effort to jump-start excavations in Mesopotamia.[14] Even before Hall's return to England, C. B. Gordon, director of the

University Museum (as it was then called), had had discussions with Sir Frederic Kenyon, director of the British Museum, concerning the possibility of the University Museum's resuming archaeological work in Iraq. Before leaving England, Gordon wrote Kenyon to summarize the substance of their conversation. In his letter, he proposed that Nippur be "reserved and set aside as a locality on which the University Museum has a prior claim for the right to excavate" and that the British Museum and the University Museum form a joint expedition to excavate Ur. Any objects found and allotted to the joint expedition were "to be divided between the two Institutions by mutual agreement."[15]

By early 1922, the Mesopotamian administration was prepared to issue permits for archaeological work, and by June, Gordon and Kenyon had agreed to a joint expedition that would begin work in the fall, with C. Leonard Woolley as director. Woolley was well known to both Gordon and Kenyon. He had worked for the University Museum in Nubia and in Italy in 1910, and he had been in Philadelphia for a short period of time writing up the results of the excavations. He had worked for the British Museum at Carchemish just prior to and immediately after World War I, before political and military conflicts between the French and the Kemalist Turks had forced him to abandon the excavations.[16]

Which site to excavate still remained an open question. Kenyon proposed completing the excavation of Tell al-Ubaid, "where Hall had obtained his best results," and continuing work at Tell Abu Shahrain and Tell al-Muqayyar. However, he recognized that Gordon might prefer to resume the University Museum's excavation at Nippur.[17] Gordon traveled to London to work out the final details in August 1922, but even before sailing he had agreed to Kenyon's suggestion:

With regard to the actual site for work, I should suppose that it might safely be left in some measure to Mr. Woolley's discretion and judgment. Otherwise I am quite in accord with your suggestion looking toward the complete excavation of Tell Obeid [al-Ubaid] and a further exploration of Ur and Eridu. Nippur I presume would always be available in case for any reason it should be decided to resume work at that place.[18]

Gordon held out hope of returning to Nippur for several more years. But during the fourth season at Ur, he wrote Woolley asking him to clear out a storeroom that the University Museum had been renting in Hillah since the close of the Nippur excavations in 1900 and settle the accounts.[19]

Woolley sailed from London bound for Basra on September 26, 1922. He was accompanied by F. G. Newton, the excavation's architect, and Sydney Smith, the epigrapher. Paul Hunter, a young docent at the University Museum, was also slated to join the project, but he never made it to Ur. He became embroiled in a series of disturbing incidents in France and London and was remanded to a psychiatric hospital for observation.[20]

The party reached Port Said by October 8, where it was joined by Hamoudi, Woolley's colorful work foreman from the Carchemish excavations (fig. 8). They landed at Basra on October 23[21] and departed for Ur on October 26. Leaving Newton and Smith to take care of the preliminaries, Woolley traveled on to Baghdad. In the capital, he met with King Feisal, the British high commissioner, and various Cabinet ministers and with Gertrude Bell, Oriental secretary to the British high commissioner and honorary director of archaeology under Sabih Bey, minister of public works.

Gertrude Bell was a well-known traveler and had achieved some notoriety for her two books *Syria: The Desert and the Sown*

(1907) and *Amurath to Amurath* (1911). She was also an archaeologist and had excavated the Abbasid fortress, Ukaidir, before World War I.[22] She had previously crossed paths with Woolley in November 1915, while passing through Port Said on her way to Cairo to join the Arab Bureau. Woolley, then with the Intelligence Office, was stationed in Port Said. Bell referred to her meetings with Woolley in a letter to her father, which Bell's mother tactfully edited for publication, cutting out the first clause of a sentence. The restored passage reads, "I've been figuring in my capacity as Director of Archaeology. Mr. Woolley arrived on Sunday. He's a tiresome little man, but a first class digger and archaeologist after my own heart—i.e., he entirely backs me up in the way I'm conducting the Department."[23] Whatever Bell's impression

Fig. 8. Leonard Woolley with his foreman, Hamoudi, at Ur in 1930. Photo: University of Pennsylvania Museum Archives.

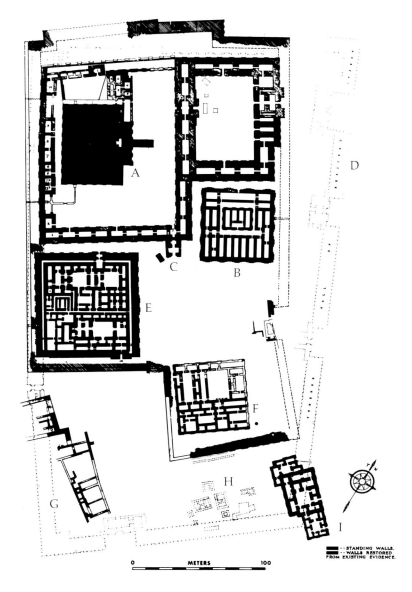

A

D

C

B

E

F

H

I

G

⬛ · STANDING WALLS.
▬ · WALLS RESTORED
FROM EXISTING EVIDENCE.

0   METERS   100

Fig. 9. Plan of the late-third-millennium Nanna temple complex. Trial Trench B lay to the east of the ziggurat (A) and cut across É-nun-mah (B). Other buildings and areas mentioned in the text include É-dub-lal-mah (C), Nebuchadnezzar's *temenos* wall (D), *giparu* (E), Building B or É-hur-sag (F), Area EH (G), royal tombs (H), and Mausoleums of the Kings of the Third Dynasty of Ur (I). Reprinted from Woolley 1974: pl. 53.

of Woolley, the minister gave him a provisional permit that provided for a division of finds: half would go to Iraq, and half to the excavators. The Antiquities Law, which Bell had authored, had not yet been formally approved.[24] Woolley returned to Ur on November 2, ready to begin the excavations.

WOOLLEY'S EXCAVATIONS AT UR
In various letters and reports, Woolley repeatedly emphasized that his goal for the first season's excavations was "to obtain as clear an idea as possible of the topography of the site, so as to guide future excavations and to economize labor by identifying beforehand its more important sections."[25] He began by digging two long, narrow trial trenches, designated A and B. Trial Trench A ran almost due south from a substantial buttressed wall immediately south of Hall's Building B and cut across the cemetery area that would yield such spectacular finds in later seasons. Woolley in fact uncovered intact and broken burials of various periods, including the late Early Dynastic and Akkadian periods, in his first season there. However, he was far more interested in the more coherent architectural remains uncovered in Trial Trench B, located east of the ziggurat (fig. 9). Trial Trench B cut across a building Woolley identified as É-nun-mah, probably a large storehouse (fig. 10).[26] He expanded the operation there to uncover much of the building in various phases of its history. When excavations had to be temporarily halted until a narrow-gauge railway could provide more efficient dumping of excavated debris, Woolley turned to tracing Nebuchadnezzar's *temenos*, first exposed by Hall in 1919. He would later put a positive spin on his decision not to follow up the Trial Trench A finds at that time by noting that the work of digging burials "could not be done satisfactorily with the absolutely untrained gang [of workers] which we had just enrolled."[27] His decision to expand Trial Trench B actually signaled his intention to focus his efforts on the principal buildings at Ur, which he reasoned would likely be located within the *temenos*.[28]

In the earlier part of the second season (1923–24), Woolley continued Hall's work at Tell al-Ubaid (an excavation originally planned for 1922–23 but abandoned for lack of funds[29]). For four years thereafter, he concentrated his efforts on buildings within Nebuchadnezzar's enclosure wall. In the second field season (1923–24), he cleared the ziggurat (fig. 11). In the third season (1924–25), he tackled É-dub-lal-mah, a building first uncovered by Taylor

Fig. 10. View of É-nun-mah taken from the southeast. The still largely unexcavated ziggurat is in the background, with its partially cleared southwest facade visible on the left. Photo: University of Pennsylvania Museum Archives.

Fig. 11. The Ur ziggurat at the end of the second season's excavations, with the workmen arrayed on the stairways. Photo: University of Pennsylvania Museum Archives.

Fig. 12. Members of the third season's expedition on the steps of É-dub-lal-mah. The young man on the left is probably archaeologist and registrar J. Linnell. In the center are Katherine Keeling, who later became Mrs. Woolley, and Charles Leonard Woolley. On the right is Leon Legrain, the expedition's epigrapher in both the third and fourth seasons. Photo: University of Pennsylvania Museum Archives.

Fig. 13. General view to the southeast from the top of the ziggurat. In the foreground is *giparu*, in the background, area EH. December 31, 1921. Photo: University of Pennsylvania Museum Archives.

(fig. 12). The building was perhaps originally a gateway into the ziggurat complex; in the building's courtyard, Woolley found the Stele of Ur-Namma, currently in the University of Pennsylvania Museum. He also excavated É-gi$_6$-pàr, or *giparu*, temple of Nanna's wife, Ningal, and residence and burial place of the *entu*-priestess (fig. 13). In the fourth season (1925–26), Woolley went back to Hall's Building B, É-hur-sag, apparently a palace. He also worked in two areas to the southeast: area EH, just within Nebuchadnezzar's enclosure wall, where he uncovered the fragmentary remains of a late-third-millennium BC temple to Nimin-tabba, a goddess closely associated with the moon god, Nanna; and area EM, just outside the *temenos* wall, where he uncovered private houses of the early second millennium BC. Woolley continued excavations in area EM in the first part of the fifth field season (1926–27). By the middle of that season's excavation, he was back where he had started, the southeastern corner of Nebuchadnezzar's *temenos*

Fig. 14. The northeast end of the cemetery during the last days of work in 1927. Photo: University of Pennsylvania Museum Archives.

Fig. 15. Dagger in its sheath of gold from PG 580. L. 37.3 cm (U.9361). Photo: University of Pennsylvania Museum Archives.

wall. It was the only area within the enclosure wall that still lay largely unexcavated, and the place where he had located Trial Trench A four years previously.

Woolley began his investigations of the area by running two long, narrow trenches off Trial Trench A, one extending toward the east angle of the *temenos* and the other running southwest toward a gate in Nebuchadnezzar's wall. He uncovered little in the first trench, but when he hit burials in the second trench he expanded it until a large area was cleared.[30] In all, he uncovered some six hundred burials in less than three months (fig. 14).

By the end of the season, he had recognized that the burials had been cut into irregular and sloping ground and that the "cemetery" represented a considerable period of time, with the burials falling into distinct periods. A burial (PG 580) of the earlier group, only partially excavated by the end of the season, was particularly large and rich. With the exception of the skulls of several oxen, Woolley found no bones, but he uncovered a considerable number of artifacts that apparently had

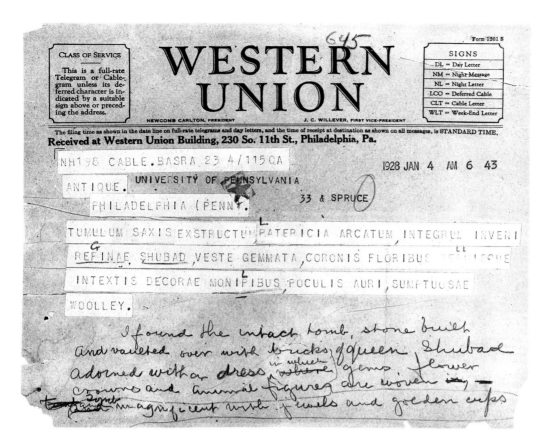

Fig. 16. Woolley's telegram in Latin to the University Museum announcing his discovery of the tomb of Queen Shubad (Puabi). Photo: University of Pennsylvania Museum Archives.

been sealed between two layers of reed matting spread over an area measuring 7 by 4 meters. The artifacts included a gold reticule containing gold toilet implements and a dagger with electrum blade and lapis handle studded with gold, in an elaborate gold sheath (fig. 15).[31]

The cemetery dominated excavations in the succeeding seasons: 300 graves were uncovered in nine months in the seventh field season (1927–28); 454 in three months during the eighth season (1928–29); and an additional 350 graves in the ninth season (1929–30). Richest of all the burials were three uncovered in 1927–28 and 1928–29: PG 789; PG 800, belonging to a royal woman named Puabi (previously read as Sumerian Shub-ad); and PG 1237. They included stone-built tomb chambers set at the bottom of pits, evidence of an elaborate burial ritual that included "human sacrifice," and countless artifacts made of semiprecious stones, gold, and silver. The tombs' wealth was such that Woolley felt

Fig. 17. Beginning excavations at the northeast edge of the cemetery in 1931. Woolley is on the right. Photo: University of Pennsylvania Museum Archives.

Fig. 18a–c. Sequence of photographs showing the progress of excavations in Pit X in 1933–34. To gauge the scale of Woolley's efforts, consider that this sounding required moving more than 13,000 cubic meters of soil. Photo: University of Pennsylvania Museum Archives.

compelled to compose his telegrams to Kenyon and Gordon announcing his spectacular finds in Latin so that the news would not be intercepted (fig. 16).

The 1927–28 season convinced Woolley that he was excavating a cemetery with royal tombs. He abandoned the cemetery site in 1930–31 while he worked on his final report, but he returned in 1931–32 to investigate additional burials that he thought significant in terms of their dating (fig. 17). He uncovered hundreds of additional burials in a deep sounding (Pit X) to the south of the cemetery area in 1933–34 (fig. 18a–c), after the final report on the cemetery had gone to press.

In the later years of excavations at Ur, Woolley continued to carry out extensive excavations at various locations around the site. The most important of his later discoveries are the Mausoleums of the Kings of the Third Dynasty of Ur, located at the northeastern edge of the Royal Cemetery, and an extensive area (AH) of private houses predominantly of Isin-Larsa/Old Babylonian and later dates in the south-central part of the site. As Woolley himself noted, however, with the discovery of the Royal Cemetery, he was committed to investigating the earlier levels of the mound.[32]

Already in 1928–29, with the excavation of the cemetery having provided a large area cleared to a depth of 10 to 13 meters, Woolley made the opportunistic decision to continue digging in a number of small soundings below the floor levels of excavated burials.[33] He made a startling discovery, perhaps second in importance only to the Royal Cemetery: a thick layer of water-laid clay that sealed strata containing the by then well-known black-painted pottery of the Ubaid period, the earliest phase of occupation on the southern floodplain. Woolley quickly associated the clay stratum with the flood known from the Sumerian King List and the Bible. However, the excavators of Kish, in the northern portion of the floodplain near Babylon, raced him to press with a flood of their own.[34]

Woolley undertook additional soundings in 1929–30, 1932–33, and 1933–34.[35] His excavations in the prehistoric strata were intrinsically interesting, but they were also relevant to his understanding of the Royal Cemetery. His excavations through those strata yielded evidence regarding the stratification of the cemetery area, as well as tablets and seals from the debris layers into which the graves were cut. These tablets and impressions provided a terminus post quem for the royal tombs. Woolley's soundings also revealed the remains of an even earlier cemetery dating to the Jamdat Nasr period (ca. 3100–2900 BC).

By the early 1930s, Woolley's longtime friends and supporters Sir Frederic Kenyon and G. B. Gordon were retired or dead, and the directors of the British Museum (Sir George Hill) and the University Museum (Horace H. F. Jayne) were facing a world radically changed. The University Museum had been particularly hard hit by the Great Depression and a wildly fluctuating dollar. On the advice of the University Museum's board of managers and its president (John Story Jenks), Jayne wrote Woolley on May 9, 1933, suggesting ending the excavations with the 1932–33 field season. Jayne presented three reasons for his request. First, he noted that the Carnegie Foundation had provided the British and University Museums with a grant of $25,000 in 1931 to cover the costs of publication and therefore full publication of the results of the excavations was an imperative. Further excavations would only increase the backlog of unpublished material. Second, he suggested that the "possibilities of the site were nearing exhaustion, at least for our generation" and that something should be left for future archaeologists. Jayne stated almost parenthetically that the last three field seasons had not "yielded richly," although he openly admitted that the royal tombs rendered the results of succeeding seasons "drab" by comparison. He also protested somewhat sheepishly that, of course, he did not want to minimize the importance of scientific data just because striking exhibits did not come to light. Third, Jayne suggested that Woolley himself might need a break after ten years of strenuous fieldwork. The deferential tone of Jayne's letter was very different from the tone of the first letters that had passed from Kenyon and Gordon to Woolley, clearly showing that the young Woolley now had an equal, if not the upper, hand in their relationship.

Woolley convinced the British and University Museums to provide funds for one more field season in order to uncover material needed for the final publication. Woolley's twelfth and final season ended on February 25, 1934. By that time, he had become, as the *Illustrated London News* termed him in a March 1, 1930, story, a "famous archaeologist," with his own series on BBC radio. In the following year, he was awarded a knighthood, announced in the Birthday Honors List of June 1935.[36]

CHAPTER THREE

The Royal Cemetery of Ur

Richard L. Zettler

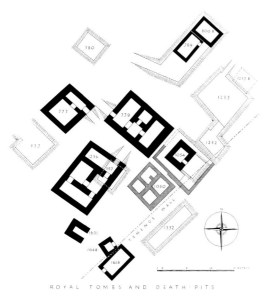

ROYAL TOMBS AND DEATH·PITS

Fig. 20. Detail of the Royal Cemetery showing the sixteen tombs deemed "royal" by Woolley. Reprinted from Woolley 1934b: pl. 273.

OPPOSITE Fig. 19. Aerial photograph taken March 12, 1930, showing excavations of the Royal Cemetery at the southeast corner of the Nanna temple complex (bottom of photograph). Photo: University of Pennsylvania Museum Archives.

The cemetery Woolley uncovered in the late 1920s included some 1,850 intact burials[1] spread over an area approximately 70 by 55 meters underneath the southeast corner of Nebuchadnezzar's *temenos* and partly beneath and outside its enclosure wall (figs. 19, 20). Woolley estimated that perhaps two or three times that number of burials originally existed in the area.[2]

As Woolley reconstructed it, the burials had been cut into irregular and sloping ground; heaps of rubbish spread out from the prehistoric town, whose center lay to the southwest, sloping down to the northeast and southeast. An earlier group of burials was separated from a later group by additional debris layers that varied in thickness, from 1 to 3 meters, as well as in composition. In most places, the debris was gray in color and made up of decomposed mud bricks, but in some places it contained pottery or a combination of pottery, brick rubble, and lime.[3]

Woolley dubbed the debris layers in the cemetery "Seal Impression Strata" (SIS) because of the large number of clay sealings recovered from them. Archaic tablets[4] and seal impressions[5] from the earlier SIS 8-5, dated to the earlier part of the Early Dynastic period (Early Dynastic I), provided a terminus post quem for the earlier group of burials. A lapis lazuli cylinder seal belonging to Ninbanda, the queen and wife of Mesannepada (see cat. no. 25), and impressions of seals naming Mesannepada king of Kish and Ninbanda the queen (see fig. 44) were found in strata that sealed the earlier burials and provided a terminus ante quem for them.[6] The Sumerian King List names Mesannepada as first king of the First Dynasty of Ur; he is commonly thought to be a contemporary of Eannatum, third king of the better attested Lagash dynasty.[7] The earlier graves, then, can be dated to the period conventionally known as Early Dynastic IIIA.[8]

According to Woolley, the cemetery's later burials could be securely attributed to the Sargonic period by inscribed cylinder seals found in two of the graves. These seals refer to officials of

21

Enheduanna, daughter of Sargon, founder of the Dynasty of Akkad.

Woolley assigned fifteen graves on the northeast edge of the cemetery to a time period intermediate between the earlier and Sargonic graves, the Second Dynasty of Ur. He did so because their artifacts seemingly shared characteristics of both groups of burials. Reexamination of the diagnostic pottery and cylinder seals, however, indicates that the "Second Dynasty" burials are Akkadian in date or later.[9]

As for the relative chronology of the burials, Woolley realized that absolute elevations provided little help because graves had been cut into uneven ground. In the cemetery's crowded conditions, later burials commonly overlaid, and not uncommonly cut and disturbed, earlier ones, and Woolley recognized groupings of as many as five, ten, and even twenty superimposed burials. Using only those groups with more than five burials, he devised a developmental sequence of artifacts such as pottery, stone and metal vessels, and metal tools and weapons. Using this developmental sequence, he could look at artifact inventories in other tombs and place those tombs too in a relative sequence. Woolley's methodology was seemingly solid, but questions remain. Beginning with Hans

Nissen's *Zur Datierung des Königsfriedhofes von Ur,* which appeared in 1966, more than thirty years after Woolley's final report, various studies continue to examine the stratigraphy and relative dating of the cemetery's thousands of burials.

THE EARLY DYNASTIC IIIA ROYAL CEMETERY

Woolley assigned 660 burials to the Early Dynastic Royal Cemetery. The overwhelming majority were simple inhumations (fig. 21),[10] in which the body, wrapped in reed matting or placed in a coffin, was set at the bottom of a rectangular pit that varied in size but averaged 1.50 by 0.70 meters. The body was invariably placed on its side, with the legs slightly flexed and the arms and hands in front of the breast at about the level of the mouth. Clothed and accompanied by his/her personal belongings—for example, jewelry, cylinder seal, and dagger —the deceased generally held a cup, and a jar and bowl were placed nearby. Other utilitarian goods such as bowls and jars containing foodstuffs, weapons and tools, and so on might be distributed around the pit, the quantity probably reflecting wealth and social status. Of the 660 burials, 16 stood apart from the simple inhumations in terms of their wealth, peculiarities of structure, and evidence of ritual. Woolley termed these "royal tombs," assuming that they contained Ur's deceased kings and queens. A cylinder seal inscribed "Meskalamdug, the king," along with a second seal inscribed "Akalamdug, king of Ur, Ashusikildingir (is) his wife," seemingly confirmed Woolley's assumption.

Royal tombs consisted of a vaulted or domed stone tomb chamber set at the bottom of a deep pit, to which a ramp provided access. The principal body lay in the chamber, buried with substantial quantities of goods, sometimes including a sled or wheeled vehicles pulled by oxen or equids. Personal and household attendants lay in the tomb chamber with the deceased king

Fig. 21. Simple inhumation, PG 622. Although probably late Akkadian or later in date, this tomb resembles those of the Early Dynastic period. Photo: University of Pennsylvania Museum Archives.

or queen and in the pit outside, which Woolley consequently termed the "death pit." Although no trace remained, Woolley felt certain that the tombs would have been marked on the surface by some sort of chapel.

In Woolley's reconstruction, the royal tombs constituted the nucleus around which the cemetery grew: the first royal tomb to be dug into the old rubbish tips set a precedent that was followed by other members of the royal house(s). In time, a double row of royal tombs came to exist, running from southwest to northeast across the cemetery area. From the beginning, the graves of private individuals encroached on the royal burial grounds, at first clustering around the tombs of the kings and queens and eventually even cutting down into the filling of the pits and into one another.[11]

Some of the royal tombs uncovered by Woolley had been partially destroyed, presumably by later tomb digging. Nearly all of the royal tombs had been robbed in antiquity.

Woolley recognized a considerable variation in the royal tombs, in both their architecture and their wealth, number of retainers, ratio of genders, and so on.[12] In terms of their architecture, for example, PG 789 and PG 800 (see Chapter 4) had tomb chambers and extensive death pits. PG 777/779 and PG 1236 consisted of multiple-room chambers that occupied the entire grave pit (fig. 22). PG 1050 and PG 1054 each held a single-room chamber-tomb apparently set at the bottom of a deep shaft. Both had additional chambers in the fill of the shafts; the floors associated with the chambers contained simple subsidiary burials. PG 1618/1631/1648 (fig. 23) might represent yet another distinct tomb type: small single-room chamber-tombs set at the bottom of a small pit.

Some of the royal tombs contained large numbers of retainers. PG 789 held sixty-three, the majority women, in the pit.

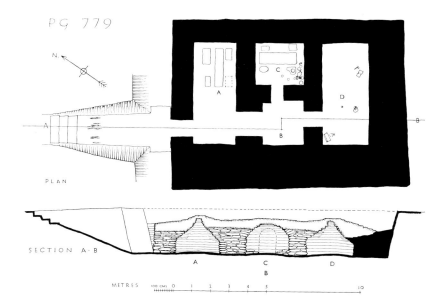

TOP Fig. 22. Plan and cross-section of PG 779, a multiple-room chamber-tomb with no death pit. Reprinted from Woolley 1934b: pl. 24.

BOTTOM Fig. 23. Plan of PG 1648, a small single-room chamber-tomb. Reprinted from Woolley 1934b: fig. 26.

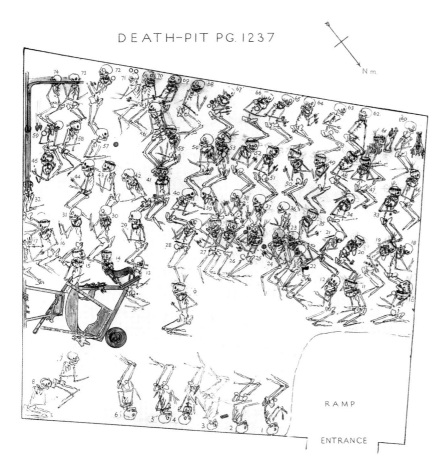

DEATH-PIT PG. 1237

N m.

RAMP

ENTRANCE

cut partly in the shaft of Royal Tomb PG 779.[13] Although Woolley speculated that the depth of the shaft had been at least 5 meters, his only evidence was a spear, approximately 1.80 meters long, that apparently had been standing vertically in the tomb; therefore, the shaft might have been as little as 2 meters deep. A coffin was placed against the northeast side of the pit. The body in the coffin was that of a male, described as a strongly built, powerful man about 5½ feet in height and under thirty at the time of his death.[14]

PG 755 was unique among the simple inhumations "in the extraordinary richness of its furniture" (fig. 26).[15] Behind the deceased's head, for example, was a gold helmet. He held in his hands a gold bowl inscribed with the name Meskalamdug. Around his waist was a silver belt, from which was suspended a gold dagger in a silver sheath, a lapis lazuli whetstone with a gold ring, a largely decayed shell cylinder seal, and perhaps a silver toilet reticule. Both the coffin and the tomb pit were filled

ABOVE Fig. 24. Plan of PG 1237, the "Great Death Pit," so called because in it lay the bodies of seventy-three retainers. Reprinted from Woolley 1934b: pl. 71.

RIGHT Fig. 25. Plan of PG 755, unique among simple inhumations for its wealth of grave goods. Reprinted from Woolley 1934b: fig. 35.

PG 1237 (fig. 24) contained seventy-three retainers, apparently five men and sixty-eight women. (Woolley called this the "Great Death Pit," because of the large numbers of retainers and because the tomb chamber itself had been destroyed.) Other tombs contained fewer but still substantial numbers of retainers. PG 1050 apparently had forty bodies in a death pit found below the floor of the chamber. PG 800 held two bodies in the tomb chamber and twenty-one in the pit. Still other burials, such as PG 1618 and PG 1648, contained fewer than five bodies. Unfortunately, the reasons for these variations are as poorly understood today as when Woolley originally uncovered the cemetery.

One particularly rich tomb that Woolley did not include among the royal tombs, in large part because it did not have a tomb chamber or retainers, nevertheless stands out. PG 755 (fig. 25) consisted of a rectangular pit measuring 2.50 by 1.50 meters,

N.

with artifacts the likes of which Woolley had found only in royal tombs. In the coffin, for example, were gold and silver lamps, a second gold bowl inscribed with the name Meskalamdug, and electrum ax heads. On the northeast side opposite the upper part of the body was a substantial collection of jewelry, including a copper pin like that normally worn by women in the royal tombs, with a head in the form of a squatting monkey. Perhaps the jewelry was a gift to be presented to underworld deities (see p. 28). Outside the coffin were, as Woolley noted, a "bewildering" number of artifacts, including metal vessels inscribed with the names Meskalamdug and Ninbanda, the queen.[16]

The identity of the young man buried with such wealth in PG 755 remains an open question. His seal, which might have been expected to be inscribed with his name, was apparently in very bad condition and not kept. Woolley assumed him to be named Meskalamdug, in large part because of the bowls inscribed with that name found in the tomb. Originally, Woolley thought the name referred to Meskalamdug the king, whose seal was found in a box in a subsidiary burial in the shaft of PG 1054. Later he apparently changed his mind, deciding that PG 755's Meskalamdug was not King Meskalamdug but a lesser person of the same name.[17]

From an inscription on a lapis lazuli bead found at Mari, we know the royal Meskalamdug took the title king of Kish and was the father of Mesannepada. Mesannepada, in turn, was the first king of the First Dynasty of Ur, according to the Sumerian King List.[18] As noted, however, one vessel from the young man's grave was inscribed with the name Ninbanda. Her identification is problematic. She is called "queen," but was she the wife of Meskalamdug the king? Or was she the wife of Mesannepada, as reported on the seal found in the debris separating the earlier and later burials at Ur? If this

Fig. 26. The gold helmet found along with gold dagger, bowls, and other riches in PG 755. Photo: University of Pennsylvania Museum Archives.

Meskalamdug was the son of Mesannepada and Ninbanda, we would have to assume that he was buried with a legacy from his grandfather.[19]

HUMAN SACRIFICE

For Woolley, the deaths of the retainers and their burial with kings and queens was an integral element of the royal tombs. The absence of such retainers in PG 755 was one of the reasons Woolley did not think it a royal burial, in spite of its bewildering wealth. For the media, "human sacrifice" had a certain lurid appeal, which the *Illustrated London News* implicitly recognized when it published two reconstructions of PG 789. One, which ultimately made its way into Woolley's final report on the excavations, showed the scene in the death pit just after the tomb chamber had been closed (see fig. 35). The second, apparently never reproduced, showed the "shambles" in the death pit after the royal retainers had drunk the poison and the oxen had been slaughtered.[20]

In the absence of any archaeological evidence paralleling what he had uncovered or any written sources hinting at such practices, Woolley was left to explain the phenomenon.[21] Using a little circular logic, he suggested that sacrifice implied "godhead." He knew that the kings of the Third Dynasty of Ur were deified during and after their lifetimes; the Early Dynastic kings of

Death and Burial in Early Mesopotamia: The View from the Texts

Steve Tinney

Among the most valuable artifacts to have come down to us from ancient Mesopotamia are hundreds of thousands of unassuming clay tablets inscribed with a kaleidoscopic array of subject matter. The great majority are mundane documents from daily operations of institutions or individuals: receipts for incoming goods, records of disbursements, contracts for loans, and accounts of dowries, to name but a few. As a class of texts, Assyriologists label these "administrative" or "economic, legal, and administrative." Relatively few texts (although still numbering in the thousands) stem from the education of scribes: from basic writing exercises, to lengthy and complex lists of signs and words, to literary texts that themselves range from the simple to the advanced. Thousands more texts represent the training and reference materials of generations of diviners, exorcists, liturgists, and astronomers, and another major corpus comprises dedicatory and narrative inscriptions left for posterity by the ancient rulers. All in all, a textual gold mine.

Exploiting this mine, however, is fraught with problems. For one thing, we do not have a steady, constant supply of documents from all places and all times; instead, we have clumps of anything from scattered odd texts to tens of thousands of tablets from specific places at specific times. For another, the texts we have are not uniformly intelligible to us; early texts, from before about 2600 BC, are often nearly opaque despite the great strides that have been made in understanding in recent years, and administrative texts often utilize a code that modern bureaucrats would be proud of. In addition, the questions we would like to answer are often not those to which the texts were

intended to speak; reconstructing complex social-psychological phenomena from administrative texts is difficult at best, and perhaps impossible. Finally, as a matter of principle, the written culture of ancient Mesopotamia tends to record the unexpected and the unusual rather than the well known and normal; what was well known could be left unwritten (taken as read). The implications of this fact for our study of the ancient cultures of the Near East are staggering: by definition, we should expect that textual records select the less obvious for description. Understandings based on these texts are guaranteed to be skewed.

Bearing in mind these reservations, then, let's review the literary texts that correlate with and, in some ways, shed light on the burials in the tombs of Ur: in modern parlance, *The Death of Gilgamesh* and *The Death of Ur-Namma*.

THE DEATH OF GILGAMESH

The Death of Gilgamesh describes the death and burial of the heroic early ruler of the city of Uruk. Whether Gilgamesh ever actually lived is to some extent a moot point, as he was certainly considered a real king in Sumerian tradition. Gilgamesh was believed to have been born to a mortal father, Lugalbanda, and a divine mother,

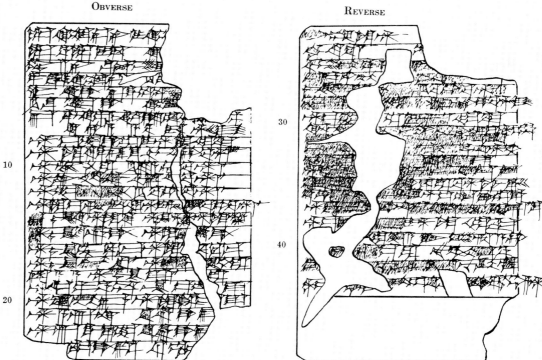

OBVERSE · REVERSE

10

20

30

40

Clay tablet recording in cuneiform script a literary text known as *The Death of Gilgamesh*. Ca. 1800 BC. UPM 29-16-86.

Ninsun. Several Sumerian tales tell of Gilgamesh's exploits. If Gilgamesh lived, we would place him around 2600 BC; the tablets on which the tale of his death is preserved all date to about 1800 BC.

The Death of Gilgamesh opens with the hero on his deathbed, mortally ill. In a dream, his fate is revealed to him: he has reached the end of his appointed time on earth and will become a lord of the underworld on a par with Dumuzi and Ningishzida. After Gilgamesh succumbs, the text turns to a description of his burial, which might equally apply to the tombs of Ur:

> His beloved wife, his beloved son,
> His beloved favorite wife and junior wife,
>   His beloved singer, cup-bearer and . . . ,
>   His beloved barber, his beloved . . . ,
> His beloved attendants who all served
>   (in) the palace,
>   His beloved consignments—
> When they had lain down in their place with
>   (him), as in the pure palace in Uruk,
>   Gilgamesh, son of Ninsun,
> Weighed out the meeting-gifts for
>   Ereshkigal, Weighed out the presents
>   of Namtar.

The text continues with similar brief descriptions of offerings being made to a series of about twenty deities and to several kinds of priestly functionaries, all of whom are dead.

THE DEATH OF UR-NAMMA

Ur-Namma was the first king of the third dynasty of Ur (Ur III). He ruled from 2112 to 2094 BC; the literary text describing his death and journey to the underworld is known from tablets dating to about 1800 BC and evidently circulated in slightly different versions.

The text opens with doom and gloom: Ur-Namma, a true shepherd king, has left the city, and the people cower in their dwellings. The gods have reneged on the happy fate promised for King Ur-Namma; the moon god, Nanna, has frowned in divine displeasure, and the sun god, Utu, has not risen in the heavens; wailing fills the broad streets, where play is the norm. Ur-Namma, having died in battle, is brought to Ur, and the soldiers who marched with him into battle now follow him toward the underworld in tears. Ur-Namma's donkey and chariot are buried, and the path to his grave is disguised so that no one can approach it. As the renowned king presents his offerings to the seven gatekeepers of the underworld, the news of his death spreads throughout the realm of the dead. Ur-Namma understands that the food of the underworld is bitter and that the water of the underworld is brackish; he understands the rituals that are required of him, and he goes about carrying them out. First he sacrifices all the oxen, kids, and sheep that he has brought with him. Then he proceeds to the palace of each of the underworld deities in turn and presents them with the appropriate offerings.

Some of these offerings are symbolic of the role of the recipient. Dumuzi, "beloved spouse of Inanna" and erstwhile ruler of Uruk, receives a "golden royal scepter." Gilgamesh and Nergal, both warriors in addition to other roles, receive weapons; for Nergal, the "Enlil of the underworld," these gifts include a bow, a quiver, a skillfully crafted knife, and a leather hip pouch. Female deities also receive appropriate gifts from Ur-Namma. Hushbisa, spouse of Namtar, receives a spindle whorl decorated with lapis lazuli and "a comb, a fitting thing for a woman." Geshtinanna, scribe of the underworld, is given "a copper stylus and everything needed for the scribal art; a shining measuring rope and measuring rod." Other offerings include various kinds of jewelry, textiles, clothing, and other objects. In some cases, these objects are less clearly symbolic and may be presented because they are precious or useful.

Having completed the offerings, Ur-Namma is seated on a great dais by the gods of the underworld. Although not explicitly mentioned in the preserved portions of this broken passage, it is likely that he too is provided with a palace, since he takes his place on a par with "his brother Gilgamesh" to sit in judgment of the dead.

The scene then shifts to the lamentation of the people of Sumer for their dead king, "who will never come to enjoy the new palace that will go unbuilt, who will never again take pleasure in the lap of his wife, and whose children will not grow up on his knee." Next Inanna appears, furious at the death of the king, lamenting his passing, and extolling the achievements of his reign, and here the text concludes.

ADMINISTRATIVE TEXTS
Some very few of the thousands of preserved administrative texts also shed some light on early burial practices. The most important are two lists, probably of grave goods intended for burial with high-ranking members of society. Both lists include jewelry and other objects, as well as a chariot and donkey team and, in one case, a slave-girl. Assuming these lists give the items intended for interment, as is likely, we have here further textual correlations with the practices evidenced in the Royal Tombs, correlations that, in the case of these administrative texts, date to within a century of the tombs themselves.

*　*　*

Although it would be naive to take either of these literary texts as straightforward descriptions of the burial practices evidenced by the Royal Tombs of Ur, obvious points of comparison exist, and the texts may offer clues to further understanding of the tombs. For instance, we learn from both *The Death of Gilgamesh* and *The Death of Ur-Namma* that deities and kings could have palaces in the underworld and that the burial of the retinue was intended to enable the king to continue living in the style to which he was accustomed. This concept fits well with the major multiple burials in the royal tombs.

Another important piece of information concerns the reasons for burying so much wealth with an individual. Of course, one reason must have been that these were the possessions that belonged in a palace. Also significant, however, is the notion that many objects may have been intended as gifts to the gods of the underworld. This notion may also explain a puzzling feature of the Royal Tombs: the inventory of items found in male burials includes many examples of female accoutrements, jewelry especially. Given that usually these gifts are appropriate to the recipients' needs and interests and that several goddesses receive gifts from Ur-Namma, it should not be surprising that gifts for the goddesses accompany males in the Royal Cemetery on their journey to the underworld. (For further reading, see Bottéro 1992: 268–86.)

that city might likewise have been "divine kings." When the kings and queens of Ur died, they were accompanied by whatever they would need for their palaces in the netherworld, including those persons who had attended them in life. The retainers who were buried with the kings and queens were thereby assured of a "less nebulous and miserable existence in the afterworld than was the lot of men dying in the ordinary way."[22]

In a more recent study, S. Pollock followed one facet of Woolley's explanation, emphasizing the inclusion of retainers in the burials of the kings and queens as an "extreme form of display of the power of certain individuals . . . over the lives of others."[23] Other scholars turned to religious rituals to explain the inclusion of retainers in the burials of Ur's kings and queens. Anton Moortgat, for example, drew on the myths of the dying fertility god Tammuz, so well known from the Mediterranean world, in arguing that the occupants of Ur's royal tombs may well have been kings and queens who had taken the parts of Dumuzi and Inanna in the New Year's sacred marriage rites. The purpose of the sacred marriage was to assure the fertility of the land.[24] As P. R. S. Moorey writes, "The key to these graves at Ur . . . may not lie so much with matters of 'royalty or monarchy' as we today conceive them, as with a cult practice special to Ur, relating particularly to the god Nanna."[25]

Some surviving written sources purport to describe the deaths of kings and the construction of palaces in the netherworld, as do texts that include slaves along with other goods and commodities buried with high-ranking persons (see p. 28). Nevertheless, no evidence exists for the deification of Early Dynastic kings, and with the exception of a few short royal inscriptions, little is known about Ur's Early Dynastic rulers or its particular traditions of kingship, including, for example, the royal relationship to the cult of the moon

god, Nanna. The sacred marriage remains poorly understood as a phenomenon. Moreover, Early Dynastic rulers may or may not have taken part in the sacred marriage. Later inscriptions indicate that certain of Uruk's Early Dynastic rulers participated in the ritual, but those references may well be anachronistic.[26]

Charles Redman proposed a somewhat different explanation for the Royal Cemetery's elaborate burials. He suggested that the Royal Cemetery reflected changes in the organization of Early Dynastic city-states. In the earlier part of the Early Dynastic and the preceding Jamdat Nasr periods, temple elites held power; by the later Early Dynastic period, written evidence and the appearance of palaces suggest that a secular elite was becoming dominant. At such a critical juncture in the evolution of leadership, kings may have been powerful enough to accumulate great wealth during their reigns, but kingship as an institution was not sufficiently strong and regularized to maintain itself. Rituals were needed to maintain the authority of the king during periods of succession. The ritual destruction of great wealth (human, animal, and artifactual) would have brought recognition to the survivors and heirs and helped to maintain their elite social status.[27] Redman's explanation is interesting, but it remains speculative. Although historians and archaeologists commonly accept that the Mesopotamian palace is a later development than the temple, the evidence for such an assertion is equivocal. Even if the existence of palaces could be demonstrated, that fact in and of itself would say little about the evolution of leadership in early Mesopotamia.[28]

If no particular explanation of the Royal Cemetery of Ur is completely convincing in our state of ignorance about early Mesopotamian society, it is perhaps worth emphasizing that similar practices are widely attested in human cultures across time and space. For Early Dynastic Egypt,[29]

his account.[36] Nor was the practice confined to the Old World, as pre-Columbian finds at Sitio Conte in Panama attest.[37] The burials of retainers with elites was likewise a deeply rooted Andean tradition, and perhaps best illustrated by the royal tombs of Sipan.[38] A cross-cultural study might well lead to a better understanding of Ur's royal tombs.

※　※　※

The Ur excavations are a remarkable story, and Woolley's prize find, the Early Dynastic Royal Cemetery, is one of the greatest archaeological discoveries ever made. Its excavation was no easy task. The soil matrix into which the tombs were cut was composed of dumped rubbish, soft and unstable. The sides of excavation pits collapsed on more than one occasion, once burying two workmen, killing one.[39] An area like the Royal Cemetery, which had been continually dug up and backfilled over a long period of time, would present any excavator with a stratigraphic nightmare of pits within pits within pits. In reading Woolley's field notes, reports, and publications, we might legitimately raise questions. Nevertheless, Woolley's recovery of artifacts from the cemetery's royal tombs still stands as an extraordinary technical achievement, all the more remarkable when one realizes that Woolley and his wife, Katherine, or one other assistant did all the detailed digging themselves (fig. 27). Woolley's own words perhaps best tell the tale:

> The clearing of the vast cemetery kept us busy for many months and from beginning to end there was not a day which would not have been a red-letter day in an ordinary excavation; if one remembers specially the royal tombs it was not so much because others were unexciting as because of the extra labor involved. . . .
>
> . . . In one death-pit there were laid

Fig. 27. Katherine and Leonard Woolley (top left) cleaning the lyres in PG 1237. Photo: University of Pennsylvania Museum Archives.

for example, the tombs located on Umm al-Qa'ab at Abydos provide particularly convincing evidence of a royal entourage buried with the king.[30] This burial arrangement is likewise documented at Kerma in Nubia, for a time period contemporary with the Egyptian Middle Kingdom;[31] in Sudan in the Middle Ages;[32] and all over west and central Africa, apparently until as late as the nineteenth century.[33] In Early Dynastic China, many of those buried with Shang kings and queens may represent the human sacrifices so abundantly recorded in oracle bone inscriptions, although some— for example, those with halberds and dogs placed at the bottom of the burial pit, below the wooden tomb chamber—could plausibly be interpreted as guards.[34] Herodotus described the practice among the Scythians;[35] an unlooted tomb of a Scythian chieftain found recently in the Ukraine and dated to the mid-fourth century BC has provided vivid confirmation of out in rows the bodies of sixty-four court ladies. . . . We did not know how many of them there were, but the sides of the pit had been traced and then at the bottom, strands of gold ribbon showed, first in one spot and then in another.

Most of the workmen were sent away and the few pickmen who were left were told to clear away the earth down to the gold, but no farther, and then they too were sent off so that the final work with knives and brushes could be done by my wife and myself in comparative peace. For ten days the two of us spent most of the time from sunrise to sunset lying on our tummies brushing and blowing and threading beads in their order as they lay. . . . You might suppose that to find three-score women all richly be-decked with jewelry would be a very thrilling experience, and so it is, in retro-spect, but I'm afraid that at the moment one is much more conscious of the toil than of the thrill.[40]

Woolley was a genius not only at get-ting artifacts out of the ground (fig. 28), but also at reconstructing them. H. R. Hall bragged of Woolley's reconstruction of the "ram-in-a-thicket" in a letter to Horace Jayne:

You will I think like your share of last years finds, especially the lyre with the silver stag among the copper 'bul-rushes', which is my favorite among your things: I was sorry to let it go! The 'ram' (really a goat, of the markhor type) 'in the thicket' (I think it is really eating a plant in the usual goat-fashion,

but then I am not romantic) is a really wonderful piece of construction (or rather re-conditioning) of Woolley's: he is easily first in the way he produces his things for exhibition, and so far as tech-nique is concerned I consider him the first of our excavators. He will restore our goat in the same way.[41]

Woolley was a man of legendary stam-ina; he routinely stayed in his office at Ur until 2 or 3 AM when he had to be back on the mound half an hour after sunrise.[42] In a real sense, the Royal Cemetery, a previously unknown chapter in Ur's long history, exists today not just because of the effective collaboration between two museums but also because of Woolley's extraordinary energy and talent.

Fig. 28. Perhaps nothing better demonstrates Wool-ley's skill in getting artifacts out of the ground than the plaster lyre from the simple inhumation PG 1151. Imme-diately against the foot of the grave's wooden coffin, Woolley noticed two rectan-gular holes, about 85 centi-meters apart, angling down into the soil for about 80 centimeters and connected at the top by a horizontal hole, round in section and slightly curved. He inserted wooden sticks and wires and poured liquid plaster around them. When he cleared the soil from around the hardened plaster, he uncovered a complete lyre, with the copper head of a cow and a shell plaque at-tached to the sound box. The plaster even reproduced the instrument's ten strings, although the wind quickly blew all trace of them away. Photo: University of Penn-sylvania Museum Archives.

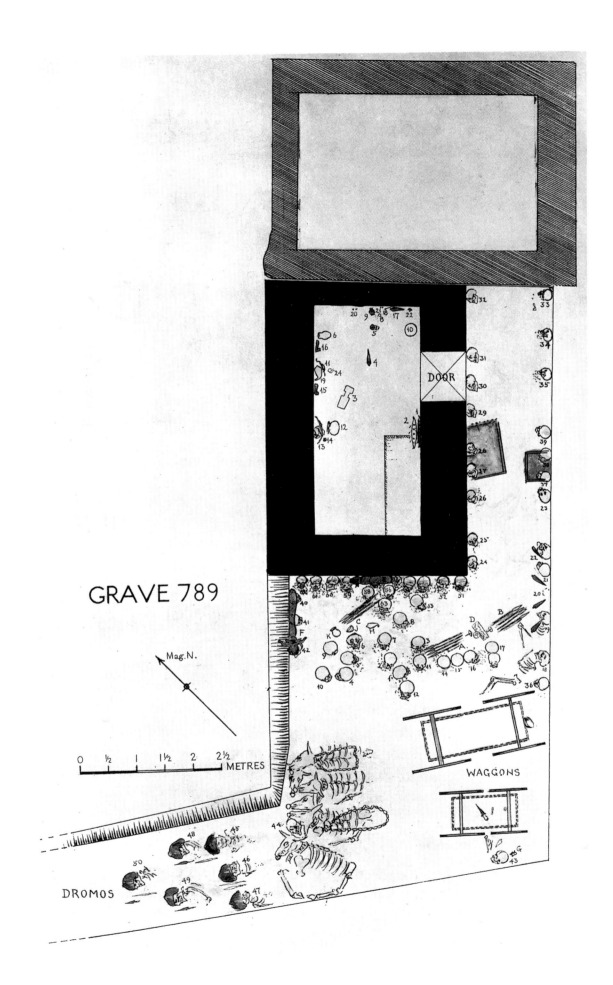

GRAVE 789

Mag.N.

0 ½ 1 1½ 2 2½
METRES

DOOR

WAGGONS

DROMOS

CHAPTER FOUR

The Burials of a King and Queen

Richard L. Zettler

Fig. 30. Southeast wall of the tomb chamber of PG 789 seen from the outside. The brick arch of the blocked doorway is visible in the front of the photograph; the remains of the brick vaulting of the tomb chamber are visible in the upper center. Photo: University of Pennsylvania Museum Archives.

OPPOSITE Fig. 29. Plan of PG 789, called by Woolley the "King's Grave." The hatched rectangle at the top of the plan shows the location of Puabi's tomb chamber. Reprinted from Woolley 1934b: pl. 29.

Many of the most important artifacts described in this catalogue come from just two of the royal burials, PG 789 and PG 800. Relatively well preserved and with rich material inventories, they typified for Woolley the Early Dynastic royal tombs. We now know that the relationship between these tombs and their death pits is questionable, but we still recognize the tombs as the final resting places of royalty. PG 789 may indeed have held a king, whose name we will never be certain of; PG 800 held a queen named Puabi.

The burials, with their adjacent tomb chambers and overlapping death pits, come from the northeast end of the cemetery. PG 789's pit, oriented northeast by southwest, was a rectangle measuring 10 by 5 meters.[1] It was entered via a ramp on the northwest side at the west corner; Woolley's plan (fig. 29) indicates that the ramp was preserved and traced for a length of approximately 3.60 meters. The floor of the pit lay 8.30 meters below the surface. The earthen sides of the open pit were hidden by a dado of reed matting, which also covered the floor. (Although reed matting is seldom preserved, it is sometimes recognizable in digging as a fine white powder that preserves impressions of the reeds.) Woolley does not say to what height the sides of the pit were preserved. The tomb chamber proper stood in the north corner, against the northwest side of the pit. It consisted of a single room measuring 4.00 by 1.80 meters, with a door in the southeast wall. Its walls were made of limestone rubble, plastered both inside and out with mud. The chamber's roof, made of baked bricks, consisted for the most part of a barrel vault formed by contiguous ring arches, but the ends were apsidal half-domes supported on pendentives (fig. 30). The doorway was arched with baked brick.

PG 789's tomb chamber had been robbed in antiquity and was thoroughly looted, probably, as Woolley postulated, at the time of the construction of PG 800. Among the artifacts left by the robbers were a silver model boat (U.10566) and a gaming

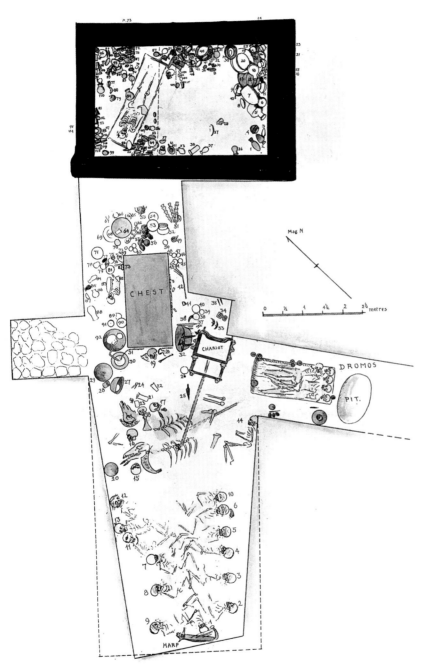

board (U.10557), both now in the Iraq Museum.

PG 789's death pit was undisturbed. At the foot of the access ramp were the bodies of six soldiers, wearing copper helmets and carrying spears. In the pit just in front of the entrance were two wagons, each drawn by three oxen. The wagons had apparently been backed down the ramp, as the oxen faced the entry to the pit. By the animals' heads was a body, identified by Woolley as a groom. To the side of one wagon and behind the other were two additional bodies, presumably the drivers. To the northeast of the wagons, the floor of the pit was covered with bodies, fifty-four in all. Half-leaning against the southwest wall of the pit was a row of women, described by Woolley as the "most richly adorned of all in the pit." Of the rest, many were women, but others, especially those who lined the narrow passage to the door of the tomb chamber, were men. Few of the bodies were well preserved, and Woolley based his identification of gender largely on accoutrements found with the bodies. Animal bones found in the center of the passage to the tomb chamber door presumably represented the remains of food offerings. Finds of particular importance in the tomb pit included what Woolley identified as a copper shield, found with two sets of spears; its repoussé relief shows lions trampling fallen enemies (cat. no. 13). A wooden lyre rested on the head of one of the women found against the southwest wall of the tomb chamber. A second stood over the tops of the bodies at the northwest side of the pit. The sounding box of the second lyre was decorated with the head of a bearded bull in gold and lapis lazuli, below which were shell plaques (cat. no. 3). Large lumps of unworked lapis lazuli lay in the south corner of the pit.

What Woolley identified as PG 800's death pit (fig. 31) lay directly over PG 789. It would presumably have been cut down into the shaft of PG 789. The pit was

Fig. 31. Plan of PG 800, Puabi's tomb. The tomb chamber, containing Puabi's bier, body, and three attendants, is at the top of the plan; the death pit, with wooden chest or wardrobe, chariot, oxen, and more attendants, is at the bottom. Reprinted from Woolley 1934b: pl. 36.

oriented northeast to southwest and approximated a rectangle measuring 11.75 by 4.00 meters.[2] Although Woolley's sketch section shows the sides of the death pit preserved quite high (2–3 meters at the southwest end of the pit and 4–5 meters at the northeast end), his description states that "the outlines of the shaft were extremely difficult to follow and were defined . . . by the position of objects in the pit."[3] The floor of the pit sloped down approximately 50 centimeters from northeast to southwest. The pit floor had been covered by mats. A dado of reed mats existed on the sides of the pit, but as Woolley was quick to note, traces could be found only in the few spots where the sides themselves could be distinguished. Traces of reed matting were also found over the artifacts and people in the pit. The pit was entered via a ramp leading down from the southsoutheast. Woolley's plan of PG 800 shows the ramp preserved for a maximum length of approximately 4.75 meters.

The tomb chamber Woolley associated with PG 800's death pit was located to the northeast, but unlike PG 789's tomb chamber, its floor was not on the same level as the death pit. Its floor was in fact 1.70 meters below the floor of the death pit, meaning that the tomb chamber's roof was flush with the floor of the death pit. PG 800's tomb chamber had been built abutting that of PG 789. As Woolley's monthly reports make clear, he first discovered PG 800's death pit, and in excavating it, he discovered PG 789. In the process of excavating PG 789, he uncovered the tomb chamber he later associated with PG 800's death pit.

PG 800's tomb chamber, similar to PG 789's in terms of construction, measured 4.35 by 2.80 meters. Woolley was unable to find a doorway in its walls and so accessed it through the largely collapsed roof. According to Sir Arthur Keith, one of Britain's premier physical anthropologists of the time, the principal body was that of a

woman just under five feet tall and roughly forty at the time of her death.[4] She was apparently on a bier that lay askew across the northwestern end of the chamber. Her body was adorned with an elaborate headdress (fig. 32, cat. no. 29); the whole of her upper body was covered with beads of gold, silver, lapis lazuli, carnelian, and agate— the remains of a beaded cape (cat. no. 31); a broad belt of gold, carnelian, and lapis lazuli tubular beads, from which were suspended gold rings, lay at her waist. Against her upper right arm were three pins, which probably secured a garment. With the pins were amulets and three cylinder seals, one of which had an inscription that identified her as Puabi, the queen. On Puabi's fingers were ten gold rings; around her right knee was a garter. To the left of the bier and near her head, on what Woolley suggested might be a shelf or small table, was a diadem or belt made of small lapis lazuli beads that had been decorated with gold ornaments (cat. no. 30). Placed across her body was a silver pouring cup.

Three attendants were in the tomb with Puabi. One, near the side of the bier, was perhaps a male, judging by the daggers and whetstone found with the body. Another, near the foot of the bier, was likely

Fig. 33. Field photograph of the northeast end of Puabi's death pit. The outline of the wooden wardrobe chest is visible in the left center of the photograph; some of the artifacts that surrounded the chest such as the calcite spouted jar (cat. no. 129), silver bowls, and tumblers are visible in the center of the photograph. Photo: University of Pennsylvania Museum Archives.

a woman. The fragmentary skull of the third attendant was against the southwest wall of the tomb chamber.

An enormous array of artifacts existed around three sides of the chamber; only the south corner was uncluttered. Woolley speculated that some objects had been placed on the floor. He argued that others had been stacked on shelves, since he found them high up in the fill of the chamber.

Puabi's death pit presented a scene similar to that of PG 789. On the ramp leading into the pit were the bodies of five men, presumably guards, with copper daggers, a razor, and seven pottery cups. In the middle of the pit, in front of the ramp down which it had apparently been driven, was a sled pulled by what Woolley originally identified as two asses, but which have more recently been identified as two oxen.[5] Mixed with the animals' bones were those of four grooms, three of whom wore either a beaded necklace or headband and a single gold or silver earring. Each carried a dagger and/or razor and a whetstone. The fourth body had a beaded headband and a cylinder seal inscribed with the name Lugal-shà-pà-da; he carried a spear. A fifth body lay

near the equids' hooves, against the corner of the entrance.

In the middle of the northeast end of the pit were the remains of a wooden chest measuring 2.25 by 1.10 meters, decorated with lapis lazuli and shell inlay. The wood of the chest had decayed, as had its contents—no doubt because, as Woolley probably correctly speculated, they had been made of organic materials. The chest had probably contained textiles. Against the wardrobe's southeast end was the body of a man wearing a single gold earring and a headband composed of gold chains and gold and carnelian beads. He had with him a dagger and two whetstones. Woolley speculated that he may have been the keeper of the wardrobe. Bodies with no personal possessions lay near the north corner and at the northeast end of the chest. An enormous array of goods surrounded the wardrobe (fig. 33)—in fact, these constituted the overwhelming majority of artifacts in the death pit. Some of these objects are included in this catalogue: gold and silver vessels, including the electrum tumbler (cat. no. 105) and gold spouted bowl (cat. no. 96); a spouted cup made of lapis lazuli (cat. no. 120) and a carved steatite bowl (cat. no. 121); silver heads of lions (cat. no. 1) that had originally decorated a piece of furniture; a lapis lazuli cylinder seal inscribed with the name A-bára-ge (cat. no. 18); and a cosmetic box with inlaid lid (cat. no. 12) showing a lion attacking a goat.

When Woolley cleared the northeast end of PG 800's death pit, directly under the wardrobe chest he found the broken roof of PG 789's tomb chamber. He described the find and his conclusions in one of his monthly reports:

> In my last report I described a large grave area which yielded many fine objects, but failed to produce the actual tomb and body of the principal person: among these objects was a wooden chest which I assumed to be a clothes-box. When the box was removed there were found below it bricks which proved to come from the arched roof of a stone and brick-built tomb; it had been plundered from above and the box served to conceal the hole made by the plunderers.[6]

Woolley was confident that PG 789 had been robbed during the construction of PG 800. His conclusion raises the possibility that many of the artifacts surrounding the wardrobe chest in PG 800's death pit had originally been in PG 789's tomb chamber and had been conveniently recycled.

At the southwest end of PG 800's death pit lay the bodies of ten women. These women, all of whom wore elaborate headdresses, had apparently been positioned in two rows facing each other. Musical instruments were found with the women. Woolley originally suggested that one of the women lay with the bones of her hands actually in place on the strings of a harp. Reconsideration of the curious instrument Woolley had reconstructed showed that he had actually uncovered not a harp but a harp and a lyre that had collapsed into one (fig. 34).[7]

Woolley explained PG 800's configuration with his usual ingenuity. The plundered tomb, PG 789, had been that of a distant and unknown king of Ur. PG 800 was that of his queen, Puabi, who died after him, but who so loved him in life that she wanted to be near him in death. She was herself important enough that her burial still had to have an independent shaft and individual sacrifices.

PG 789 and PG 800 provided the grist for Woolley's accounts of what happened at the death of Ur's kings and queens:

> We must imagine the burial in the chamber to be complete and the door sealed; there remains the open pit with its mat-lined walls and mat-covered floor, empty and unfurnished. Now down the sloping passage comes a procession of people, the members of the court, soldiers, men-servants, and women, the latter in all their finery of brightly colored garments and headdresses of lapis-lazuli and silver and gold, and with them musicians bearing harps or lyres, cymbals, and sistra; they take up their positions in the farther part of the pit and then there are driven or backed down the slope the chariots

Fig. 34. A harp and the sound box of a lyre found collapsed into each other against the southwest wall of Puabi's death pit. Woolley mistook the two for a single instrument. Photo: University of Pennsylvania Museum Archives.

Fig. 35. Reconstruction of
the scene in PG 789 just
before the death of the
royal retainers. *Illustrated
London News,* June 23, 1928,
pp. 1172–74.

drawn by oxen or by asses, the drivers in
the cars, the grooms holding the heads
of the draught animals, and these too
are marshaled in the pit. Each man and
woman brought a little cup of clay or
stone or metal, the only equipment required for the rite that was to follow.
Some kind of service there must have
been at the bottom of the shaft, at least
it is evident that the musicians played
up to the last, and that each drank from
the cup; either they brought the potion
with them or they found it prepared for
them on the spot—in PG 1237 there was
in the middle of the pit a great copper
pot into which they could have dipped—
and they composed themselves for
death. Then someone came down and

killed the animals and perhaps arranged
the drugged bodies, and when that was
done earth was flung from above on
them, and the filling-in of the grave
shaft was begun.[8]

Woolley skillfully unraveled the archaeological facts presented by PG 789
(fig. 35) and the death pit and tomb chamber he dubbed PG 800. Nevertheless, his
interpretation of those facts and his en-
dearing tale about the relationship of the
occupants of the two tombs is not beyond
question (see p. 39). In many ways, the
tombs of Ur's Early Dynastic Royal Cemetery remain as much a puzzle to archaeologists today as when they were first
uncovered.

Two Tombs or Three?

Paul Zimmerman

Woolley's reconstruction of the relationship between tombs PG 789 and PG 800 tells a touching tale, but in fact no evidence exists to support a connection between PG 800's death pit and the tomb chamber Woolley associated with it. The floor of the PG 800 death pit lay 1.70 meters above the floor of the PG 800 tomb chamber—the top of the chamber was at about the same elevation as the floor of the death pit. The floor of PG 800's chamber, was 40 centimeters lower than the floor of PG 789's death pit and chamber (Woolley 1934b). Woolley first uncovered the death pit he assigned to PG 800, then PG 789's tomb chamber and death pit, and last the chamber he associated with PG 800's death pit—PG 800's tomb chamber was discovered because of its relationship with PG 789, not because of its relationship with its supposed death pit.

Woolley admitted that he had difficulty in defining the edges of PG 800's death pit (Woolley 1934b: 73). Excavation of the pit stopped about 50 centimeters from the outermost edge of the southwestern wall of the chamber. In the northeastern end of the death pit, excavation ceased 1.10 meters from the easternmost corner of the wardrobe box. Although the earth between this stopping point and the chamber was later cleared, Woolley does not mention any artifacts as having come from it.

Woolley found no doorway into PG 800's tomb chamber and assumed that access was from above, with the roof being constructed only after Puabi's interment. He recounts evidence of mud brick and a possible arch in the "west end of the south-west side" of the chamber (Woolley 1934b: 831). This must be a typographical error, because his notes show mud brick in the southern end of the southwestern wall. Woolley probably meant either "west face of the south-west side" or "south end of the south-west side" of the chamber. His notes state that bricks set "slantwise on edge" were found in this location. What Woolley had perhaps discovered and not recognized was a collapsed arch over the doorway and/or a blocking of the door similar to that of PG 789's tomb chamber (Woolley 1934b: 63).

A doorway near the southern end of the southwestern wall of PG 800 is further supported by the distribution of artifacts within the tomb chamber (see Woolley 1934b: pl. 36). Artifacts were piled high along the northeastern and southeastern walls but relatively few were in the western corner of the tomb chamber.

If there is a doorway in PG 800's chamber, it would not have provided direct access to the death pit that lay 1.70 meters above. A doorway would not have provided access without disturbing the bodies in PG 789's death pit. Therefore, PG 800's chamber must predate PG 789's.

If PG 800's death pit and chamber did not belong together, where was Puabi's tomb's death pit? Since the floor of PG 800's tomb is 40 centimeters lower than that of PG 789 (Woolley 1934b: 84), the floor of its real death pit may have been at the same level below the floor of PG 789's pit. Woolley never excavated below the floor of PG 789's death pit. Although 40 centimeters is not a great depth, it is sufficient to conceal skeletons and all but the largest artifacts.

If Woolley's reconstruction is not correct, what was the relationship between PG 789 and PG 800? Based on their architectural similarity and their spatial juxtaposition, we can assume, as Woolley had, that these two tomb chambers are close in time and might belong to a king and queen. The doorway and lower floor in PG 800's chamber suggest that this tomb predates PG 789 and that its death pit remains unexcavated. PG 800's death pit then would not be Puabi's, but would belong to an undiscovered or destroyed tomb of some unknown royal person. Woolley's PG 789 and PG 800 then provide a sequence of not two but three royal burials.

CATALOGUE

The rosette to the left of the catalogue
entry title indicates an object from PG 800,
Queen Puabi's tomb.

Art

Art of the Royal Tombs of Ur: A Brief Interpretation

Donald P. Hansen

Without the Royal Cemetery of Ur, our knowledge of the art of the Sumerians in the middle of the third millennium BC would be severely limited. This art, which sometimes appears flamboyant and at other times seems sublime, is composed of objects manufactured from different raw materials. Since these objects were intended to accompany the dead on the route to the underworld and in the afterlife, many were probably made specifically for the burials or tombs in which they were found. These include weapons and headgear of a ceremonial nature as well as an inordinate amount of jewelry that not only decorated the body of the deceased and affirmed status but was also intended as necessary gifts to assuage the wants and needs of the demons and gods residing in the netherworld. Other objects differ little from those found in nonburial contexts; they were placed in the graves to assist in the maintenance of an afterlife. Many are identical to votive gifts found in contemporary temples. All art from the Royal Cemetery is best seen as functional art: it was used as adornment for the body and as decoration on containers used to hold food and drink; it was added to furniture or enhanced magnificent musical instruments used to accompany the chanting of hymns or songs of praise.

Whether one chooses to view the cemetery as the burials of members of the royal families, or as interments of participants in rites connected with the moon god, Nanna, the main god and owner of the city of Ur, or as some combination of the above, this is an art associated with a very elite class of residents of Ur. Efficacy of intent and heightened awareness of content is achieved through the use of extremely precious materials such as gold, silver, lapis lazuli, agate, carnelian, conch shells, and copper obtainable only through a complex system of trade and barter that linked Sumer to such distant fringes of the known world as Egypt, Anatolia, Iran, the Gulf regions (including the Gulf of Oman), the Indus, and even Central Asia.

Some of the most spectacular works of art preserved from

Fig. 36a,b. The Standard of Ur. Shell, lapis lazuli, and red limestone. L. 47 cm, H. 20 cm. British Museum WA 121201 (U.11164). Courtesy of the British Museum.

Sumerian times are found in this cemetery. The artists had a particular adeptness in depicting fauna, whether these creatures be of the tamed domestic type, the beasts of the wild, or those imaginative, evocative creations of composite human and animal. These artists developed the skills that abstracted the essence of an individual species and presented the forms in an impeccable blend of abstract shapes coupled with naturalistic observation and detail. Perfect examples are the silver lion head (cat. no. 1) and silver bull head (cat. no. 2) from Puabi's tomb—life is infused into these heads by

the visually demanding contrast of lapis lazuli and shell that inlay the eyes, the seat of vitality and life. A long tradition stands behind these naturalistic sculptures, going back to the beginnings of Sumerian art during the Uruk and Jamdat Nasr periods, a time when writing first developed, large city-states came into existence, and an art evolved that focused on real observations of different aspects of the bodies of humans and animals. This development occurred primarily in the city of Uruk toward the end of the fourth millennium BC and remained a strong element in the art that followed. Almost subsumed by a new interest in abstract art in the second quarter of the third millennium BC that curiously seems to have evolved from techniques inherent in carving images in clay, the Sumerian artists never lost command of this naturalistic bent. Although the more angular abstract style, with sharp transitions between planes, coexisted for some time with the more naturalistic, it is not represented to any real degree in the art of the Royal Cemetery.

The ability to translate keen observations of the animal and human worlds into art in media other than sculpture in the round is evidenced by the artists' use of cutout pieces of shell with incised drawings. These shell pieces were used either as complete individual panels or as part of larger compositions in the form of mosaics. The former is best represented by the magnificent front panel from the Great Lyre of PG 789 (cat. no. 3). Animals such as the lion, the hyena, the jackal, the bear, and the wild ass are represented with an assured deftness and are defined with a great economy of means. These beasts are the creatures of the wild, of unknown and distant realms, and they are depicted in the form of human actors in the weighty drama of the underworld. This banquet is found in more human and abbreviated form on the small lyre from PG 1332 (cat. no. 5), on which the main participant is shown seated and approached by attendants of a lesser rank dressed in simpler garments. Here the individual shell pieces function as inlays and are fitted into a background of variously shaped fragments of vivid, deep blue lapis lazuli.

The most detailed and compositionally involved object created using this mosaic technique is the so-called Standard of Ur[1] (fig. 36a,b), found in tomb PG 779 in the Royal Cemetery. It is one of the most important objects from the cemetery. The two side panels and both ends of this originally wooden box were covered with three regis-

ters of both figurative and geometric mosaics formed of pieces of shell, lapis lazuli, and red limestone set into bitumen. The box is of irregular shape; the end pieces are truncated triangles, making the box wider at the bottom than at the top. Because it was found lying close to the shoulder of a man who may have held the object on a pole, it was called a "standard" by Woolley, and this name has remained associated with the box even though there is no real evidence to support this assumption.

One side panel (fig. 36a) depicts aspects of a battle and its aftermath. The most important person, probably the ruler, is shown in the center of the top register. His importance is signified by the fact that he is taller than the rest of the figures in the scene; indeed, his height is emphasized by the way his head projects appropriately out of the register into the framing geometric border above. Behind him is his chariot, drawn by four onagers, or wild asses, and before him nude and bound prisoners are presented by a few of his soldiers. In the second register, a phalanx of almost identical armed soldiers creating a repetitive rhythm are contrasted with soldiers in a variety of poses dispatching enemies and leading off prisoners. The king's chariotry is depicted in the lower register. Each four-wheeled chariot carries a charioteer and a warrior and is drawn by four onagers, indicated by the parallel lines that echo the tails, heads, and legs of the nearest animals. In representing harnessed animals, Sumerian artists usually emphasized and exaggerated the terret, or rein ring, which could be either plain, as shown on the Standard of Ur and elsewhere (see, for example, cat. no. 139), or could be topped by an animal, as is seen on the rein ring of Puabi in the British Museum (see fig. 52). The latter terret of silver has a magnificently executed onager in electrum surmounting the double ring.[2] On the "standard," a rhythm is established by the change of gait of the asses from left to right: the onagers on the left are walking, the next group is cantering, and the final group proceeds at a full gallop. The more rapidly moving chariots all show a naked and dead enemy lying prone beneath the legs of the asses, a compositional scheme so effective that it lasted as a signifier of impending victory both in war and in the royal hunt into the first millennium BC. Their nakedness, as well as that of the prisoners in the registers above, signifies that these figures are degraded, deprived of identity, and impotent. Their debasement is further emphasized by the large, bleeding gashes on their chests and thighs, a simple but effective device indicating defeat.

The other side of the "standard" presents a completely different theme. The turbulence of battle and variety of rhythms on the one side is set against the serenity and slow progression of men and animals on the other. A banquet is depicted in the upper register, but it is not a funeral banquet. A variety of banquets were celebrated for different but related purposes in the cult dramas of Sumer, and this one held in association with men bringing forth produce and animals had a specific meaning. The organization of this side of the "standard" places the primary cultic scene in the top register, above other registers showing

men, animals, and foodstuff. This arrangement naturally brings to mind the ordering of the registers in a much older cult object, the great vase of Protoliterate Uruk made at the end of the fourth millennium BC (fig. 37a,b); both the vase and this side of the "standard" deal with variants of the same central concerns of life in Sumer. On the vase, all nature—represented visually along the bottom of the vase as water, essential for the fecundity of the flora and fauna above it—is dependent on the enactment of the marriage between the goddess and her consort shown symbolically on the top. The goddess, or her priestly representative, receives her bridegroom at the door of the storehouse dwelling, an act that anticipates the consummation on which life is dependent. Whether the female figure is the goddess herself or her representative is unimportant; in an enactment of the drama, the participant becomes the godhead.

The principal banqueter on the "standard" is joined by seven other participants, all of whom hold cups in their right hands.[3] Three standing attendants administer to the banqueters, who enjoy the accompanying music of the lyre and perhaps the intoned words of a figure with long hair who may be a singer. The main figure is distinguished from the others, who are intended to be seen as seated before him in either a straight line or a partial circle, again by his larger size and by his flounced or fleecy skirt. It seems reasonable to assume that this figure represents the same ruler depicted on the other side of the "standard"; there he is shown in battle dress and helmet, and here he is shown bald-headed and partaking in a banquet with distinct religious overtones. It is of interest that the ruler of Lagash, Enmetena, whose statue was found at Ur, had himself portrayed in sculpture in the round dressed only in a flounced skirt in an attitude of prayer before the god Enlil.[4]

Fig. 37a,b. Carved alabaster vase (with detail of top register) from Protoliterate Uruk, late fourth millennium BC. H. 92 cm. Iraq Museum, Baghdad. IM19606. Courtesy of Hirmer Verlag, Munich.

The second register introduces the bountifulness of the land with bald-headed Sumerians wearing full, fringed skirts leading bulls and other animals and carrying fish. These animals symbolize the pasturelands and the marshes, distinct regions of southern Sumer ruled over by gods of fertility. A male figure standing behind the bull on the left-hand side of the register has a beard and a full head of black hair topped by a scalloped headdress. His skirt is short, and his belt differs from the belts on the other figures to his right. The implication is that he and the damaged figures behind him are the vanguard of the remainder of the procession in the bottom register. These men for the most part are differently dressed and coiffed. Some carry produce in bags on their shoulders, others carry heavy backpacks supported by headbands, and still others lead asses by ropes attached to nose rings. They come from afar, from the northern parts of Sumer, and probably from the region of Kish north of Nippur. They are meant to signify another bountiful quarter of this land between the two rivers. The registers represent what later Sumerian rulers came to call ki-en-gi and ki-uri—that is, Sumer and Akkad.

The dual sides of the Standard of Ur are best seen as the visual expression of the duality of kingship as it existed in the time of the Royal Cemetery in Early Dynastic IIIA. Rulership encompassed two related but very cardinal concepts that might be expressed as "*lugal*-ship" and "*en*-ship." The former dealt with the ruler's role as warrior, the mighty male and protector of his city-state, and the latter was concerned with his role as priest and mediator between man and gods, the one responsible for the fecundity of the land. These pregnant ideas that position the ruler at the core of life are splendidly developed in the iconography of the war themes shown on the one side and the banquet and produce themes presented on the other side of this justly famed work from the Royal

Cemetery. That ideas of kingship are expressed here reinforces the idea that this is indeed a royal burial.

The love of the bright contrasting colors of precious and semiprecious materials seen in the mosaics of objects such as the Standard of Ur or in the commanding bull's head of the Great Lyre (cat. no. 3) naturally also found expression in articles chosen for the decoration of the body in the form of necklaces, earrings, bracelets, and other types of jewelry made of gold, silver, copper, lapis lazuli, carnelian, agate, shell, and copper. Although most of the jewelry was worn by the principal figures and their attendants, much was carried by the deceased into the netherworld to be used as gifts and bribes for the gods and demons who inhabited these otherworldly regions. Many pieces were of a "grand" design, such as the cape of Puabi, which was made of multiple strands of beads (cat. no. 31) that, if worn as regal paraphernalia by a living queen, would have shimmered delightfully and emitted a gentle sound produced by the beads striking together as she walked. Some of the headdresses had complex wreaths of gold imitations of poplar and willow leaves; other jewelry sets were made of gold amulets representing plant and floral elements.

The richness of the precious articles worn for the passing into the underworld is overwhelming. Certain pieces of jewelry can be associated with images derived from myth, for example, the necklace with gold and lapis lazuli flies (cat. no. 69) mentioned in the Atrahasis myth concerning the flood. The goddess states: "Let these flies be lapis around my neck."[5] The flies seem to be associated with death, but for the most part we cannot ascertain a definite meaning for the individual stones used by the artisans in Early Dynastic Sumer. That jewels could be miraculous, inspiring, and beautiful is evidenced in *The Epic of Gilgamesh* by the special garden at the gate of sunrise with trees of precious stones bearing their fruits.

Fig. 38a,b. Seal (with modern impression) of the Uruk period, supposedly from near Uruk. Berlin VA 10537. Courtesy of the Vorderasiatisches Museum, Berlin.

The carnelian bears its fruit;
It is hung with vines good to look at.
The lapis bears *foliage;*
It, too, bears fruit lush to behold.[6]

Furthermore, the jewelry of Inanna, the great goddess of fertility and battle —encompassing the dual aspects of kingship—was very special. In her descent into the netherworld, Inanna discards at each of the seven gates her crown, necklaces, stones worn at her breast, and other items of her precious apparel, emblems of her identity.

We know that in much later times, particular stones had certain magical qualities, and that some even had medicinal healing powers. Perhaps the early Sumerians believed in this potency of stones. During the somewhat later Third Dynasty of Ur, toward the end of the third millennium BC, chips of the same stones used for the jewelry were placed in the foundation boxes of temples along with a statue of the king shown as builder.[7] In the Old Babylonian period, prior to the reconstruction of the Bagara temple of Ningirsu at Lagash, the ground was leveled and then purified by scattering semiprecious stone chips over the prepared surface.[8] Such rituals clearly indicate that the individual kinds of stone had significance and suggest that the precious materials of the jewelry likewise had a function other than a solely decorative one.

The iconography of the art in the Royal Cemetery is complex. Since we do not have contemporary textual materials that might aid in elucidating what the Sumerian artists intended in their representations and designs, much of the meaning remains opaque. Undoubtedly, a variety of connotations were attached to certain works and a plurality of associated perceptions were possible, depending on the artists who made the objects and the positions held by viewers from diverse social strata of elite Sumerian society. The iconography also appears to be composed of several fused and overlapping concepts, so any precise definition of a particular work might be entirely misleading or even naively simplistic. Nevertheless, certain basic concepts emerged in Sumerian art at the end of the fourth millennium BC, long before the advent of the Royal Cemetery, that remained constant, although altered, throughout the third millennium.

Sumer and the beginnings of complex societies arose in a flat alluvial land devoid of sufficient rainfall for intense cultivation. An intricate system of canals was established whereby enough water was distributed for agricultural needs, but humans and land were still subjected to drought, storms of fearful intensity, and other devastations of the region. Life focused on the problems of producing enough foodstuff such as grains, vegetables, and fruits as well as the animals necessary for sustaining life. The gods were gods concerned with fertility, and the art that evolved was also focused on the visual expression of fertility abstractions. The vase of Uruk mentioned earlier is a major example; a cylinder seal of exceptionally fine carving in Berlin (fig. 38a,b), supposedly acquired near Uruk and dating from the Uruk period, clearly encapsulates the basic concept of fertility as conceived by humans in relation to their gods. On this seal, a grouping of a man and two animals is framed by gateposts with streamers, symbols of the goddess Inanna, that designate the space as one belonging to the goddess and mark the location as one infused with the female principle of creation. The male principle is represented by the central figure—usually identified as a ruler figure, the *en*, or lord—who is clothed in an article of cult significance, the net skirt. No designation or special marking for divinity appears in the art of this period; indeed, the world of humankind and the world of the gods were fused and inseparable, so this figure may well also be Inanna's consort and lover, Dumuzi, a god who was thought to die and resurrect each spring. The bulls, rising on their hind legs, feed on flowers attached to branches held and offered by this male figure. The flowers, or rosettes, are also indicative of the presence of the goddess. Arranged in an exceptionally clear antithetical composition, the duplication of the pictorial elements of gateposts, bulls, and branches (each with four rosettes) serves to intensify the visual impact and meaning of the image. The plant symbolizes the perpetual regeneration of life. The results of this fusion of male and female signifiers is suggested by the jars for the storage of food and by the newborn calf nestled between the backs of Inanna's gateposts.

The beauty of the artist's vision of this fundamental concept—the necessary continuation of plant and animal as well as human life achieved through the powers of the divine—is materialized with great skill through a relatively simple iconographic scheme. Linear and plastic forms are neatly balanced and contrasted. Although the seal probably was used by a special temple office comprised of a group of temple personnel, it is clear that many seals had amuletic and magical properties in their own right. The rolling of the cylinder was efficacious in the sense that it helped to produce the desired message expressed in the carving, or at least the seal impression generated a heightened awareness of the basic concept, much as prayer wheels in other cultures.

In the art of the Royal Cemetery, this idea of plant and animal fertility remained a central concern but usually was expressed in less explicit or condensed representations. A shell plaque in the British Museum (fig. 39), for example, shows two ibex rearing on either side of a tree that emerges from the symbol for earth or mountain. The top of the plant is capped with the rosette of the goddess, and the branches end in ovoid-shaped buds or perhaps fruit, suggesting a stage in the cycle of renewal born of the fusion of the male and female principles. It could be expressed in even simpler form—for example, on the shell pieces of gaming boards (see cat. no. 6), depicting a striding animal or man-animal placed before a plant with enormous buds.

The linking of flora and fauna with the idea of regeneration is most fervently expressed in the composite sculpture of a standing goat physically tied to the golden plant of life by a silver chain (cat. no. 8). This remarkable, multicolored sculpture, often referred to as the "ram caught in a thicket" because it is reminiscent of a biblical image described in the sacrifice of Isaac, shows a rearing male goat, the procreative "ram," with his front legs resting on the branches of a tree or plant. The ends of the branches are alternating rosettes and buds. The same idea underlying the Uruk period seal is implied in this sculpture, one of the most compelling images surviving from ancient Sumer.

Thorkild Jacobsen, in his extraordinarily perceptive analysis of Mesopotamian religion, has pointed out that in literature preserved from later periods it is possible to discern the existence of three major cult dramas: the sacred marriage by which fertility is ensured, lamentations for the loss of fertility with the arrival of the summer and the ensuing period of aridity, and "the battle drama in which a primeval contest for world order against the forces of chaos was refought and rewon."[9] The anxieties expressed in these dramas clearly reflect the same concerns felt by earlier Sumerians, concerns probably voiced in an oral

Fig. 39. Shell plaque from the Royal Cemetery. British Museum (U.10917a). Drawing by Jana Fisher after Woolley 1934b: pl. 100.

tradition if not in literature and poetry, but certainly articulated and made manifest in the visual arts. The focus on ideas of fertility in the first two dramas has been commented on in relation to the early iconography dealing with a variety of compositions with plants and animals. The concerns of the third drama also found expression in Sumerian art and were embodied in an iconography centered on scenes of contest or battle between "heroes," composite man-animals, and pure animals.

Some scholars have suggested that this very complicated iconography was concerned with the protection of the flock from predators, an interpretation that is partially correct but that takes little account of what is actually presented visually. The cylinder seal engravers developed scenes with a complex interlocking of groups composed of heroes, bull-men, bovines, caprids, and felines. Not all these elements need be represented at the same time, but usually a combination of grappling wild and domestic beasts was depicted. A heroic figure, or even a bull-man, either grasps an animal, holds it aloft upside down, or plunges a dagger into its body. The violent action is always shown in progress; the outcome is not in evidence; no one wins. This grouping of figures reflects the eternal and cyclical battle against chaos, between civilized and uncivilized man, between domestic animals and beasts of the wild, between periods of peaceful fecundity and the vagaries of nature, between the known and the unknown. It is probably to be viewed or comprehended on different levels with different nuances of meaning.

The contest scene was an apt choice for royal seals. It appears on the Royal Cemetery seals of Meskalamdug and Akalamdug as well as on the slightly later seals of Mesannepada and A'annepada of the First Dynasty of Ur. On a seal of Eannatum, a ruler of Lagash contemporary with Mesannepada (fig. 40), the unresolved battle between the hero and the bull-man is

probably intended on a different, more psychological plane—that is, the semi-divine hero and ruler struggles with his baser animal self. Long ago, the idea was put forth that the hero and bull-man represent Gilgamesh and his friend, the hairy Enkidu. This theory is no longer generally accepted since concrete episodes of the epic, except for the Hawawa battle, are not among the preserved visual materials. The identification is immaterial; the concept behind the heroic myth and the "hero" as represented in Sumerian art is much the same.

The finest and most beautiful drawing of the hero from the Royal Cemetery is found on the top register of the front of the sound box on the Great Lyre from PG 789 (cat. no. 3, detail p. 55). Bearded and endowed with heavy locks of hair on either side of his head, the hero is shown nude save for the ever-present belt. He grasps and holds in place two rearing bulls that have human faces exactly like his own. The animal-men are also bearded and have two long side locks. In abbreviated fashion, the idea of the contest scene is represented; the heraldic scheme signifies the control of nature, elements that need containment to ensure survival. On another level, this scheme represents mastery of the lower, physical self and is thus synonymous with an ideal of kingship. On the lyre sound box, the hero and the human-animals are set atop the funeral banquet and oversee it, thus assuring by a signifier of control the efficacy of the underworld meal. The hero and animals fused eternally together in this crystalline image best summarize Early Dynastic Sumerian concerns and their expression in art.[10]

1. SILVER HEAD OF A LION

This silver lion head is one of a pair of attachments located in the *dromos* of the tomb, close to the remains of a large

Fig. 40. Fragmentary clay sealing from al-Hiba of Eannatum, ruler of Lagash at the time of the First Dynasty of Ur. H. 5.9 cm. Al-Hiba 2H381. Drawing by Anne Searight.

1

❋ SILVER HEAD OF
A LION

Silver, lapis lazuli, and
 shell
H. 11 cm, W. 12 cm
PG 800, *dromos* of Puabi's
 tomb
B17064 (U.10465)

wooden box called a "wardrobe chest"
by Woolley.[11] Found 45 centimeters apart,
the heads were originally attached to a
wooden object. On the basis of all the
physical evidence in the ground, the excavator reasonably suggested that the heads
were protomes affixed to the arms of a
chair.[12] No contemporary representations
of a chair with animal protomes survive,
and it is not until the end of the third millennium BC that lions associated with the
goddess Inanna form part of the throne of
an Elamite goddess.[13] It is highly unlikely
that the piece of furniture in the *dromos*
with the lion heads was a chair for a deity
or cult statue; it is also highly unlikely that
the feline was used here for purely decorative purposes.

The locks of hair, although in no way
exaggerated, suggest a real mane and indicate that the sculptor intended to represent
a lion rather than a lioness. The lion was
one of the primary animals in the iconography of Sumerian art and was most often

seen as a contestant in conflicts between
lions, bulls, bull-men, and heroes. Here the
protome may well have had another significant meaning and functioned perhaps
as an apotropaion, to divert evil.

Although this lion head is only one
of the many masterpieces of art from the
Royal Cemetery, it is a particularly ex-
pressive image of leonine power. Like the
bronze bull head (cat. no. 4), it was probably cast, but the remaining silver is too
corroded to permit analysis.[14] The sculp-
tural forms are simple and the head is
boldly executed, yet the visual effect
is naturalistic. The nose is sharply defined
and the mouth is slightly open. There is a
real suggestion of the softness of the flesh
of the upper lip as well a suggestion of a
slight snarl enhanced by the incised stri-
ations on the snout. Artistically, this lion
head stands within the long tradition of
keenly observed animal representations
reaching back some five hundred years
to the Uruk and Jamdat Nasr periods.

The slanted, deeply inset eyes of lapis lazuli and shell contrast with the silver color of the head and demand the viewer's attention. These eyes, coupled with the added shadows of the nose and mouth, give to this lion head an intensity of expression rarely achieved in early Mesopotamian art.

2. SILVER HEAD OF A BULL

This bull head is made of silver, and like many Early Dynastic Sumerian sculptures, the eyes are inlaid with lapis lazuli and shell. When found in Puabi's tomb chamber, one horn was broken off from the head, and the muzzle was damaged. The horn was reattached, the muzzle repaired, and the head photographed for publication before the object was cleaned. Woolley thought that it must have been attached originally to a no longer existing wooden sound box of a lyre. He believed that two fragmentary shell plaques (fig. 41) found in close proximity to the bull head were part of the decoration of the front of the lyre, but it is curious that other shell plaques or fragments of plaques normally comprising the front of a lyre were not found in the immediate vicinity.

This head is a remarkable example of hollow-cast metal sculpture and one of the few examples that can be dated as early as the middle of the third millennium BC. Like the silver lion head (cat. no. 1), this bovine representation exhibits a masterful blend of naturalistic forms and abstract shapes. One of the great achievements of many Sumerian sculptors of the middle of the third millennium was the ability to

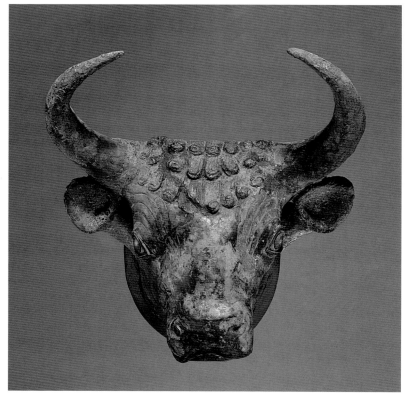

2
❋ SILVER HEAD OF
A BULL

Silver, lapis lazuli, and shell
H. 16.5 cm, W. 15.5 cm
PG 800, Puabi's tomb chamber
B17065 (U.10916)

accentuate selected naturalistic forms and to abstract them into partially decorative accents that at the same time generically define and illuminate the character of the animal species. An excellent example is the treatment of the region of the eye. In order to emphasize the openness and vitality of the eye, several stacked curving bands rounded at the ends follow the curvature of the upper eyelid. The bands are demarcated by incised lines and are raised in slight relief. The edges of the eyelids, formed of raised ridges of lapis lazuli, tightly define and securely hold in place the eyeballs and pupils, which are made of shell and lapis lazuli. The eyes bulge slightly in a naturalistic manner and impart to the sculpture a sense of presence and vivacity. These elements coupled with the erect projecting ears, the curve of the horns, and the naturalism of the muzzle convincingly portray the essence of a bull.

The hair on the upper part of the head is treated in a conventional manner for the period. Three overlapping and curving rows of hair locks fall over the forehead of the animal; a fourth row falls back from the poll onto the top of the head. Locks such as these that end in spit curls are also commonly used to represent animal hair and fleece. Often the locks are carved individually of shell, limestone, or lapis lazuli and are sometimes attached to sculptures in the round by means of a copper wire passed through a hole in the back of the lock. The beard of the bull on the sound box of the Great Lyre (cat. no. 3) is made of such individually formed locks of lapis lazuli.

3

GREAT LYRE FROM THE
"KING'S GRAVE"

Gold, silver, lapis lazuli, shell, bitumen,
and wood
H. of head 35.6 cm, H. of plaque 33 cm
PG 789
B17694 (U.10556)

3. GREAT LYRE FROM THE "KING'S GRAVE"

Lying against the northwest wall of the death pit of PG 789 was this magnificent large lyre, another of the most famous objects from the Royal Cemetery. Enigmatically, the bottom of the lyre rested on the heads of three bodies crowded along with other bodies into the corner formed by the northwest wall of the death pit and the southern wall of the tomb chamber. A second lyre now in the British Museum was also found on top of the head of one of the bodies leaning against the tomb chamber wall. On the basis of their jewelry

Fig. 41. A fragmentary shell plaque found near the silver bull head in Puabi's tomb chamber. UPM B16746 (U.10917b). Reprinted from Woolley 1934b: pl. 100.

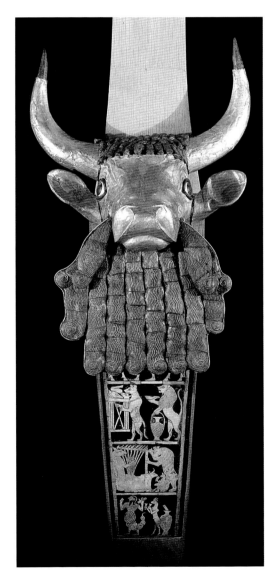

types, all the bodies beneath the lyres were identified as women. In fact, these women had the most elaborate headdresses and were the most elegantly coiffed of all the women discovered in the grave. They may well have been the lyrists and singers who took part in the celebration of the death ritual. Either the women collapsed and died during the course of the ritual or the lyres were placed atop the bodies after the celebrants died; given the consistency of the placement of the lyres, the latter seems the most likely explanation. We know that lyrists could be either male or female. A man plays a smaller lyre in the male banquet depicted on the Standard of Ur (see fig. 36b, top register, right); behind him stands a figure with long hair who may be a singer. It appears that the artist intended to suggest that a wide band or sling attached to the lyre encircled the lyrist's shoulders, thereby supporting the instrument. Since the upper part of the body is shown naked, the long hair in this case does not indicate that this figure is a woman. A female lyrist is shown playing a lyre in a feast with male and female participants on a plaque from Nippur.[15]

The bull head, made of precious materials affixed over a wooden core, was badly crushed due to the disintegration of the wood. Based on the relationship of the various parts in the ground and based on other heads of bulls from the cemetery excavations, Woolley was able to reasonably reconstruct the splendid head. Removing the lyre from the earth is an example of one of Woolley's extraordinary excavation coups,[16] but unfortunately the front upright arm was cut away before the excavator realized what was in the ground. The impression of the sound box indicated that the maximum length of the lyre was 1.40 meters, and the impression of the upright back arm was 1.17 meters. The sound box and the arms were of plain wood except for the gold and lapis lazuli bull head affixed to the front of the lyre and a series of shell

plaques that decorated the front of the sound box.

Many musical instruments accompanied the dead in the Royal Cemetery. There is some evidence that pipes, drums, cymbals, and sistra as well as harps and lyres were included. The names of the musical instruments in Sumerian are not well known. The term "balag" might simply signify a stringed instrument, denoting either a harp or a lyre, but some scholars believe that the harp was known as the "balag" instrument and the term for the lyre was probably "zà-mí," which carried the meaning of "praise." Certain types of texts were specified by the name of the musical instrument to which they were sung or recited.[17] Most of these lyres had eleven strings, and it is assumed that each string produced a different sound. Such a series of tones suggests that Sumerian music for the lyre was indeed more complicated than contemporary Egyptian music, whose lyres had only four strings.[18]

As mentioned, the bull head was composed of precious materials, including gold, silver, lapis lazuli, and shell. Most of the head and horns was formed of gold sheet worked over a wooden core. The style of the resultant bull head was very similar to the bronze bull head of the small lyre (cat. no. 4) and the silver bull head from Puabi's tomb (cat. no. 2). The eyeballs were insets of shell, and the pupils and eyelids were made of lapis lazuli. Lapis lazuli was also used for the layered tufts of hair on the forehead and on top of the head, as well as for the tips of the horns. The magnificently full and luxurious beard of twelve locks ending in tight curls was composed of many individual pieces of lapis lazuli set into a silver backing with a raised edge. For the most part, the silver was fully corroded.

Although most of the lyre was made of plain wood, the front of the sound box was fully decorated with one of the most intriguing and masterfully executed of all

Sumerian compositions. The trapezoidal shape was framed with small rectangular pieces of shell with additional pieces dividing the enclosed area into four registers. Each register was composed of a shell plaque. These plaques diminished in size from the top of the sequence to the bottom. The background in each panel was cut away so that the figures stood out clearly, and the shallow background was filled with bitumen, creating a sharp contrast between the figures and their backgrounds. When excavated, the bitumen had turned into a powder. Woolley used wax as a cohesive medium to extract the panel from the ground. This wax then affixed the bitumen in place; the panel as seen today is almost precisely as it was seen in antiquity.

The largest plaque at the top of the panel shows the heraldic scheme of a heroic figure, nude save for a belt made of a plaited material suggestive of reeds, grasping two rearing human-headed bulls. The lower part of the hero's body is in partial profile; his chest and head are frontal. He is bearded, which in this instance probably denotes his semidivine nature, and he has three large locks of hair on either side of his head. His hands, unduly large in relation to the rest of his body, hold in place the two bull-men, whose bodies are also in profile and whose heads are likewise seen *en face*. The chests of these bearded, human-faced bulls, with side locks and scalloped waves of hair on their brows, nestle snugly into the constricted waist of the hero. Their far forelegs are raised and bent, thereby framing the hero's head and aiding to develop an ingenious, interlocked design of man and animal that is fully engaging aesthetically. The human faces all have intense, engrossing expressions achieved by small, fully revealed pupils set in overly large eyes.

The intertwined hero and human-headed bulls, a concept not fully comprehended today but here related to or representing the deceased, stand physically

Detail of front panel of Great Lyre, cat. no. 3.

above and spiritually over the three lower panels, which are interrelated thematically: the scenes depict the funeral banquet celebrated in the netherworld or in preparation for the crossing into the netherworld. This banquet stands apart from others, such as that seen on the sound box of the small portable lyre (cat. no. 5), in that here the celebrants are represented as animals who perform their tasks not as actual animals but as if they were human.

A canine animal and a lion appear in the plaque immediately below the hero and bulls. The hyena stands on his rear legs facing to the left and in his very human hands holds forth a table on which are placed the heads (of a boar and perhaps a calf) and the bent leg of a bovine. The hyena functions as the butcher, indicated by the dagger stuck into his belt. The hilt of the dagger is decorated with seven black dots that represent nails, a simplified version of a dagger similar to the gold and originally wood dagger decorated with small gold nails from PG 1054 (cat. no. 146). It is difficult to know whether the haunch seen on the sacrificial table is associated with the mark or "sign" engraved on some metal bowls, stone bowls (usually chlorite), and spears from the Royal Cemetery.[19] Since the "sign" appears on different types of objects, it is difficult to discern a meaning related to the cemetery or to burial practices; it does not appear to signify ownership, as Woolley suggested.

Whereas the hyena deals with butchering and animal sacrifice, the male lion with full mane and upright tail standing behind him is concerned with drink. The lion's mouth is slightly open, as if he were speaking, and in his very human left hand he grasps the handle of a wicker basket or envelope enclosing a large jar with a narrow neck and broad rim, a type of vessel not found among the categories of metal, stone, and clay containers in the Royal Cemetery. In his extended right hand with its exaggerated thumb, he holds a pouring vessel

similar to ones of metal, stone, and shell found in many graves. (Cat. no. 112 shows two examples in copper alloy from PG 333 and PG 789.)

In the next lower plaque, an animal orchestra accompanying the banquet is illustrated. An ass is shown seated, his tail up against his back. He faces right and with spread human fingers plucks an eight-stringed lyre decorated with a bull head; therefore, the represented lyre is much like the actual lyre that it decorates. Most sound boxes of lyres exhibit a certain general resemblance in shape to the form of the body of an actual reclining bull or cow. That this similarity was intended by the Sumerian artisans is indicated by the fact that the sound box of the lyre played by the ass clearly shows the bull's tucked-under foreleg. Helping to support this large lyre is a standing male bear facing left who grasps the lyre's front upright arm and crosspiece. He might be shuffling or dancing to the music of the lyre, but such movement would be hampered by a small animal with large ears and a long bushy tail, perhaps a fox, sitting on his right foot. One can assume that this animal and the ass are male since the masculine gender of all other members of this banquet is evident. The small animal holds a sistrum in his right hand and rests his left hand on an object lying across his knees. It is tempting to suggest that the object is a tablet containing the text of the hymn or other class of literature sung at this special banquet.

In the bottom register, a scorpion-man generously endowed with long hair and beard holds undefined objects in his raised hands. Behind him is a gazelle with human shoulders, arms, and hands facing left and holding two tumblers similar in shape to the electrum and silver tumblers from Puabi's tomb chamber (see cat. nos. 105–107). Presumably, the vessels have been filled from the large pottery container behind the gazelle. Projecting from the top of this jar is an object similar to that held in the scorpion-man's left hand.

Such depictions of animals acting as humans are rare in the art of early Sumer. Frequently, animals do appear in poses unlike those assumed in nature—for example, in contest scenes—but this context is very different from animals actually performing human tasks. An elaborate singular early example of animals behaving like humans is found on a seal impression (fig. 42), also from Ur. This seal was found in the so-called Seal Impression Strata (SIS), debris into which the cemetery graves were sunk, and it dates more than a hundred years prior to the lyre shell plaques. A seated lion is feted by a caprid with a cup, and ass musicians play a harp and cymbals or clappers. Among other animals and objects included in the composition, another lion acting as butcher cuts the throat of a small bovine. This sealing is clearly an antecedent for the lyre panel, but the banquet depicted might not be funereal. Although the scene might appear to illustrate a fable, no literary evidence of such a fable survives.

The ultimate source for an iconography based on the concept of animals acting as humans is Elam, that extension of the Mesopotamian plain into what is today southwestern Iran. After an initial close relationship between the art of Elam and Sumer during the Uruk period, toward the end of the fourth millennium BC, Elamite art developed its own very distinctive character during the period known as Proto-Elamite, even though relations between Sumer and Elam remained close. Toward the end of the Proto-Elamite period, which was contemporary in part with Early Dynastic Sumer, iconography in glyptic art as well as in sculpture in the round focused on the depiction of animals engaged in a variety of activities associated with religious beliefs as well as in scenes that might appear as if they were meant to be genre. Probably for a variety of uses and at differ-

ent times, this Elamite iconography was taken over and adapted by Sumerian artists when it could best express ideas specifically Sumerian better than the iconography traditionally available to them.

F. Wiggerman has noted that the scorpion-man is a creature associated with the mountains of sunrise and sunset, distant lands of wild animals and demons, a place passed by the dead.[20] Consequently, the adaptation of an originally Elamite type of imagery adds a profound new dimension to this royal Sumerian burial. What could be more fitting than this lyre intended for the accompaniment of liturgical chants whose sounds are associated with the sounds of the divine bull and whose decorated sound box gives a glimpse of the underworld banquet?

4. BRONZE HEAD OF A BULL
5. MOSAIC PANEL FROM LYRE FRONT

This bronze bull head and the mosaic plaques are the decorative members of the front of a lyre whose sound box and upper frame were made of wood that has completely disintegrated. The original lyre would have been a much smaller version of the Great Lyre (cat. no. 3) and was similar in size to the lyres shown carried by musicians in representations on relief plaques and on seals.

Only the death pit of PG 1332 was found, not the tomb chamber of the main figure buried there. The description given by

Fig. 42. Seal impression found in the Seal Impression Strata. Reprinted from Legrain 1936: no. 384.

4
BRONZE HEAD OF A BULL

Tin-bronze, lapis lazuli,
 and shell
H. 12 cm, W. 14 cm
PG 1332
30-12-696 (U.12435)

5
MOSAIC PANEL FROM
LYRE FRONT

Lapis lazuli and shell
H. 19 cm, W. 7 cm
PG 1332
30-12-484 (U.12435)

Woolley is somewhat confusing. The burial
shaft was preserved for only 1 meter in
depth, and twenty bodies were discovered
on the floor of the pit.[21] Slightly more than
1 meter above the floor, a second layer of
twenty-three bodies was recovered. How
two layers of bodies came to be separated
by more than 1 meter of earth is not explained. Quite possibly, the upper layer of
bodies belonged to a somewhat later second
burial. The lyre was found on the floor in
the northeast end of the pit, close to a body
that may well have been a musician. Two[?]
copper objects 30 centimeters long and 4
centimeters wide were also found in the
immediate vicinity and were interpreted by
Woolley as musical clappers.

  The small bull head was cast over a
bitumen core using the lost wax process.[22]
It is modeled in the same style as the silver

bull head (cat. no. 2) but is somewhat
simpler due to its smaller scale. Like other
sculptures of bulls, the eyes are formed of
shell eyeballs and lapis lazuli pupils that
bulge out from the head below the marked
brows. A row of hair curls is positioned on
the back side of the poll of the head, and
only one row of rudimentary formed hair
locks falls down on the front of the head,
leaving space for a triangular insert of
lapis lazuli to be affixed to the cranium.
Although only this bull, among all the
animal sculptures in the Royal Cemetery,
has this triangular inlay, the use of such
inserts has a long tradition in Sumer going
back some five hundred years to works of
art created in the Uruk and Jamdat Nasr
periods.[23] Undoubtedly, the triangle had a
specific meaning beyond its use as a decorative detail. Small lapis lazuli squares and

shell triangles were apparently found near the head. Woolley suggests that these were part of a poorly preserved mosaic collar used at the juncture of the head and the wooden sound box. These pieces are preserved in the University of Pennsylvania Museum collection.

The mosaic plaques show four human figures and are one example of the several iconographic schemes for the banquet scene. In this case, all the participants are male. The scene can be interpreted as a seated main figure with three acolytes standing before him in a line or row. The banqueter seated on a stool is bald-headed and is nude from the waist up. His lower body is clothed in a fleecy garment with long, scalloped tassels or fringe at the bottom. This fleecy garment appears to be an apron worn over a plain skirt with fringe such as the skirts worn by the attendant figures; however, as this is an almost unique representation, such an interpretation may be erroneous. In his raised right hand, the banqueter holds a drinking cup, and in his lowered left hand, he grasps an object that appears to have a long, undulating tassel like a fly whisk. In other representations of the banquet scene in which the object held in either hand of a seated male figure is clearly drawn,[24] the object is a tied bud containing the pollinating strands from the male tree inserted against the female spadix; hence, in this representation the tasseled object is probably a plant form and may well be the male inflorescence of the date palm.[25]

The partially bald attendant standing before the seated figure holds his right arm up with the hand partially open; his left hand is tucked into his armpit. The other two attendant figures extend their joined hands before them. One acolyte clearly holds an unidentifiable object. A similar

enigmatic object is held in the extended right hand of a standing attendant in the upper register of the Standard of Ur. This figure tucks his left hand under his right armpit, and despite the burden of the object, he shows precisely the same purposeful gesture as that of the first attendant in the mosaic panel. Perhaps all the attendants on the mosaic panel originally held objects in their hands. Keeping in mind that such panels were essentially found loose in the soil and were subsequently reconstructed, it is easy to understand that many small pieces might have been lost and easy to see how a restorer might have substituted a bit of lapis lazuli for a similarly scaled shell object.

Lost pieces could account for the peculiarities of the bottom borders of the mosaic panel. At some point after the excavation photo was taken and published in Woolley 1934b, the fragmentary lower part of the panel was restored and regularized into its present shape. It is clear from the original photograph that the bottom is incomplete. Whether the pieces were lost during the course of the excavations or before the lyre was buried is not known. In any case, the bottom borders as presently restored seem wrong. It would make more sense to restore the bottom in a fashion similar to the top of the panel, with a border of an engraved "eye" motif set between two shell pieces incised with a woven pattern.

The "eye" as a symbolic or purely decorative element in Sumerian design was used in a variety of instances. Here it frames a variation of the banquet theme, but it was also used, for example, as a square and as a border in a gaming board. The significance of the "eye" in such contexts is unknown.

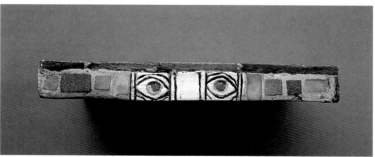

6. PIECES FROM A GAMING BOARD
7. PLAYING TILES

Various pieces of inlay from a gaming board were retrieved from the filling of a burial shaft; there was no indication of how these pieces relate to one another. Included among the finds were twelve shell plaques with incised representations of animals and plants[26] (two are broken and others chipped); five badly decayed shell plaques; seven white shell squares, each with five blue dots; three black shell squares, each with five white dots; two shell squares with incised rosettes; nine partially decayed shell strips with an incised "eye" pattern; and a variety of edging pieces of shell, red limestone, and lapis lazuli. The present arrangement of the twelve plaques and some of the edging pieces has no archaeological validity; however, similar rows of such plaques were used on a number of gaming boards from various tombs—for example, on a fairly complete board from PG 789.[27] One of the best preserved boards is from the tomb of Puabi and is now in the British Museum. The squares of Puabi's gaming board are all geometric patterns. It not known how these games were played, nor is it known how the games functioned as burial gifts. Much more is known about games in ancient Egypt because they are depicted in tomb decorations and many actual examples have been preserved from the graves.[28]

The animal decoration on these mosaic plaques includes bulls, bulls with bearded human faces, and gazelles. In each case, the animal facing left or right is placed in front of or beside a stylized plant in a manner found on other objects contemporary with the Royal Cemetery. Iconographically, this scheme is reminiscent of plant and animal depictions on cylinder seals of the much earlier Uruk and Jamdat Nasr periods.[29]

Displayed with the gaming board plaques are three playing tiles, each measuring 2.30 by 2.30 centimeters. Two are

6

PIECES FROM A
GAMING BOARD

Shell, red limestone, and
 lapis lazuli
H. 14 cm, W. 11.4 cm
PG 580
B16742 (U.9776)

7

PLAYING TILES

Lapis lazuli and shale
2.7 × 2.7 cm
Found loose in the soil
B16972a–c (U.9320)

made of lapis lazuli and one of limestone. All have five holes distributed like the five side of a modern die. One of the lapis lazuli tiles (cat. no. 7) is recorded as having been found loose in the soil without any specific provenience; there is no record of the other two tiles.

8. "RAM CAUGHT IN A THICKET"

This goat standing upright against a flowering plant and its counterpart in the British Museum are two of the most famous objects from the Royal Cemetery. They have frequently been referred to as "Ram Caught in a Thicket" because the biblical image (Gen. 22:13) so aptly fits the sculptures. They were found badly crushed and were ingeniously reconstructed by Woolley. The University of Pennsylvania Museum example had collapsed on its back and had broken in two; however, the thickness of the body was preserved. The British Museum sculpture was essentially flattened, but the outline of the body was still clear. The Conservation Department of the University of Pennsylvania Museum recently cleaned and reconstructed this example, basing the few changes on a careful study of the object as seen in the ground in the single preserved expedition photo[30] and on considerations of the internal evidence that appeared when the statue was dismantled. The only fundamental change in the reconstruction is that now the front hooves of the goat rest on the branches of the tree. When Woolley first reconstructed the goat and the plant, a mistake was made in calculating the height of the plant. The bottom of the plant stem was inserted too deeply into the base, and based on the photograph some of the gold pieces were put into place in the wrong order. The angle of the branches needed correction, and it was also necessary to readjust the angle of the forelegs in relation to the body.

Since the silver underside of the body was badly corroded, no indication of the gender of the animal was found; however, the penis sheath and gold-covered testicles were preserved on the British Museum example. It seems reasonable to assume that the goat in the University of Pennsylvania Museum Collection is also male.

Other metals and materials in addition to silver were used on various parts of the goat's body. Gold covered the face and legs, and copper was used only for the ears. The gold of the head had been broken into eighteen pieces. The horns, the beard, the

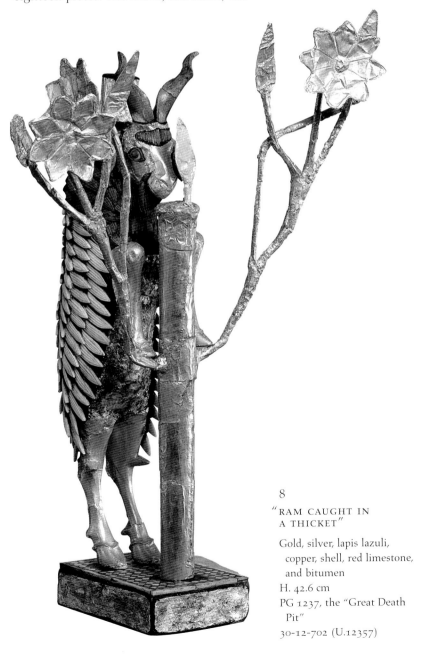

8

"RAM CAUGHT IN A THICKET"

Gold, silver, lapis lazuli, copper, shell, red limestone, and bitumen

H. 42.6 cm

PG 1237, the "Great Death Pit"

30-12-702 (U.12357)

eyebrows, the pupils, and the locks of hair on the forehead were made of lapis lazuli. Also of lapis lazuli was the fleece of the shoulders and chest; the remainder of the body fleece was formed of shell. These lapis lazuli and shell tufts, or locks, of fleece were made of individual pieces attached with bitumen to the frame of the body. This frame, originally made of wood, was not preserved. The elements that comprise the fleece probably projected out more fully from the body than they do at present.

The goat stands on a base originally made of wood that had thin silver pieces, not well preserved, attached to its sides. The top of the stand was covered with a mosaic diaper pattern of shell, lapis lazuli, and red limestone. The mosaic pieces and the edging were completely preserved. Fitted into this base is the stem, or trunk, of the plant, covered with gold foil. The stem is topped with a single vertical piece of gold in the shape of a leaf, and from the sides project two branches, also covered in gold. Each branch divides into four smaller shoots that originally ended in two leaves and two floral rosettes, but not all of these elements were preserved. These rosettes and leaves must have all faced forward. Some of these as well as some of the plant branches were bent out of shape when the object collapsed. No attempt has been made to change their positions in the new reconstruction.

As Woolley correctly pointed out, this goat and plant as well as the example in the British Museum were not intended as freestanding sculpture; instead, they should be seen as applied art in the sense that the sculpture constitutes the lower part of a stand. The upper element was not preserved, but it was originally attached to the gold-covered cylinder that projects from the back of the goat's neck. The base probably supported a small tray or tabletop similar to the representation of such a piece of furniture shown on a roughly contemporary cylinder seal in the Vorderasiatisches Museum, Berlin (fig. 43). If this conception is correct, due to the delicate nature of the plant and goat sculpture, its tray could not have supported much weight. Woolley reported that a quantity of ash was found in the soil around one of the goats, suggesting that something was burned on the stand during the course of the ritual involved with the "Great Death Pit."[31]

This small composite sculpture, with its strong contrasts of gold, silver, blue lapis lazuli, and white shell, is highly coloristic, an effect cherished by the Sumerian artists in creating sublime works for the temple or for elite burials. Color in a world of relatively drab surroundings was essential to impart life and to elevate and infuse an image with *numina*. At the same time, this combination of the goat and floral branching tree is one of the most engaging and substantive images from third millennium BC antiquity. It encapsulates in a highly symbolic manner the fundamental Sumerian concerns with the fecundity of the plant world and the fertility of the animal domain. The goat is a prime progenitor second only to the bull. He stands against the tree, a position often seen in nature when an animal reaches for the succulent leaves higher up on a plant.[32] At the same time, this is the stance of the sexual act of this perhaps ithyphallic goat. His legs rest on a highly stylized plant that has little relation to an actual plant of any time in southern Mesopotamia. Rather it is a plant that combines the

Fig. 43. Modern impression of a cylinder seal, roughly contemporary with the "Ram Caught in a Thicket," which shows a similar "ram" supporting a small tabletop or tray. VA 3878. Courtesy of the Vorderasiatisches Museum, Berlin.

9
SILVER HEAD OF
A HORNED ANIMAL

Silver
H. 6.6 cm, W. 5.8 cm
PG 55
B17716 (U.8013)

flower or rosette often seen as a symbol of the goddess Inanna with a leaf shape that does not function as a leaf on this plant. A solitary example of the latter stands upright on top of the stem, or it functions as a flower on the end of a branch or twig. It would perhaps not be wrong to view this as a simplified and stylized form of bud as yet to become the rosette or flower, or as a simple fruit, the consequence of a fertilized floral spadix. The intimate link of animal and plant life so central to Sumerian religion is powerfully implied by the fact that originally the forelegs of the goat were tied to the plant by means of a silver chain encircling a branch and the goat's fetlocks.

9. SILVER HEAD OF A HORNED ANIMAL

This small head was found in PG 55, a badly plundered and disturbed grave located relatively close to the surface of the cemetery area. It was found corroded together with a silver bracelet. Adhering to the corrosion were beads, and a cockleshell was situated between the horns of the animal head. Due to the corrosion, the head was not immediately identifiable; it was revealed only after the silver was cleaned.

How this head functioned is unclear, but it seems relatively certain that the position of the cockleshell was accidental. The head was cast of silver, and originally inlays of another material were used for the eyes. The series of eyebrows or furrows may

This gold amulet is in the form of a couchant bull. Clinging to the right side of the body near the two suspension loops on the back were four tiny gold beads; hence, the bull was originally part of a necklace of gold and came from a plundered tomb. Other gold, lapis lazuli, and carnelian beads as well as some stone vases also were found nearby in the loose soil. Woolley convincingly suggests that these fine objects came originally from the plundered PG 337. The bull is made from a thin sheet of gold formed over a bitumen core. The body is fully rounded, and the legs, tucked up on the side of the animal, are both incised and raised slightly in relief. The body is seen in profile, and the head is turned out at a right angle facing the viewer. This bull is divine and wears a heavy false beard with an attached strap that passes over the snout of the animal. Similar gold bearded bull amulets as well as a lapis lazuli example (cat. no. 33) also were found among the collection of jewelry from the tomb of Puabi. Considering its minute size, the piece is a remarkable example of goldworking. The accent of the deeply demarcated front of the muzzle coupled with the relatively enormous eyes imbues the bull with a very lively and heightened expression.

The animal viewed from the side with the head turned out toward the viewer as well as the idea of a couchant bull as an amulet are within the traditions of Sumerian art established over five hundred years earlier in the Uruk and Jamdat Nasr periods.[36] New in the art of the Early Dynastic period of Sumer is the style of rendering the animal and the concept of the divine bearded bull. The present archaeological evidence indicates that the iconographic feature of the bearded bull was first introduced in the Early Dynastic I period and is first represented on a sealing from the so-called Seal Impression Strata (SIS).

10

GOLD BULL AMULET

Gold

H. 1.5 cm, W. 1.5 cm

Found loose in the soil near PG 184

B16685 (U.8269)

also have been inlaid with another substance such as bitumen. It is difficult to identify this animal, whose distinctive horns are large, circular, and point upward at the ends. Both the ears and the horns appear to be bovine, yet the snout of the animal is very pointed and small; nevertheless, the head is most probably that of a bull. Similarly shaped horns are used on a copper sculpture of a bull with human face found loose in the soil of the Royal Cemetery.[33] It is of interest that a bull head with precisely the same type of encircling horns was found in the Barbar temple in Bahrain, pointing to the close cultural contacts known to have existed between Sumer and ancient Dilmun in the Gulf region during the middle of the third millennium BC.[34]

Woolley considered this head to be "one of the most exquisite heads of animals found in the cemetery."[35]

11. FILLET OR HEADBAND

This fillet was cut from a single sheet of gold and was probably originally attached to another object, such as a leather band, by means of the holes piercing the gold strip at each end. A small piece is missing after a repair in antiquity in which the broken gold band was reattached to its backing by sewing. Four small stitch holes are preserved on either side of the break.

the stalk of a plant with leaves and a rosette blossom; a stag, with antlers, striding to the right; a goat[?] facing left whose body is depicted as if bound in a basket; two bearded, kilted figures with flamelike hair, one facing left and one facing right, with outstretched arms holding unidentifiable objects (perhaps animal body parts) between them; an equid walking to the right surmounted by a rider with flamelike

11

FILLET OR HEADBAND
Gold
L. 32 cm, W. 2.8 cm
PG 153
B16686 (U.8173)
Drawing by Charles Henneberry

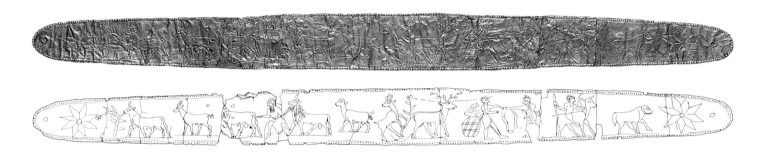

PG 153 was a simple inhumation in the earth and not a major burial. The body was covered with a reed matting and buried with the gold fillet around the head, stone bowls, a copper bowl, a copper pin with a lapis lazuli head, a cylinder seal of lapis lazuli,[37] and a variety of beads of gold, lapis lazuli, and other semiprecious stones.

Although other gold fillets were found in the Royal Cemetery of Ur (see, for example, cat. no. 53), only this fillet has a punctate pattern border, rosettes, and a series of figures of humans and animals executed by means of simple incised lines. From left to right, these images are a large eight-petaled rosette; a striding bull facing left and eating from a plant with leaves and a geometric-patterned blossom; a ram facing left; a bearded figure with flamelike hair facing left, kneeling on one knee, and grasping the tail of one bull and the beard of a second bull, both of which also face left; a ewe with udders (which are rarely depicted) facing left in the process of giving birth; a ram facing left but with its body turned to the right, its forelegs resting on

hair brandishing a weapon or tool in his right hand; a fat-tailed sheep facing right; and another large eight-petaled rosette. The ram standing upright against a plant marks the central point of the fillet design —the animals to its left move left, and those to its right move right. Although the head is turned in the opposite direction of the body, this group of ram and plant is essentially a simplified drawing of the famed "Ram Caught in a Thicket" from PG 1237, the "Great Death Pit" (cat. no. 8).

The groupings of humans and animals are undoubtedly related conceptually, but visually they remain a succession of individual elements. A standard theme in Sumerian iconography is the contest scene, in which closely interlocked groups of contesting heroes and animals are used; however, on this gold fillet a totally different dimension of the animal and human realm is presented. Although the style of the drawings is distinctly Early Dynastic III, some of the iconographic elements are very rare, if not unique. For example, a heroic figure on one knee grasping the head of one bull and the tail of another is practically unknown. Normally, both animals would face the hero in an antithetical composition. The missing head of the bull on the left of this group is due to the loss of gold in the ancient repair. Unique to Mesopotamian iconography is the butchering[?] scene, which shows an animal head projecting from a basket[?] and two human figures holding curious objects. Of particular interest is the figure riding an equid on the right side of the fillet: this might well be the earliest depiction of animal and rider in the ancient world. This long-eared animal is undoubtedly a wild ass or an onager. One other Early Dynastic or early Akkadian representation of an equid and rider survives; it occurs on a somewhat bizarre and slightly later sealing in the collection of the Ashmolean Museum.[38]

12. COSMETIC BOX WITH INLAID LID

This silver box with carved lid of lapis lazuli and shell is roughly semicircular. It was found among the large number of objects close to the "wardrobe chest" in the death pit of Puabi's tomb. Woolley identified the object as a toilet box used for holding cosmetics needed by the queen. This elaborately decorated example is unique among the cosmetic containers, which were

usually either actual cockleshells or imitations of cockleshells fashioned in gold or silver (cat. nos. 108, 109). Because the curved edge of the lid is decorated with a band of incised geometric pattern inlaid with tiny lapis lazuli disks, the straight edge that is undecorated and hence unfinished indicates that another segment of the lid is missing. The completed lid was probably oval shaped and consisted of two semicircular sections covering an oval, segmented silver box.[39]

The lid is the finest surviving example of shell carving from the Royal Cemetery. It is carved from a single piece of shell and has two incised lines filled with red and black pigment on the top that follow the curve of the box. Set into the center of the lid is another shell piece carved in relief and depicting a lion downing a horned caprid. Small lapis lazuli tesserae surround and set off the carved animals. The three-dimensional effect of the animals is heightened by the projection of the inlay above the plane of the surrounding outer edge.

The crouching lion tears at the caprid's throat. Whereas the supine caprid forms a ground line for the group, the contour of the lion's rear haunch, its erect curved tail, and especially its full mane reflect the external curve of the lid and create a highly satisfying design. The caprid has been thrown on its back. The legs that are visible point upward, and its tufts of body hair point downward, emphasizing the animal's upside-down position. The caprid's head is in profile; the lion's head is frontal, with two lines characteristically separating the top of the head from the elaborate mane. Although the style of the carving is in keeping with the best of Early Dynastic III art, the composition is unique and truly imaginative.

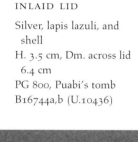

12

✳ COSMETIC BOX WITH INLAID LID

Silver, lapis lazuli, and shell

H. 3.5 cm, Dm. across lid 6.4 cm

PG 800, Puabi's tomb

B16744a,b (U.10436)

This copper relief came from one of the more important and richest tombs of the Royal Cemetery, called the "King's Grave" by the excavator. This singular relief was found on the floor in the death pit, which contained some sixty-three bodies, and was situated between two groups of four spears. The relief has a rectangular panel surmounting a roundel in the form of a ten-petaled rosette in raised relief with a raised circular boss at the center. It is not clear whether the roundel belonged in the position seen here. Much of the copper is missing, and hence the original extent and shape of the object is not known. Because it was found with spears and was originally affixed to a wooden backing, Woolley thought that it might be part of the central and upper part of a shield. The upper right corner of the copper shows a finished curved edge that is somewhat reminiscent of the shape of the front panel of a chariot;[40] however, until further comparanda are available the original purpose of this relief will remain unclear.

The rectangular panel is divided into two registers by a narrow raised band. On the upper part of the relief are two addorsed lions, striding firmly in opposite directions. Their bodies are long and their manes full. Heavy corrosion has obscured some of the chased details of the manes and faces, but many specifics can be viewed in a drawing of the relief created with the aid of an X-ray photograph. Beneath the raised band in the lower register are two nude, bald-headed enemies lying face down. Their legs are slightly apart, and their near arms, bent at the elbow, lie across their chests. Their far arms, also slightly bent, reach across their faces. Undoubtedly, the two registers are conceptually related.

Woolley considered that the relief was very close to neo-Assyrian art of the first half of the first millennium BC and thought that additional finds might establish more

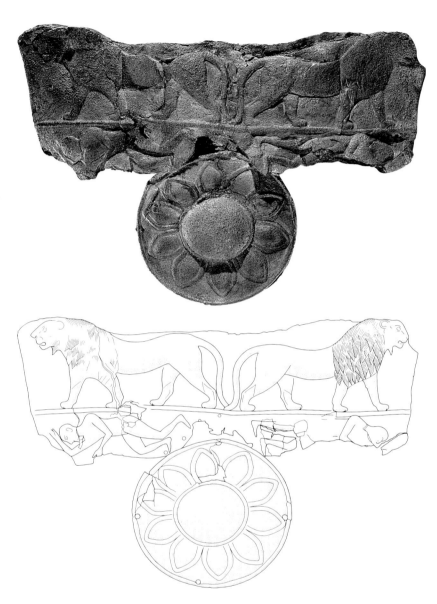

13
COPPER ALLOY RELIEF

Copper alloy
H. 31 cm, W. 45 cm
PG 789, the "King's Grave"
B17066 (U.10475)
Drawing by Veronica Socha

firmly the Sumerian antecedents for the later art of the Assyrian empire. Indeed, certain artistic motifs, themes, and interests did survive over a very long period of time, but the singular aspects of the style and iconography of this relief that set it apart from other art of the Royal Cemetery is undoubtedly the result of foreign influence, a fact that also has been noted by others.[41] The measured pace of the heavy, striding, addorsed lions as well as the association of the lions and naked fallen enemies with one arm stretched over their faces suggests that the Sumerian artist was aware of or had seen examples of Egyptian art in which the pharaoh as lion tramples his enemies. Because a contact that resulted in an artistic interaction between Egypt and Greater Mesopotamia had been established as early as the late fourth millennium BC, it seems reasonable to assume that such an interchange continued during the period of the Sumerian city-states and Egypt's Old Kingdom even if concrete examples of this contact are very rare. Interpreted in terms of Sumerian ideas, the lion might not symbolize the king, but rather a god such as the warlike Inanna, who is associated with the lion. Similarly, the lion might be associated with the warrior-god Ningirsu, who grasps his emblem, the anzu (Imdugud), a bird with outstretched wings and lion head that surmounts a net filled with naked enemies on the famous Stele of Eannatum from Girsu.[42] This particular combination of naked fallen enemy and lion as god or victorious ruler did not survive in the imagery of Sumerian art.

14. POURING VESSEL WITH RELIEF DECORATION

This vessel belongs to a class of stone bowls whose shapes imitated half shells. In addition to these stone bowls, others were made of actual shell, gold, silver, stone, and copper. Although some scholars have suggested that these vessels were lamps, none

shows any traces of burning. More likely they were used as pouring vessels, either for liquids that accompanied the dead as drink or for libations during funerary rituals. A similarly shaped vessel is carried by the lion on the shell plaque on the front of the Great Lyre from PG 789 (cat. no. 3).

The shape of this particular stone vessel is far removed from the original shell shape. Carved in relief on the side of the bowl is the body of a bull; his left front leg is raised and bent at the knee, and his other legs are drawn up beneath and directly to the side of his body. The two right legs are carved in such high relief that they appear almost in the round. The tail follows the external contour of the rear haunch, and the switch passes beneath the body of the animal and terminates lying over the rear leg in a manner almost unique in the art of the third millennium BC. The head, with the ears and horns of a bull, is carved in the round and faces outward, perpendicular to the body. The face is human and bearded, with two long curls of hair framing the sides of the face. A heavy mass of curls covers both the neck and chest. All of this hair was originally painted black, probably using bitumen; much of this color is still preserved.

Woolley assigned this piece to PG 871, one of a group of graves he called "Second Dynasty."[43] For the most part, these graves date to the Akkadian period on the basis of the pottery and seals found with the bodies. This vessel was found in the filling above the level of the grave gifts, so it is not securely dated to PG 871 and might indeed be earlier or even later than the burial. Nevertheless, the style of the sculpture with, for example, its deeply set and finely articulated eyes and precisely modeled cheeks connotes a date late in Early Dynastic IIIB or early in the Akkadian period.

Another translucent calcite vessel, now in the British Museum, having the same type of carved decoration of

a human-headed bull or bison and also painted with a black pigment, was attributed to PG 1134, a grave considered to be late in the sequence of Early Dynastic burials.[44] The carving of the face in this case is in the manner of the regional Lagash school of sculpture contemporary with Mesannepada and A'annepada of the First Dynasty of Ur and postdating most of the brilliant works of art from the royal tombs shown in this catalogue. Most likely, the vessel came from Lagash, although it might have been created at Ur in the Lagash style at a time when Ur must have come under the hegemony of Lagash, a political situation evidenced by the finding of the statue of the ruler Enmetena of Lagash at Ur.

14

POURING VESSEL WITH
RELIEF DECORATION

Calcite
L. 15 cm, W. 8.5 cm
PG 871, in filling above floor
B17087 (U.10746)

Detail of face.

15. GOLD VESSEL IN THE FORM OF AN OSTRICH EGG

This vessel, made from a single sheet of gold, was formed by hammering from the inside. It approximates the true size of an ostrich egg with the top cut off and is decorated with geometric patterns on the upper part and base. These patterns are formed by a mosaic of lapis lazuli, red limestone, and shell tesserae set into a bitumen matrix adhering to the gold. When excavated, the mosaic had fallen away from the vessel; it was reconstructed by Woolley on the basis of other better preserved eggs. Found within the same tomb was a second vessel made from a real ostrich egg as well as another in silver imitating the same form.

The original homeland of the ostrich was apparently Saharan North Africa. From there, the bird came to the Arabian Peninsula and moved farther north into Syria. Until fairly recent times, the ostrich was still seen and hunted in the Near East by the Bedouin.[45] In antiquity, the Assyrian kings and others hunted the bird, which was known for its swiftness and strength. The ninth-century BC Assyrian monarch Ashurnasirpal II, for example, boasted of having slain "200 ostriches like caged birds."[46] The physical presence of the ostrich in Syria as early as the latter part of the fourth millennium BC is attested by the finds of eggshell fragments at Tell Qannas, a site located on the upper Euphrates. Ostrich bones were excavated in Bronze Age Habuba Kabira, another site in the same region. It is probable that the ostrich eggs recovered in southern Mesopotamia came from this upper Euphrates region as well as from the Syrian steppes.

Ostrich eggs used as containers have been found as early as the aceramic phases of North Africa. In predynastic Egypt during the Badarian, Amration, and Gerzean periods, ostrich eggs were placed in the graves.[47] The eggs could be partially cut away and used as containers or placed in the grave whole. They might have been intended as food offerings for the dead, yet all the eggs were pierced at one end, indicating that the contents had been removed before the eggs were buried. Many of the Egyptian eggs were decorated with paint or with incised lines. The ostrich also appears early in Egyptian visual iconography. Clear representations occur, for example, on the late Gerzean "Hunters' palette" in the Louvre, which shows an ostrich in flight along with other animals of the desert, and on the Hieronkopolis palette in Oxford, which shows an ostrich placed between the leonine heads of two fabulous monsters with long undulating necks inspired undoubtedly by greater Mesopotamian prototypes.[48]

In Sumer, the earliest eggs found thus far date to the Early Dynastic IIIA period, the time of the Royal Cemetery of Ur. Many of the tombs, including the tomb of Puabi, were provided with ostrich eggs. Most were found smashed, so it is difficult to determine how many were whole eggs and how many were cut down as vessels or containers. The practice of furnishing graves with ostrich eggs or ostrich egg vessels was probably widespread in third-millennium BC Sumer, as is evidenced by the slightly later Cemetery A at Kish, where eggshells were found in a number of graves. These vessels, as well as their imitations in gold and silver, could have held food for the dead or been used in the ritual performed in association with the burial. Eggshell cups were also found in non-funerary contexts. Fragments were excavated in the Early Dynastic temple of Ishtarat at Mari in the middle Euphrates region and in other contexts contemporary with the Royal Cemetery.[49] Curiously, an eggshell vessel came from the excavations of the so-called Planoconvex Building at Kish, and a particularly fine example, complete with elaborate mosaic decoration, a highly favored decorative device during

15
GOLD VESSEL IN
THE FORM OF AN
OSTRICH EGG

Gold, lapis lazuli, red lime-
   stone, shell, and bitumen
H. 14.6 cm, Dm. 13 cm
PG 779
B16692 (U.11154)

Early Dynastic IIIA, was found in a room of the temple of Inanna at Nippur in Level VIIB. The latter vessel would suggest that the egg either contained food or drink for the goddess or might have been used in some type of libation ceremony.

No textual evidence survives that provides a genuine understanding of the meaning of the ostrich egg or how it functioned in a funerary or temple context; however, in a lexical text contemporary with the Royal Cemetery, an archaic forerunner to HAR-ra = hubullu, a bronze ostrich egg is cited.[50] Dating somewhat later, to the Third Dynasty of Ur toward the end of the third millennium BC, a speckled ostrich egg inlaid with gold is mentioned among a catalogue of objects adorned with metal. In texts of much later periods, ostrich eggs are listed as part of the meal served to the gods, and ostrich eggshells are used, perhaps symbolically, in the preparation of medicines.[51]

The ostrich is not depicted frequently in Mesopotamian art. No unmistakable representation of the bird is found before Akkadian times;[52] in the early second millennium BC, a man is shown riding an ostrich as part of a mythological[?] scene on a singular Old Babylonian terra-cotta plaque from Kish.[53] From the Middle Assyrian period of the late second millennium onward, however, the ostrich is depicted more often. Particularly noteworthy aesthetically is the composition of a heroic figure pursuing an adult ostrich and its offspring on a Middle Assyrian seal in the collection of the Pierpont Morgan Library.[54] In such a case, the ostrich as a creature of the steppes might be associated with the unknown, the outer limits of reality, and even with the curious monsters of the netherworld.

At some point, the ostrich egg, or the concept of the egg, became associated with regeneration and resurrection. The ostrich egg iconography passed into Christian and even Islamic art; the idea of the egg associated with new life remains with us today in the symbolism of Easter.

Cylinder Seals

Cylinder Seals

Holly Pittman

Like cuneiform script, cylinder seals are unique to the ancient civilizations of the Near East. Eleven of the cylinder seals included in this catalogue come from the time of the royal tombs; two are royal seals for the period immediately following the Royal Cemetery. One, generously loaned by the Vorderasiatisches Museum, Berlin, is included in the exhibit, although not in the catalogue, for its important iconography (see fig. 43). As the name implies, these seals are cylindrical objects made of stone or some other hard material such as gold or bronze or of man-made materials such as faience, whose curved sides are carved with a design that can be either abstract or figural. When seals are rolled across a malleable material such as damp clay, the engraved design appears in relief as a mirror image.

From their invention around 3500 BC, cylinder seals served as an important tool in ancient administration. They were rolled across still damp written documents to officially acknowledge that the contents of the documents were accurate and that responsibility was assigned. Cylinder seal impressions in lumps of clay were also used to protect containers or doors against unauthorized opening, much as customs seals or locks are used today. Many examples of these ancient locks were found in the rubbish layers into which the royal tombs were dug. In fact, so many impressions were found that the rubbish dump is called the Seal Impression Strata (fig. 44).

In addition to their administrative role, cylinder seals were also valuable as objects. Often they were deposited in temples in supplication to the deities, on whose whims the fate of both the individual and the community depended. Cylinder seals were either owned by individuals or acquired by them as insignia of social status or official position. As such, these most prized possessions were deemed necessary in the afterlife and were buried along with the other valued property of the deceased. More than four hundred cylinder seals were found in the graves excavated by Leonard Woolley in the Royal Cemetery of Ur. From the tombs

Fig. 44. Clay sealing found in Seal Impression Strata 1–2. The sealing depicts a combat scene and is inscribed with the name of the founder of the First Dynasty of Ur, Mesannepada. L. 9.5 cm. UPM 31-16-677 (U.13607).

considered to be royal burials, approximately thirty seals were found whose designs can be recognized.

The designs engraved on the sides of cylinder seals varied over time. During the Early Dynastic III period, only a few themes were used. And with rare exceptions, only two themes were found in the royal tombs: the banquet scene and the combat scene. Both scenes appear on seals as early as 3000 BC. Although their literal reference to festival and conflict are clear, the precise meaning of these themes to contemporary users is not fully understood today.

The basic format of the banquet scene includes one or two seated celebrants, in any combination of male and female. Sometimes, a table laden with foodstuff or a vessel holding beer or wine is included. In many examples, one or more serving figures carrying foodstuff approach the celebrants. Most of the banquet-theme seals found in the royal tombs had two horizontal registers. Either both scenes contained banqueting themes or one was a banqueting scene and the other was a combat scene. The few examples of single-register banquet-theme seals, although engraved in lapis lazuli or marble, tend to be crudely carved and iconographically condensed.

The earliest combat scenes show a hero with a dagger protecting a domesticated cow or goat against an attacking lion. A sense of actual struggle is conveyed, perhaps referring to the constant threat of the wild and untamed animals against the valuable domesticated livestock of the early city-states. Carried to a metaphorical level, the struggle of order over chaos is embodied in this powerful theme. In these early scenes, arranged in a horizontal composition, each figure is easy to distinguish from the other combatants. While the basic subject matter remained unchanged, the organization of the combat scenes found in the Royal Cemetery cylinder seals changed radically, becoming far more decorative. In these combat scenes, a "figure band" contains five or six figures shown in overlapping struggle. The sense of urgent combat has been replaced by a decorative band that might represent the idea of the balance between the uncontrollable forces of nature embodied in the lion and the order of civilization embodied by the domesticated animals. Although the hero is often described as "Gilgamesh," he must be understood as a generic heroic figure without specific identity.

The cylinder seals of the Royal Cemetery are made of the same colorful and precious materials used for the other small objects of personal adornment. Gold and lapis lazuli are the most precious materials. White limestone and shell are also used. Studies have shown a coincidence suggesting that certain scenes tended to be carved on seals of certain materials: combat scenes are more often carved in a white material, either shell or calcite, whereas banquet scenes are more often rendered in lapis lazuli. Other studies have suggested that the scene was not chosen by its owner at random, but that it in some way reflected the owner's role in the court or social hierarchy. Double-register banquet scenes seem more often associated with women involved in the internal workings of the court; banquet scenes combined with a combat scene have been related to individuals involved in the economic workings of the court or the secular sphere; and single-register combat scenes seem to be associated with men who, judging by their remains, appear to be closely tied to military activities.

When they are found in situ in close association with their owners, we can see that cylinder seals were worn as objects of personal adornment. Sometimes the seals were suspended at the bottom of a series of stone plaques strung together as a pendant (fig. 45); at other times, they were suspended from the long pin that served to close a heavy woolen cloak. Other seals were worn either at the wrist or suspended from a belt.[1]

Fig. 45. Shell inlay from Mari depicting a woman with plaques and a cylinder seal suspended from her cloak pin. Drawing by Jana Fisher after Parrot 1962: pl. XI.

16. CYLINDER SEAL

This schematic design engraved by a cutting wheel closely resembles seals of the earlier Jamdat Nasr period. However, the material (lapis lazuli) and the double line separating the two registers of the composition, as well as the distinctive triangular rendering of the animal heads, are characteristic of seals dating to the period of the Royal Cemetery, even though this example was found in the fill, without clear archaeological context. This design is not common among the cemetery seals, but it appears in a few other examples.

17. CYLINDER SEAL

This dark blue lapis lazuli cylinder seal was found leaning against the right upper arm of a queen. On it is engraved a double-register banquet scene with only female participants. All of the women wear a skirt or a dress with a long fringe, and their long hair is drawn together at the nape of the neck in a bun. In the upper register, two females sit on identical folding stools facing each other and raising their conical drinking cups. Between them, two standing servants gesture with raised

16A
CYLINDER SEAL
Lapis lazuli
H. 4 cm, Dm. 2.3 cm
Found loose in the soil
30-12-13 (U.11757)

16B
MODERN IMPRESSION

17A
✳ CYLINDER SEAL
Lapis lazuli
H. 4 cm, Dm. 2 cm
PG 800, Puabi's tomb chamber
B16728 (U.10872)

17B
MODERN IMPRESSION

Fig. 46a,b. Modern impressions of two seals found near Puabi's body in PG 800. British Museum, (a) WA 121545 (U.10871); (b) WA 121544 (U. 10939). Courtesy of the British Museum.

hands, and to the far left a third servant stands gently waving a square fan. In a second banquet vignette in the lower register, a single female celebrant sits on a stool facing a high table laden with breads and a haunch of meat and is flanked by servants. Behind her, a woman holds a handled jar and raises a cup, perhaps offering a portion of beer to drink with the meal. To the side, a separate scene depicts a musical performance, in which one woman plays a small four-stringed instrument accompanied by two women who clap cymbals and perhaps sing.

Two similar cylinder seals were found close to the body of the queen. On one, the banqueters drink from straws that draw down liquid from a large jar (fig. 46a). The other carries an inscription Pù-abi, nin designating the owner as Puabi, the queen (fig. 46b). It is this seal that makes Puabi's identity certain.

18A

✳ CYLINDER SEAL

Lapis lazuli
H. 4.2 cm, Dm. 2.6 cm
Inscribed: A-bára-ge
PG 800, pit
B16727 (U.10448)

18B

MODERN IMPRESSION

18. CYLINDER SEAL

Woolley reported that this double-register banquet scene was found against the end of the "wardrobe box," in the fill above the floor. This cylinder seal differs from cat. no. 17 in two aspects: here both male and female participants are depicted, and there is no musical performance. A personal name read in Sumerian as A-bára-ge is inscribed in three vertically arranged cuneiform signs to the side of the scene in the upper register. When attempting to identify the occupants of the royal burials, Woolley conjectured that this cylinder belonged to the husband of Queen Puabi, a king buried in the contiguous PG 789. Other scholars have not accepted Woolley's hypothesis, arguing that the name Abarage is neither certainly male nor certainly royal. Moorey believes that this example could be another seal belonging to Puabi or that it might have belonged to one of her ladies-in-waiting.[2]

19. CYLINDER SEAL

The other seal from PG 1237 shown in this catalogue is also unusual. It was found under the body of "individual no. 7," who was collapsed in the corner of the death pit near the cluster of three magnificent lyres—one of gold, one of silver, and one a large bull effigy lyre of mixed materials. In addition to the seal, the victim was rather sedately adorned, wearing only gold earrings, hair wires, a gold pin with a fluted lapis lazuli ball head, three gold finger rings, a "dog collar" necklace of gold and lapis lazuli, and a lapis lazuli bead necklace. The seal is a finely carved double-register banquet scene that carries an inscription giving a title and personal name Dumu-kisal. Combining elements of other banquet seals, here three seated celebrants are shown in the upper register: two face each other and drink through tubes from a large vessel; the other raises her hand in a gesture to a standing servant. Curiously, the inscription is placed between these two figures, without regard for their obvious narrative coherence. Across the lower register is an elaborate scene of dancing, singing, and musical performance. From the left, a man carrying a staff over his shoulder is preceded by two females clapping cymbals. This group faces a woman playing a bull lyre. Beneath the instrument, two small figures dance; their diminutive size has been interpreted either as a portrayal

of dwarfs or as an attempt to show the figures in front of the musical instrument. Facing the performers is a group of three additional female figures with cymbals.

20. CYLINDER SEAL

PG 337 was the first royal tomb found by Woolley, and although it was small and had been plundered in antiquity, he determined from its contents that it was clearly a royal grave. In addition to the bodies of three victims, the tomb contained a pile of personal jewelry that was essentially identical to that of the most elaborately adorned women found in tombs uncovered later. Among the personal adornments Woolley found was this cylinder seal, carved of lapis lazuli with a double-register banquet scene. Apart from the fineness of its carving, the virtually identical images in the two registers distinguish this seal. In both registers, seated male celebrants gesture with raised cups toward standing servants. Unique to the lower register is a tall table bearing breads and a haunch of meat.

19A
CYLINDER SEAL
Lapis lazuli
H. 4.5 cm, Dm. 1.5 cm
Inscribed: Dumu-kisal
PG 1237, the "Great Death Pit," Body no. 7
30-12-2 (U.12374)

19B
MODERN IMPRESSION

20A
CYLINDER SEAL
Lapis lazuli
H. 4.2 cm, Dm. 2 cm
PG 337
B16828 (U.8615)

20B
MODERN IMPRESSION

21A

✳ CYLINDER SEAL

Shell
H. 3.1 cm, Dm. 1.6 cm
Inscribed: Lugal-shà-pà-da
PG 800, on the body of a
   groom in the pit (Body
   no. 18)
B16747 (U.10530)

21B

MODERN IMPRESSION

22A

CYLINDER SEAL

Shell
H. 3.4 cm, Dm. 1.6 cm
PG 1054, near a skeleton
30-12-8 (U.11528)

22B

MODERN IMPRESSION

21. CYLINDER SEAL

This seal was found with one of the grooms in the tomb pit of Puabi. Unlike the other four seals found in her tomb, this seal, carved from shell, carries a depiction of a combat scene—a fine example of the typical Early Dynastic IIIA combat scene, consisting of an unbroken figure band made up of five struggling figures. To the left, a hero is shown wearing only a wrestling belt and with hair standing on end in large backward-turning curls. He wields a dagger and grapples a lion, who grasps a rampant cervid in his forelegs. The lion's head is rendered as if seen from the top, indicating that he has turned his head to the side in order to take a bite out of the animal's neck. Overlapping the lion is a second rampant lion with a very full mane, which attacks a long-haired goat from behind. Beneath the goat's chin is a small scorpion, and above his head, separated from the scene by two incised horizontal lines, is an inscription giving a male personal name, Lugal-shà-pà-da.

22. CYLINDER SEAL

This shell seal is engraved with a simplified combat scene in which the hero stands to the side of two rampant lions that attack a reversed-horned animal. The undistinguished carving on this seal is heavily worn.

23. CYLINDER SEAL

When it was first cut, this shell seal would have been a fine example of a combat scene. The main group of combatants is a pair of rampant lions attacking a rearing long-haired goat. Crossing behind the left-most lion is a second caprid rampant toward a two-tiered composition that replaces the nude hero. Each register has two distinct groupings. In the upper register to the left, the personal name Lugal-anzu$_x$ is inscribed; to the right, a pair of rampant crossed bulls is shown. In the lower register, a heroic master of animals dominates a pair of felines, holding them upside down by their back legs. Next to this group is an elaborate snake interlace. These three scenes, shown in miniature in association with the inscription, are all used on other seals at full scale. Although there is no narrative association between these motifs, each one must have significance, perhaps in reference to the seal's owner.

Although this simple inhumation had been plundered, Woolley found remnants of the kind of assemblage often associated with military men. Along with the cylinder seal were cockleshells with cosmetic paint, copper razors, remnants of a wooden gaming board, a bronze ax with remains of the haft, other weapons, and copper and stone vessels.

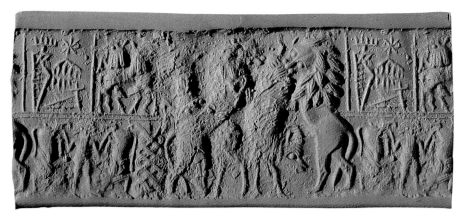

23A
CYLINDER SEAL
Shell
H. 4.5 cm, Dm. 2.7 cm
Inscribed: Lugal-anzu$_x$ ^{mushen}
PG 261
B16869 (U.8513)

23B
MODERN IMPRESSION

24. CYLINDER SEAL

This fine example of a six-animal combat scene shows three lions attacking a caprid and a human-headed bull; a second caprid stands rampant to the side. The style of carving of this seal is characteristic of the Royal Cemetery period. The figures are fully modeled, and the manes of the lions are very full, the hair rendered in a flame-like pattern. The heads of the lions are shown from the top, and the human-headed bull turns his heavily bearded face frontally, looking out with wide-open drilled eyes. In the field are a seven-petaled rosette or star and a moon crescent with disk. A corroded silver wire still runs through the suspension hole of the seal, indicating that it was once worn suspended, perhaps from its owner's belt. This private grave included another seal carved in lapis lazuli with an overall lozenge-and-dot pattern as well as silver earrings, a pin, an ax, six vessels of various materials, and a shell lamp.

24A
CYLINDER SEAL
Lapis lazuli
H. 2.6 cm, Dm. 1.6 cm
PG 1382
30-12-4 (U.12674)

24B
MODERN IMPRESSION

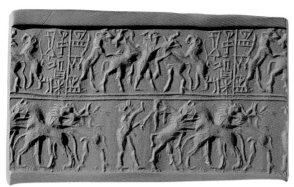

25. CYLINDER SEAL

Woolley was very lucky to find this seal in the loose soil above the royal tombs because through its inscription, Ninbanda, the wife of Mesannepada, we have a historical record of the first queen of the First Dynasty of Ur. It is interesting that the imagery of Ninbanda's seal is also a combat scene, like that of her husband (fig. 44), but of a very different style. Ninbanda's seal, cut from lapis lazuli, is a double-register composition. The lower register shows a five-combatant composition typical of the Royal Cemetery period, but in the upper register the composition has changed. Here the hero is in the middle, protecting two rampant bovids who are being attacked from each side by lions. The sense of a decorative band is still present, but the figures do not overlap. The quality of the carving on this seal is not as fine as on that of her husband, Mesannepada.

26. CYLINDER SEAL

This double-register lapis lazuli seal was found in a simple inhumation of a single deceased wrapped in matting. It lay in front of the face, close to a copper pin with a lapis lazuli head. Each of the registers carries two separate combat compositions. Across the top, two groups of five combatants struggle; in the bottom register, one group of five and one group of four combatants engage in battle. The larger struggles are arranged around a hero with upward-pointing curls who protects rampant caprids attacked by felines. The scenes are staggered so that there is an unbroken band of violence between the two registers. Unlike in earlier combat scenes, here the bodies of the struggling figures do not overlap, indicating that this seal belongs to the Early Dynastic IIIB period, just following the Royal Cemetery period. It is close in composition to the seal of Barnamtara, the wife of Lugalbanda, found at Ur in SIS-1.

Woolley reported that this grave intruded into the "Great Death Pit" of PG 1237, strengthening the idea that it is somewhat later than the royal tombs. Another lapis lazuli seal found in the grave attached by a silver wire to a silver bracelet is engraved with interlocking lozenges.

27. CYLINDER SEAL

This lapis lazuli seal was found associated
with one of the most elaborately adorned
of the sixty-eight female victims in the
"Great Death Pit." She wore the full com-
plement of gold, lapis lazuli, carnelian, and
marble headgear and jewelry. In addition,
a gold pin with a lapis lazuli ball head and
a silver pin with a lapis lazuli head held
her cloak together. Perhaps this lapis lazuli
cylinder seal was suspended from one of
these. Next to her was a silver tumbler.

This double-register cylinder seal shows
a summarily carved composition. In the top
register, an unusual version of the banquet
scene is depicted, showing two seated female celebrants, both facing left, each raising a vessel. A servant stands behind a
table holding breads. In the lower register,
an animal combat scene is shown. The
combination of banquet and combat scenes
is unusual but not unique on cylinder seals
and other artifacts. The significance of the
association is unknown. It has been suggested that these seals designated offices
responsible for the economies both inside and outside of the court, but it is unclear what the elaborate adornment of the
seal's owner can tell us about her official
responsibilities.

27A
CYLINDER SEAL
Lapis lazuli
H. 4.5 cm, Dm. 2 cm
PG 1237, the "Great Death
  Pit," Body no. 61
30-12-3 (U.12380)

27B
MODERN IMPRESSION

 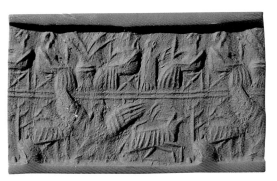

28. CYLINDER SEAL

This double-register shell seal is engraved
with yet another combination of scenes. In
the top register is a banquet scene in which
a pair of celebrants drink through tubes
from a vessel, while another seated celebrant raises a cup toward a standing
servant. In the lower register is a spread-
winged eagle that dominates a goat with its
talons. This heraldic theme, which appears
early in the Early Dynastic period, is used
both on seals and as large-scale ornament
engraved on the base of large votive figures
or on votive plaques. Like the other combat
scenes, its precise meaning eludes us, but it
may be associated with a deity or an institution as well as having a more general
metaphorical meaning.

Jewelry

Jewelry

Holly Pittman

The jewelry worn by the occupants of the Royal Cemetery, more than any other item, conveys the compelling sense of unified purpose and belief that brought so many people together in their final moments. Rather than setting individuals apart, a function now familiar for precious and colorful jewelry, both attendants and primary occupants wore ensembles that differed from each other in degree but not in kind. Many of the individuals buried in the elaborate tombs at Ur were dressed and bejeweled for the same special occasion, participating as members of a single troupe in a powerful ritual drama enacted by each for the last, if not the only, time. The uncovered remains suggest that each burial occasioned a public spectacle that first ritually displayed wealth, accompanied by feasting and celebration, and then permanently removed human beings, animals, and precious material resources from circulation in human society.

The unity of the occasion communicated by the jewelry is embedded in the rich materials, their texture and vibrant colors, and the use of bold and distinctive forms. For the most part, only the upper body was adorned with jewelry, perhaps arranged over brightly colored textiles. Rarely—for example, the band of beads that Woolley described as a garter (cat. no. 31)—is jewelry worn below the waistline. Heads, both of women and of men, were the most highly decorated part of the body, often in a manner that disguised as well as enhanced the wearer. Many of the bejeweled women wore a version of a headdress that finds its most elaborate form on Puabi (see below). At their most modest, simple ribbons of silver or gold held a wig or plaited hair in place. The more ornate head embellishments included wreaths with pendant leaves or circlets of gold laid on top of the ribbons. The most constructed headdresses, in gold or silver, dubbed by Woolley "Spanish combs," had three, five, or even seven open rosettes on long stems rising from a plate embedded in the hair. Earrings and hair rings framed the face, and many strings of beads were draped around the neck or wrists or even around the shoulders as a cape.

While the role of individual participants was undoubtedly coded in the details of their jewelry, the overall themes and materials are remarkably unified for both men and women as well as for attendants and primary burial occupants. Unlike the shell plaque compositions, the jewelry contains no discernible narrative content. Rather, the imagery seems to be entirely symbolic. Plants are the most frequent subject matter; less often, animals are depicted—most notably among the pendants associated with the so-called diadem of Puabi (cat. no. 30) and on amuletic pendants suspended from strands of beads (cat. no. 33). Among the floral forms, the open eight-petaled rosette appears often, as do poplar and willow leaves, both trees that lined the banks of the rivers and canals.[1] The rosette of the Royal Cemetery is so similar to that used in the earlier Protoliterate period that a general continuity of meaning seems likely. Flat leaves and small fruits appear in the iconographic repertoire for the first time in the Royal Cemetery.

Although we tend to associate these natural phenomena with fertility, their metaphorical meaning was probably far more complex. From the texts, we know that garments, and especially jewelry, played an important role in the ritual associated with the entry of the deceased into the underworld. In the poem *Descent of Inanna,* we are told that the goddess was required to remove her ornaments and insignia of power one by one, rendering her entirely naked by the time she finally enters the underworld. In *The Death of Ur-Namma,* we are told that the deceased must offer gifts to the gods in order to gain entry to the underworld (see pp. 27–28). Jewelry figures prominently in the list of appropriate offerings, which might explain the pile of jewelry found next to the final resting place of Meskalamdug in PG 755, or the "diadem" resting on the table next

to Puabi. Although we will never be certain of its purpose, the Royal Cemetery jewelry would have made spectacular votive gifts. This kind of accoutrement, combined with the presence of attendants, musicians, dancers, and musical instruments, suggests that the royal burials preserved at Ur serve an additional purpose: along with the texts, they convey the notion of ritual associated with the moon god, Nanna.[2]

The striking appearance of the jewelry comes from the use of strong colors in complementary combinations. This effect is achieved through a deliberate selection of both stones and metals. These materials, which were also employed in other works of art found in the Royal Cemetery, include deep blue lapis lazuli, bright yellow gold, shimmering white silver, and red-orange carnelian. Their abundant repetition gives an overwhelming sense of rich contrasting color within a highly unified aesthetic and symbolic system. Although for this early period we do not know the precise meanings of these wonderful materials, later texts tell us that many of them had powerful magical as well as predictive functions. At the most obvious level, each of the materials evoked far distant lands because none of them are native to southern Mesopotamia. The Sumerian myth *Enmerkar and the Lord of Aratta*[3] paints a vivid picture of the kind of relationship that might have existed in the mid-third millennium BC between such Mesopotamian city-states as Ur and the distant communities that could deliver these precious materials so valued in the urban centers.

To judge from the forms of various jewels, virtually all of the material was imported into southern Mesopotamia in either raw or semiprocessed state. From sites in eastern Iran and on the Iranian plateau comes evidence for the bulk production of blanks for beads, and perhaps even for cylinder seals, but the final production was certainly done in Sumerian workshops. Such a conclusion is based both on the fact that no comparable objects are found at sites where the materials were initially processed and on the fact that these forms were also used in other cities in southern Mesopotamia. Of Puabi's jewelry, only the so-called etched carnelian beads, strung with other types of beads, can be positively identified as imports. These beads were made using a complex firing technique developed in the Indus Valley centers. The white lines were made on the surface of the carnelian following patterns traced in an alkali mixture and then subjected to heat. After several additional steps, this process eventually caused the affected area to lose its color and translucency and become opaque white.[4] The presence of imported artifacts from the Harappan civilization lends credibility to the more tenuous suggestions of intercultural contact found in the figural arts.[5]

A variety of metallurgical techniques were used to create gold and silver jewelry. For the most part, metal jewelry was made from sheet metal hammered over a wooden or bitumen core. Often these formed sheets were soldered together, as in the case of the two lobes on a pair of large lunate earrings (cat. no. 59). On rare occasions, filigree was used—in particular, on finger rings and gold pendants. The cloisonné technique of inlay was used to secure colorful stones to a gold or silver matrix. One of the most important techniques that has sometimes been attributed to the Royal Cemetery is gold granulation. This technique,[6] so highly developed by the second millennium BC, cannot be confidently identified among the Early Dynastic grave goods, but several examples from this early phase have been described as protogranulation. In addition to the gold dagger handle (cat. no. 146), which uses hemispherical nail heads to simulate granulated balls, one of the "dog collar" chokers was made of large gold spheres soldered together onto a gold backplate. Very little casting of precious

metal jewelry pieces is evident, suggesting that the goldsmiths were careful to conserve their materials whenever possible.

29. PUABI'S HEADDRESS

The body of Queen Puabi was laid to rest adorned with the finest jewelry found in the Royal Cemetery. For the most part, hers was an elaborate version of the ensembles worn by the women who accompanied her to the grave: the theme of vegetation conveyed by rosettes, the combination of precious and semiprecious materials, and the striking combination of blue, gold, and red were consistent. Woolley reported using particular care in removing the jewelry from this royal body; he seemed confident that the original relationships between the clusters of jewels had been preserved.[7]

As did her handmaidens, Puabi wore a complex coiffure that either was formed from her natural hair supported by some kind of padding or was a wig onto which the elaborate headdress of gold and precious stones was arranged. Because the organic material does not remain, the best evidence of the Sumerians' treatment of hair comes from statues (fig. 47) and incised plaques, which show women wearing

Fig. 47. Alabaster statuette from Khafajah of a woman with braided hair. Early Dynastic period. UPM 38-10-51.

their long hair dressed in thick braids that were wrapped in a circle around the crown of the head[8] or were brought together into a large chignon at the back of the head. Some examples show that additional large braided rolls were sometimes formed over the ears; others show a support used to lift the hair at the back of the head. Sometimes locks of hair would fall down in front of the ears. The fastening and support apparatus of the jewelry would have been embedded in the hair mass and would have provided support for the weight of the hair arrangement.

Puabi's headdress was constructed from hundreds of individual pieces arranged in a fashion similar to the headdresses of her handmaidens. In Woolley's reconstruction, a long gold ribbon overlaid with wreaths and frontlets was draped across the forehead, ending somewhere close to the ears before being buried in the dense hair roll. The gold ribbon was wound around so that the strands crossed each other at the crown and then swung down to form staggered festoons on either side of Puabi's head. At the back of the head, the strands of ribbon crossed each other again, most of them between the head and the hair bun, although Woolley thought it possible that one or two of them might have secured the hair roll in place. Over all of this layering of what was originally one long ribbon lay a frontlet of lapis lazuli and carnelian beads supporting gold ring pendants. Over the frontlet was a wreath of lapis lazuli cylindrical beads and pendant poplar leaves made of sheet gold with a carnelian bead surrounding each tip. Over this lay a third lapis-and-carnelian wreath from which groups of three gold willow leaves hung, similarly tipped with carnelian beads. Between the willow leaf clusters were gold rosettes whose petals were inlaid with lapis and white paste. Over all of this lay a series of large ovoid lapis beads, but Woolley was unsure how these beads were arranged on the queen's head.

29
PUABI'S HEADDRESS

✳ COMB
   Gold
   H. 36 cm
   PG 800, Puabi's tomb
      chamber, with Puabi
   B16693 (U.10937)

✳ HAIR RINGS
   Gold
   Dm. 2.7 cm
   PG 800, Puabi's tomb
      chamber, with Puabi
   B16992 (U.10890)

✳ WREATH
   Gold, lapis lazuli, and
      carnelian
   PG 800, Puabi's tomb
      chamber, with Puabi
   B17709 (U.10935a)

✳ WREATH
   Gold, lapis lazuli, and
      carnelian
   PG 800, Puabi's tomb
      chamber, with Puabi
   B17710 (U.10935a)

✳ WREATH
   Gold, lapis lazuli, and
      carnelian
   PG 800, Puabi's tomb
      chamber, with Puabi
   B17711 (U.10936)

✳ HAIR RIBBON
   Gold
   PG 800, Puabi's tomb
      chamber, with Puabi
   B17711a (U.10934)

✳ EARRINGS
   Gold
   Dm. 11 cm
   PG 800, Puabi's tomb
      chamber, with Puabi
   B17712 (U.10933)

At the back of Puabi's head, a substantial gold hair ornament was buried in her abundant hair. Although in many reconstructions the gold triangular body of the ornament is shown high above the head, it almost certainly was not visible when it was worn. Instead, this thick gold sheet served to support the mass of hair that had to be held in place. Rising from the top of the plate were seven stems, each ending in a rosette of gold with a lapis center. The stems of each rosette were bent forward, causing the seven rosettes to droop languidly over the crown of the head.

The splendor of Puabi's headgear was completed by a set of great gold double-lunate earrings; these were supported by four spiral twists of gold wire set in locks of hair somewhere close to the ears.

30. "DIADEM"

The most magnificent and enigmatic item of jewelry associated with Puabi is the "diadem," reconstructed by Woolley as a wide band of tiny lapis lazuli beads to which are attached animal and floral figures made from hammered gold. This remarkable object was not found on Puabi's body; it lay to the left of her bier, near her head, on the remains of a wooden surface that Woolley interpreted as a shelf or a small table. Woolley assumed that this pile of more than one thousand tiny lapis beads and gold amulets was a single object that had been sewn onto a fabric or leather backing. However, close examination suggests that this collection of beads and amulets was not a singular object but as many as six discrete items that might have been intended as elements in a coordinated ensemble. Rather than attempting to re-create another pastiche, here the types of amulets are described according to their subject and according to the size and nature of their modes of attachment.

Four pairs of animal amulet pendants

were found: long-hair sheep, cervids, bearded bulls, and antelope. This pairing is clearly suggested by the fact that each set consists of two recumbent animals facing each other. Each animal was originally modeled in bitumen; the form was then covered with gold foil and chased with details. Each amulet has a double suspension loop made of copper covered with gold. All eight animals are of the same scale, are made using the same techniques, and appear to belong to a single object of adornment, perhaps a bracelet. These animals are familiar subjects from the incised plaques and must have carried some specific symbolic imagery.

The remainder of the pendants or attachments depict floral elements or fruits. One pendant type of approximately the same scale as the animals is a branch with oval fruit made of lapis or carnelian or gold. While Woolley attached leaves to several of these branches, it seems more likely that they carried only fruit and not leaves. Six very finely made, slightly bending stalks, with up to twenty stacked grains of wheat or millet,[9] hung from double loops that are somewhat smaller than those from which the animals or fruit-laden branches depended.

Another fruit theme consists of bunches of berries (identified as pomegranates by Woolley). Each cluster of three round fruits with pointed tips ends in a carnelian bead. Above the fruit cluster are three full leaves. The pieces are held together by double suspension loops, some of which are the same size as those used to secure the animals and branches and some of which are slightly smaller.

A unique type of pendant consists of gold wire twisted around a nine-peg form and a long twisted stem ending in a double suspension loop. It is possible that these twisted wires represented fruit, but it is also possible that they are an abstract pattern. Finally, the least substantial of the

30
✳ "DIADEM"

Gold and lapis lazuli
L. 88 cm
PG 800, Puabi's tomb chamber
B16684 (U.10984)
(as reconstructed by Woolley)

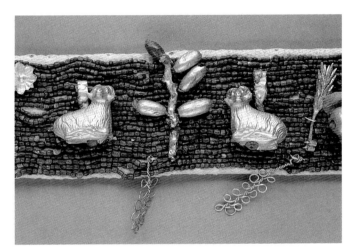
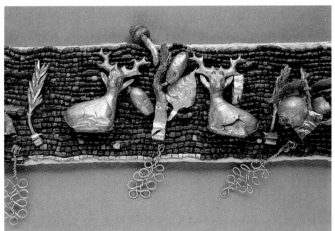

ornaments associated with the "diadem" are seventeen gold leaf rosettes, each with a small gold loop on the back for attachment.

Deciphering the meaning of this ensemble would require pure speculation revolving around fertility, reproduction, and productivity. If these jewels were indeed meant as gifts of passage into the underworld, carrying the "diadem" would have ensured that Puabi would have been allowed to enter without delay.

31. PUABI'S BEADED CAPE AND JEWELRY

Unique among Puabi's jewelry was a "garment" made of strung beads. Between Puabi's neck and waist, Woolley found some fifty strands of beads, which he determined could not have been necklaces because in no case did a horizontal bead connect two vertical strands—that is, none of the strands formed a closed loop. Further, Woolley reported that these straight strands were found completely surround-

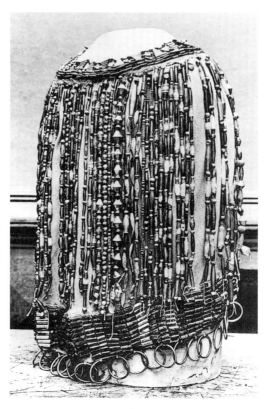

Fig. 48. Woolley's restoration of Puabi's cape. Reprinted from Woolley 1934b: pl. 130.

ing the upper body, forming what he described as a cape of beads. Although unusual and certainly heavy, this cape of carnelian, agate, lapis lazuli, silver, and gold beads must have been stunning. It would have moved and shimmered as the queen moved, much like the long leather fringes on traditional Native American clothing. Although the order of the beads was somewhat disturbed, Woolley felt certain that some of the individual strands of beads could be followed. He reported that below the cape, across the body at the level of the waist, ran a broad belt of beads, tubes of gold, carnelian, and lapis lazuli in ten rows of alternating colors. From this, gold wire rings were suspended. He believed that these beads were sewn on a cloth or leather backing. On other, less elaborately dressed individuals, shell rings were sometimes found at the waist, and Woolley suggested that these also were pendant from belts. At the top of the cape, a group of triangular beads identical to those used in the "dog collar" chokers worn by handmaidens was found. According to Woolley, these alternating triangles separated by three small round beads were attached to the cape and served as the finished edge for the neck opening.

Around her neck, Puabi wore a necklace of three strands of small round gold and lapis beads. A very fine openwork gold rosette was pendent in the middle. The queen wore ten gold rings: eight were plain gold, decorated with a cable pattern made of twisted wire; the other two were inlaid with lapis lazuli. Around her right knee was a garter made of flat rectangular beads of gold and lapis with one carnelian ball. A gold pin was found resting on the edge of her wooden bier.

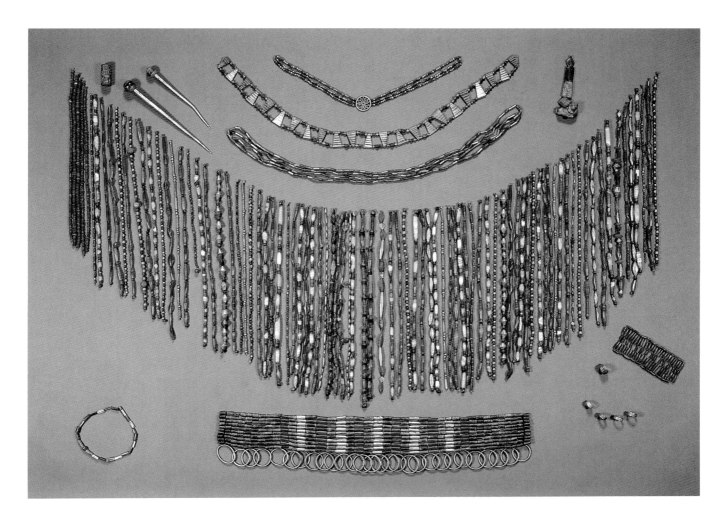

31
PUABI'S BEADED CAPE
AND JEWELRY

TOP:

❋ CYLINDER SEAL

(see cat. no. 17)

❋ PIN

Gold and lapis lazuli
L. 21.1 cm
PG 800, Puabi's tomb chamber,
 with Puabi
B16729 (U.10940)

PIN

Gold and lapis lazuli
L. 16 cm
PG 1064 (but similar to U.10941,
 found with Puabi)
30-12-552 (U.11553)

❋ STRING OF BEADS
 WITH ROSETTE

(see cat. no. 34)

❋ BEADS AND AMULET

(see cat. no. 33)

MIDDLE:

❋ CHOKER, STRING OF BEADS,
 AND BEADED CAPE

Gold and various stones
PG 800, Puabi's tomb chamber, with Puabi
83-7-1 (no single U. number)

BOTTOM:

❋ GARTER

Gold, lapis lazuli, and carnelian
L. 38 cm
PG 800, Puabi's tomb chamber, with Puabi
B16783 (U.10979)

❋ BELT

Gold, lapis lazuli, and carnelian
PG 800, Puabi's tomb chamber, with Puabi
B17063 (U.10867)

❋ FINGER RINGS

Gold
Dm. 2 to 2.2 cm
PG 800, Puabi's tomb chamber, with Puabi
B16717–16720 (U.10877a–d)
B16721 (U.10878)

❋ CUFF

Lapis lazuli and carnelian
L. 14.5 cm
PG 800, Puabi's tomb chamber, with Puabi
B17292 (no U. number)

32. PIN OR HAIR ORNAMENT

This object, hammered from heavy sheet gold, probably served as a support for a mass of hair brought together at the back of the head. It probably functioned similarly to the "Spanish combs" and perhaps had organic materials threaded through the rolled top. It was found on Puabi's wooden bier, to the left of her waist.

33. BEADS AND AMULET

This string of two flat and two rhomboidal beads from which an amulet depends was found next to the queen's left shoulder. The amulet is in the form of a recumbent bearded bull sculpted in the round, with his head turned out from his body. His tail is tucked under his hind leg. Small amulets in the shape of lion-headed eagles, bearded bulls, and double-bearded bulls whose heads or wing tips often were made of gold were found in the jewelry hoard in the so-called Akkadian palace at Tell Asmar.[10] Similar amulets were found in the Treasure of Mari[11] and were thought by Max Mallowan[12] to be the dowry for the marriage of a princess. Such amulets are shown on incised plaques from Mari and from Nippur suspended with cylinder seals from rings attached to cloak pins (fig. 45).

In addition to this bull amulet, three fish amulets of gold and lapis and an amulet of recumbent gazelles hung from three gold pins found against the queen's right upper arm. Three lapis lazuli cylinder seals were suspended from the pins as well. Next to the right shoulder was a reclining calf figure carved of lapis that was strung together with three large beads of lapis and agate.

32

❋ PIN OR HAIR ORNAMENT

Gold
L. 12.8 cm
PG 800, Puabi's tomb
  chamber
B16908 (U.10938)

33

❋ BEADS AND AMULET

Lapis lazuli and carnelian
L. 12.3 cm
PG 800, Puabi's tomb
  chamber, with Puabi
B16726 (U.10985)

34
❋ STRING OF BEADS
   WITH ROSETTE

Gold and lapis lazuli
L. 43 cm
PG 800, Puabi's tomb
   chamber, with Puabi
B16694 (U.10982)

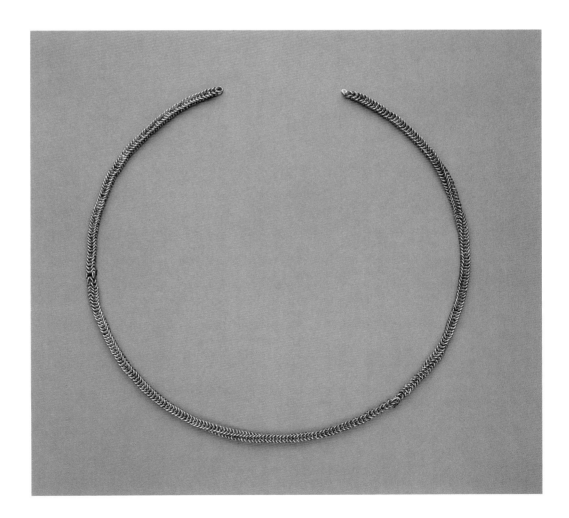

35
❋ CHAIN

Gold
L. 44 cm
PG 800, Puabi's tomb
   chamber, with Puabi
B16761 (U.10875)

36
PIN

Gold, silver, and
  lapis lazuli
L. 17.8 cm
PG 1237, the "Great
  Death Pit"
30-12-732 (U.12406)

PIN

Copper alloy and
  lapis lazuli
L. 23 cm
12th Expedition
35-1-481 (no U. number)

HAIR RINGS

Gold
Dm. 2.5 to 3 cm
PG 1284
30-12-634 and 30-12-635
  (U.12186)

✳ STRING OF BEADS

Gold, lapis lazuli,
  and carnelian
Arbitrarily strung
L. 56 cm
PG 800, Puabi's tomb
  chamber, with attendant
  at foot of bier
B16735 (U.10889)

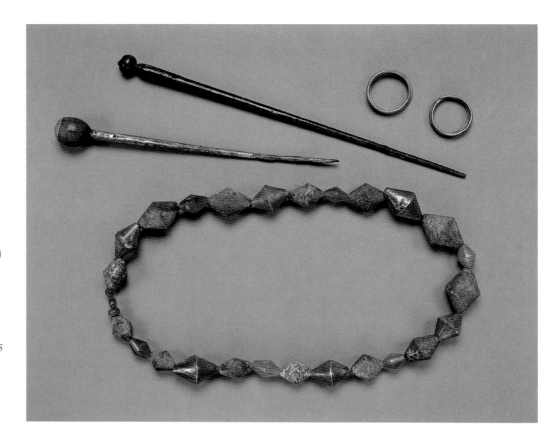

36–43. PUABI'S ATTENDANTS' JEWELRY

The items in cat. no. 36 were (or are similar to) those found with the body of the female attendant crouched at the foot of Puabi's bier. Of the female attendants in Puabi's death pit, Body no. 1 was adorned with a gold hair ribbon, a gold wreath with pendent poplar leaves (cat. no. 38), silver hair rings, gold earrings (cat. no. 37), a straight silver pin with a lapis lazuli head, a thin silver fillet found on the head, a necklace of silver and lapis lazuli beads, and two small clay pots and a clay saucer. Body no. 7 was bedecked with a gold hair ribbon, a wreath with gold poplar pendants, a silver hair ring, gold earrings, a silver pin with lapis lazuli head, a necklace of gold, lapis lazuli, and carnelian (cat. no. 40), and a

silver finger ring. A cockleshell with green paint was found close to the body.

Body no. 15 was one of three grooms found near the head of the oxen attached to Puabi's cart. With him were beads and a whetstone, a single silver earring (cat. no. 41), and a copper alloy dagger. Body no. 18, also one of the grooms, was found with a string of beads (cat. no. 42), a shell cylinder seal inscribed with the name Lugal-shà-pà-da (cat. no. 21), a bronze spear, and three beads of gold and lapis lazuli which originally formed a brim. Body no. 19 lay crouched against the short end of Puabi's wardrobe. He wore a brim (cat. no. 43) and a gold lunate earring, and carried a dagger and two whetstones.

37

❋ EARRING

Gold
Dm. 7.3 cm
PG 800, Puabi's death pit,
  with female attendant
  (Body no. 1)
B16777a (U.9977)

❋ EARRING

Gold
Dm. 7.5 cm
PG 800, Puabi's death pit,
  with female attendant
  (Body no. 1)
B16777b (U.9977)

38

❋ WREATH

Gold, lapis lazuli, and
  carnelian
L. 40 cm
PG 800, Puabi's death pit,
  with female attendant
  (Body no. 1)
B16705 (U.9979)

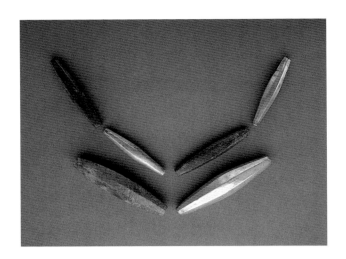

39

❋ BEADS

Gold and lapis lazuli
Lengths range from 6.7
 to 9 cm
PG 800, Puabi's death pit
B16733a–f (U.10424)

40

❋ STRING OF BEADS

Gold, lapis lazuli, and
 carnelian
L. 36 cm
PG 800, Puabi's death pit,
 with female attendant
 (Body no. 7)
B17642 (U.9985)

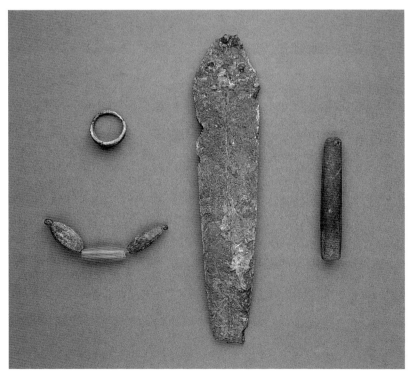

41

❋ EARRING

Silver
Dm. 2.1 cm
PG 800, Puabi's death pit,
 with groom (Body no. 15)
B17561 (U.10535)

❋ BRIM

Lapis lazuli and carnelian
L. 9.5 cm
PG 800, Puabi's death pit,
 with groom (Body no. 15)
B16784 (U.10532)

DAGGER

Copper alloy
L. 18.7 cm
Similar to one found in PG
 800, Puabi's death pit, with
 groom (Body no. 15)
30-12-292 (no U. number)

❋ WHETSTONE

Stone
L. 7.5 cm
PG 800, Puabi's death
 pit, with groom
 (Body no. 15)
B16993 (U.10533)

42

❉ STRING OF BEADS

Gold and lapis lazuli
L. 25.2 cm
PG 800, Puabi's death pit,
  with groom (Body no. 18)
B16754 (U.10544)

43

❉ BRIM

Gold, carnelian, and
  lapis lazuli
L. 41.5 cm
PG 800, Puabi's death pit,
  with male attendant
  (Body no. 19)
B17568 (U.10449)

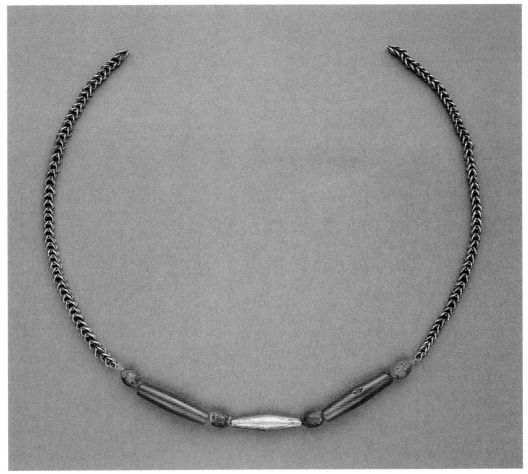

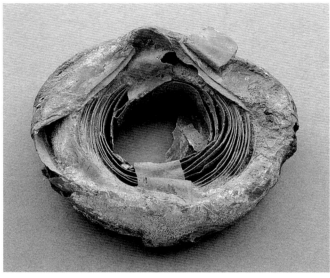

44
HAIR RIBBON
Gold
Dm. 15 cm
PG 1054
30-12-757 (U.11905)

45
HAIR RIBBONS
Gold
L. 76 cm, L. 190 cm
PG 1237, the "Great Death Pit"
30-12-742 (U.12420a)

46
HAIR RIBBON
Silver
Dm. 8 cm
PG 1237, the "Great Death Pit"
30-12-611 (U.12425a)

JEWELRY FROM THE ROYAL CEMETERY

44–46. HAIR RIBBONS

Whether simple or elaborate, all the head-dresses apparently included hair ribbons. Made either of thin gold or silver sheet, these ribbons were laid over the head, across the crown. They were coiled at each end into a small loop through which either a pin or a thread was passed to fasten the ribbon to the hair. Because Woolley found short silver pins on the head but never actually in the loop, loops in fact might have been used to secure a string or a tie of some organic material. However it was secured, the ribbon was then draped in festoons on either side of the head. Woolley believed that the large size of Puabi's festoons indicated that her hair was padded or else was a wig. Often the hair at the back was drawn together into a chignon within which the fastenings of the "wreaths" and frontlets would be hidden. Among the attendants in the death pit of PG 1237, one long ribbon of silver was found coiled into a very tight spiral and clutched in the hand of a young girl. Woolley created a wonderful fantasy of the girl being late for her fateful last performance and running to her place before she was able to finish the final touches to her costume.

47

WREATH

Gold, lapis lazuli, and
 carnelian
L. 42.7 cm
PG 1237, the "Great
 Death Pit"
30-12-714 (U.12366c)

48

WREATH

Gold, lapis lazuli, and
 carnelian
L. 33.1 cm
PG 1237, the "Great
 Death Pit"
30-12-725 (U.12423)

47–51. WREATHS AND FRONTLETS

Overlaying the ribbons of the headdresses were a type of bead and pendant combination that Woolley termed "wreaths." These wreaths for the most part consisted of a double string of lapis lazuli beads and carnelian rings that separated leaf-shaped pendants cut from gold sheet and engraved with veining. These leaves had two basic shapes: long narrow leaves grouped in units of three, probably meant to represent willow leaves, and broader, almost heart-shaped leaves. Woolley called these broader leaves beech leaves even though the beech

tree is not native to the riverbanks of the Middle East. It is much more likely that the broad leaves were intended to represent the leaves of poplar trees, which along with the willows are very common close to the riverbanks of the Tigris and the Euphrates. Indeed, this leaf type gets its name from *Poplar euphraticus*.[13] On the most elaborate of these wreaths, the tips of the leaves are bent around a small carnelian bead. Woolley reported that the "beech leaf" wreath was always part of the headdress. Other wreathlike elements called "frontlets" could be combined with the wreath but

49

WREATH

Gold, lapis lazuli, and
  carnelian
L. 55 cm
PG 1054
30-12-755 (U.11907)

would not replace it. Although a single
wreath was the norm, as many as four
wreaths could be worn at once.

Identical in function to the wreaths,
frontlets were constructed of two strands
of tubular lapis beads separated by carnelian disks. From these disks were pendent several different types of ornaments,
most commonly solid gold rings but also
gold rings with lapis hemispherical centers.
Some frontlets had pendants hung from
their beaded strands.

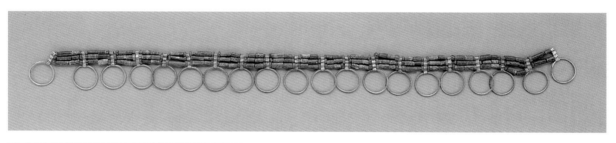

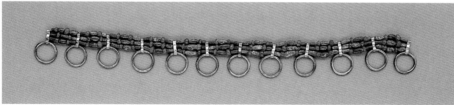

50

FRONTLET

Gold, lapis lazuli, and
  carnelian
L. 56 cm
PG 1054
30-12-759 (U.11908)

FRONTLET

Silver, lapis lazuli, and
  carnelian
L. 37.7 cm
PG 159
B16704 (U.8214)

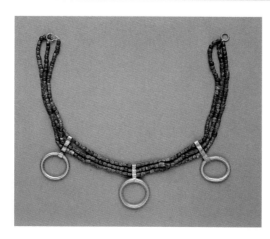

51

FRONTLET

Gold and lapis lazuli
L. 21.5 cm
6th Expedition
B17657 (no U. number)

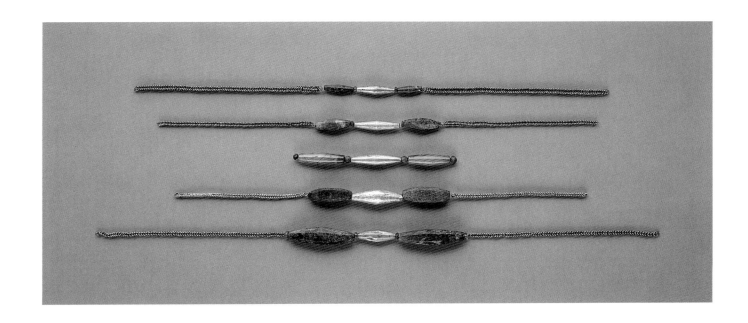

52
BRIM

Gold, lapis lazuli, and
  carnelian
L. 36.5 cm
PG 1133
30-12-619 (U.11809)

BRIM

Gold, lapis lazuli, and
  carnelian
L. 12.4 cm
PG 1237, the "Great
  Death Pit"
30-12-467 (U.12377)

BRIM

Gold and lapis lazuli
L. 31.6 cm
PG 429
B16798 (U.8693)

BRIM

Gold, lapis lazuli, and
  carnelian
L. 33.5 cm
PG 1133
30-12-756 (U.11809)

BRIM

Gold and lapis lazuli
L. 43 cm
PG 1195
30-12-652 (U.11962)

52. BRIMS

Woolley identified the single strands of
beads joined by braided gold wire as the
headband used by men to keep a head cloth
in place; his reasoning for this identification is primarily ethnographic. These
strands were always found near the heads
of the deceased, and often the body would
be associated with weapons or other trap-
pings that Woolley associated with men
rather than women. These headbands are
usually made of three long, faceted beads
of lapis lazuli, gold, or less frequently carnelian that were separated by small disk-
shaped beads of contrasting color. These
beads were connected on each end to a
heavy, braided gold wire chain that would
have been joined into a circle at the back of
the head. It is indeed curious if Woolley is
correct that we have no representations of
such a device among the numerous depictions of men shown in a wide variety of
social roles—king, priest, guard, warrior,
prisoner, wrestler, singer, and the like. In
graves having poorer goods, similar headbands made of prosaic materials were also
found, suggesting some widespread function that crossed social, economic, and
probably ritual lines.

54
COMB

Gold and silver
H. 28 cm
PG 1237, the "Great Death
    Pit"
30-12-436 (U.12423)

55
COMB

Gold, silver, shell, and
    lapis lazuli
H. 21 cm
PG 1237, the "Great Death
    Pit"
30-12-437 (U.12420)

54–55. COMBS

Many headdresses were rather modest, having only ribbons, earrings, and perhaps a single wreath. Others had all of the constituent parts, including the magnificent "Spanish combs" that would have been used to support a mass of hair at the back of the head while at the same time projecting numerous large-petaled rosettes over the head in an array of flowers.

Queen Puabi's comb was made of gold and had seven flowers. The more modest combs were made of silver and had three or five flowers. The petals were inlaid with gold, shell, lapis lazuli, and red limestone. Originally, each of the three rosettes in

cat. no. 54 had eight petals of alternating gold leaf and frit ovals fitted into a silver support. The center of each flower was originally made of lapis. One silver comb is unique, with five points ending in balls of lapis.

An interesting but enigmatic parallel is the presence of rosettes in the hair of figurines from the Harappan sites in India. Although these figurines are crudely rendered in terra-cotta, this parallel has been offered as evidence of close contact between the two civilizations that involved not only the movement of goods but also the movement of people.[14]

56–59. EARRINGS

Many of the women of the Royal Cemetery, both the primary deceased and the accompanying handmaidens, wore elaborate decorations pendent from their ears. The most remarkable of these are the lunate-shaped earrings hammered from sheets of gold or, less commonly, silver. Among the several pairs of earrings found in the Royal Cemetery, this one is the largest. They are constructed of two tapering, crescent-shaped lobes of thin hammered metal soldered together side by side. A solid loop curves up from one crescent, from which the earring would have been pendent either from a hole pierced through the ear or, more likely, from around the ear itself.[15] Smaller versions of this crescent earring appear later; the type continues long into the first millennium BC.

56
EARRING
Gold
Dm. 1.8 cm
PG 1133
30-12-758b (U.11810)

EARRING
Gold
Dm. 1.3 cm
PG 1195
30-12-662 (U.11965)

57
EARRINGS
Gold
Dm. 6.5 cm
PG 1237, the "Great
    Death Pit"
30-12-715a–b (U.12366b)

58
EARRINGS
Gold
Dm. 7.5 cm
PG 1237, the "Great
    Death Pit"
30-12-691a–b (U.12362)

59
EARRINGS
Gold
Dm. 11 cm
PG 1237, the "Great
    Death Pit"
30-12-716a–b (U.12374)

60–62. HAIR RINGS

Objects made of three spiral twists of gold or silver wire are usually thought to be hair rings, although we do not have any definitive evidence to confirm this use. These rings were always found on the head and close to the ears. Woolley thought that they had been twisted around a lock of hair. Some were actually inside the large earrings. Others were found on the shoulder, as if they had held a lock of hair that hung down to the breast. In other instances, they were used without large earrings and were found close to the ear, suggesting that they might have been worn as earrings either in the lobe of the ear or suspended by a lock of hair that was secured close to the ear.

60

HAIR RINGS

Gold
Dm. 2.2 cm
PG 1651
31-17-75a–b (U.14091)

61

HAIR RINGS

Gold
Dm. 2.2 cm, Dm 2.5 cm
PG 1237, the "Great Death Pit"
B16841 (U.12374)

62

HAIR RING

Silver
Dm. 3 cm
PG 1237, the "Great Death Pit"
30-12-614 (U.12425e)

HAIR RING

Silver
Dm. 3 cm
PG 1237, the "Great Death Pit"
30-12-615 (U.12425d)

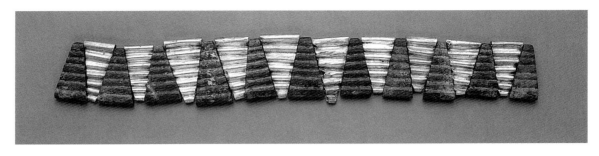

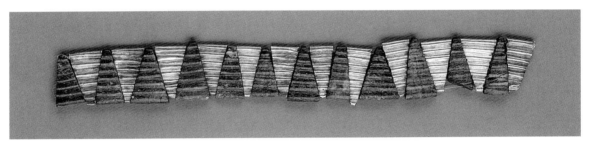

63–65. CHOKERS

Unlike many of the necklace types, this distinctive neck choker, called a "dog collar" by Woolley, seems to be restricted to the period of the Royal Cemetery at Ur.[16] These necklaces typically consisted of between thirteen and eighteen lapis lazuli and gold triangular beads strung together in an alternating pattern that enhanced their contrasting colors. The lapis beads are cut from a single piece of stone, their front and back surface textured by six rounded channels through which six horizontally drilled string holes pass. Woolley described the gold triangles as made from sheet metal folded in half over parallel rods and beaten to produce channels for the strings. The two sides of the gold bead were usually, but not always, soldered together.

This necklace type was worn by certain of the female attendants to the deceased in the Royal Cemetery. An expanded version served as the collar for the elaborate cape of beads that surrounded Puabi's upper body. A unique representation of what might be a cult image found on a painted terra-cotta plaque from the site of Ashur shows a naked and heavily bejeweled female figure wearing such a striking piece of jewelry (fig. 49).

Fig. 49. Painted terra-cotta relief from Ashur. Reprinted from Andrae 1922: pl. 28c.

63

CHOKER

Gold and lapis lazuli
L. 21.6 cm
30-12-706 (no U. number)

64

CHOKER

Gold and lapis lazuli
L. 33.5 cm
PG 1237, the "Great Death Pit"
30-12-722 (U.12403b)

65

CHOKER

Gold and lapis lazuli
L. 21 cm
PG 1237, the "Great Death Pit"
30-12-443 (U.12380e)

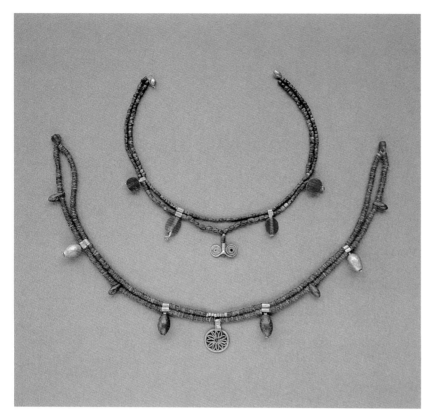

66

STRING OF BEADS

Gold, lapis lazuli, and
  carnelian
Arbitrarily strung
L. 30.2 cm
PG 580
B16804 (U.9351)

STRING OF BEADS

Gold, lapis lazuli, and
  carnelian
Arbitrarily strung
L. 24.5 cm
6th Expedition
B17636 (no U. number)

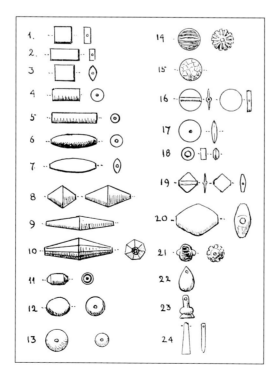

Fig. 50. Typology developed by Woolley for beads
from the Royal Cemetery. Reprinted from Woolley 1934b: fig. 70.

66–83. STRINGS OF BEADS

Beads are the fundamental building blocks
of the Royal Cemetery jewelry. Virtually
every type of ornament except finger rings
used beads as a constituent part. Beads
were made from precious metals as well
as from stones, including lapis lazuli and
carnelian. Only rarely are beads from the
Early Dynastic graves made of agate—for
example, in Puabi's tomb—but during the
later Akkadian period, beads of this banded
quartz are rather common.

In order to describe them systematically,
Woolley established a typology of bead
shapes (fig. 50) that includes more than
twenty distinct forms ranging from square
and rectangular to spherical. Among the
most common shapes is one that he associ-
ates with a date, round in section and tapering toward each end. Another frequently
occurring shape is the double conoid.
Spherical beads were treated in a number
of different ways: they were entirely
smooth, fluted vertically, or faceted.

Beads were pierced and strung together
using organic material that has long since
disintegrated, meaning that beads were
rarely recovered in an undisturbed state.
In the case of Puabi's grave, Woolley felt
quite confident that he was able to reconstruct the order of many of the beads. But
in other instances, beads were found only
generally associated with bodies. Thus,
we are in no case certain that the order in
which the beads are strung, or indeed their
associations, are correct. Many strands are
constructed from beads without a secure
primary findspot and are combined according to twentieth-century aesthetic criteria.

One arbitrarily strung single strand of
beads (cat. no. 69) includes an unusual type
made from lapis and gold in the form of
flies seen at rest from above. The fly is an
unusual image during this early period,
appearing in rare instances engraved on
cylinder seals and on zoomorphic stamp
seals, where it is associated with horned

animals. References in the texts suggest the meaning of the fly image within the context of the Royal Cemetery.[17] In the Old Babylonian *Atrahasis* and in *The Epic of Gilgamesh,* the Mother Goddess wears a necklace of lapis lazuli flies to commemorate the death of her children in the Great Flood. Other textual references refer to flies in contexts that relate to death and dead things. Flies also play an important role in the Inanna and Dumuzi texts, which might shed light on the significance of the royal tombs at Ur.

Another arbitrarily strung double strand of beads (cat. no. 68, top) has suspended from it two ovoid lapis lazuli pendants and five carnelian beads with an etched design in the form of a figure eight. Of all the beads found in the Royal Cemetery, this etched type is the only type that can be identified with certainty as imported—in this case, from a Harappan center in the Indus Valley.

67

STRING OF BEADS WITH
GOLD PENDANT (TOP)

Gold and lapis lazuli
Arbitrarily strung
L. 19.2 cm
PG 580
B16794 (U.9351)

STRING OF BEADS
WITH GOLD PENDANT
(BOTTOM LEFT)

Gold, lapis lazuli, and carnelian
Arbitrarily strung
L. 14.5 cm
6th Expedition
B17650 (no U. number)

STRING OF BEADS
WITH GOLD PENDANT
(BOTTOM RIGHT)

Gold, lapis lazuli, and carnelian
Arbitrarily strung
L. 11.2 cm
6th Expedition
B16716 (no U. number)

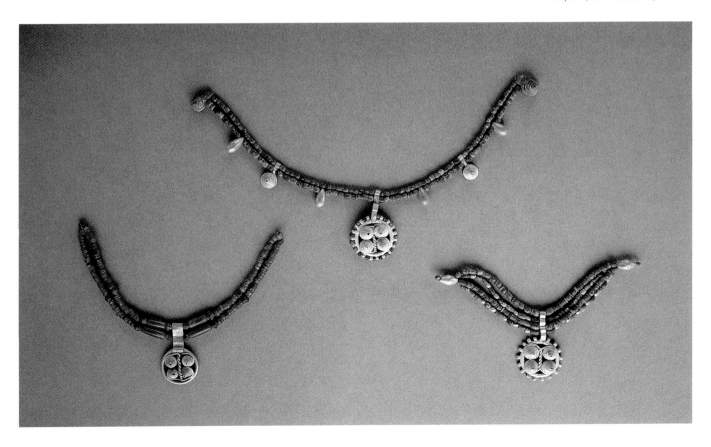

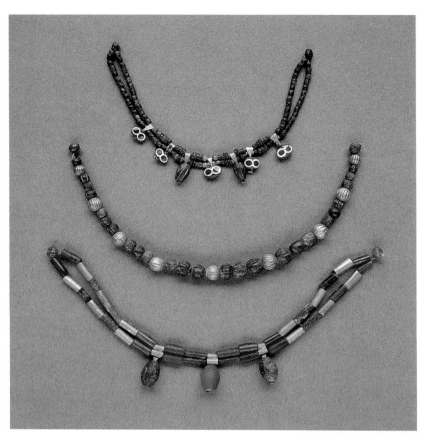

68

STRING OF BEADS

Gold, etched carnelian, carnelian,
and lapis lazuli
Arbitrarily strung
L. 14 cm
PG 453
B16799 (U.8931b)

STRING OF BEADS

Gold and lapis lazuli
Arbitrarily strung
L. 17.5 cm
PG 580
B16800 (U.9351)

STRING OF BEADS

Gold, lapis lazuli, and carnelian
Arbitrarily strung
L. 16.7 cm
6th Expedition
B17649 (no U. number)

69

STRING OF BEADS

Gold and lapis lazuli
Arbitrarily strung
L. 22.7 cm
PG 1284
30-12-570 (U.12187)

70

STRING OF BEADS

Gold and carnelian
Arbitrarily strung
L. 25.3 cm
PG 580
B16819 (U.9351)

STRING OF BEADS

Gold, etched carnelian, and
 carnelian
Arbitrarily strung
L. 27.5 cm
PG 580, in fill near the north-
 east side of the grave shaft
B17655 (U.9780)

STRING OF BEADS

Gold and carnelian
Arbitrarily strung
L. 40 cm
PG 580, in fill near the north-
 east side of the grave shaft
B17654 (U.9780)

71

STRING OF BEADS

Gold, etched carnelian, and
 lapis lazuli
L. 10.5 cm
7th Expedition
30-12-573 (no U. number)

72
STRING OF BEADS
Gold, agate, carnelian, jasper,
  and marble
Arbitrarily strung
L. 91 cm
PG 1847, Burial R
32-40-227 (U.17813e)

73
**STRING OF BEADS WITH
CARNELIAN PENDANT**
Gold and carnelian
L. 15 cm
1st Expedition
B15583 (no U. number)

STRING OF BEADS
Gold, carnelian, and lapis
  lazuli
L. 61 cm
PG 1845
31-17-61 (U.15381)

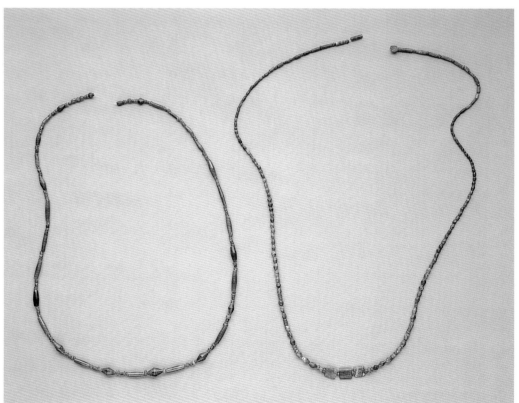

74
STRING OF BEADS
Carnelian, lapis lazuli, and
  chalcedony[?]
L. 90.5 cm
PG 1170
30-12-610 (U.11894)

STRING OF BEADS
Lapis lazuli and carnelian
Arbitrarily strung
L. 108.5 cm
PG 453
B16797 (U.8931a)

75

STRING OF BEADS

Gold, jasper, chalcedony, agate,
sard, marble, carnelian, and
other stones
L. 117 cm
PG 1422
30-12-567 (U.12474)

76

STRING OF BEADS

Silver, lapis lazuli, and
chalcedony[?]
L. 66 cm
PG 789
B17679 (U.10594a)

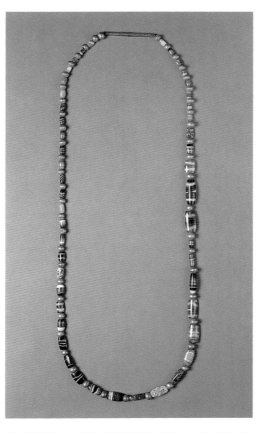

77

STRING OF BEADS

Gold, lapis lazuli, and rock
crystal
Arbitrarily strung
L. 198 cm
PG 789
B16779 (U.10824a)

78

STRING OF BEADS

Gold and lapis lazuli
L. 148 cm
PG 1237, the "Great
Death Pit"
30-12-704 (U.12374)

79
STRING OF BEADS

Gold and carnelian
L. 111.5 cm
PG 1054
30-12-562 (U.11910)

80
STRING OF BEADS

Gold, lapis lazuli, and
 carnelian
L. 88.5 cm
PG 1116
30-12-561 (U.11728)

81
STRING OF BEADS

Lapis lazuli
L. 93 cm
PG 1237, the "Great Death Pit"
30-12-575 (U.12362)

82

CLOCKWISE FROM LEFT:

STRING OF BEADS

Gold, lapis lazuli, and carnelian
L. 121.4 cm
PG 1237, the "Great Death Pit"
30-12-685 (U.12426e)

STRING OF BEADS

Gold, lapis lazuli, and carnelian
L. 91.2 cm
PG 1237, the "Great Death Pit"
30-12-713 (U.12366)

STRING OF BEADS

Gold, lapis lazuli, and carnelian
L. 65.5 cm
PG 57
B16792 (U.8097)

STRING OF BEADS

Gold, lapis lazuli, and carnelian
L. 34.8 cm
PG 1054, Burial C
30-12-449 (U.11743)

STRING OF BEADS

Silver and lapis lazuli
L. 82 cm
6th Expedition and PG 1054
B17713 (no U. numbers)

83

STRING OF BEADS WITH
CYLINDER SEAL

Gold and lapis lazuli
L. 17.3 cm
PG 337
B16829 (U.8614)
Cylinder seal is cat. no. 20

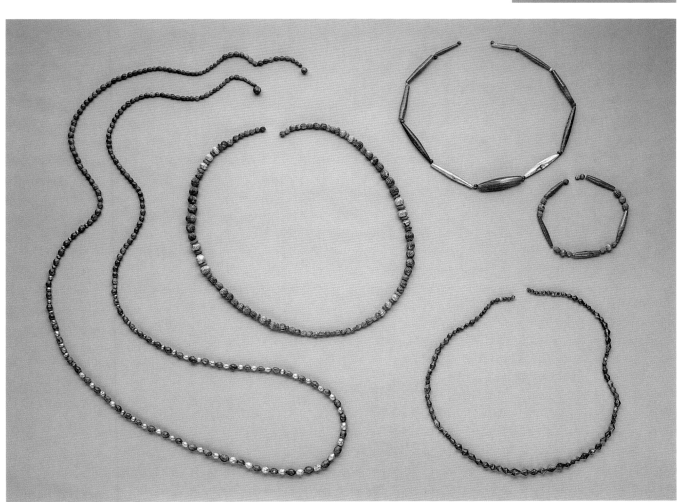

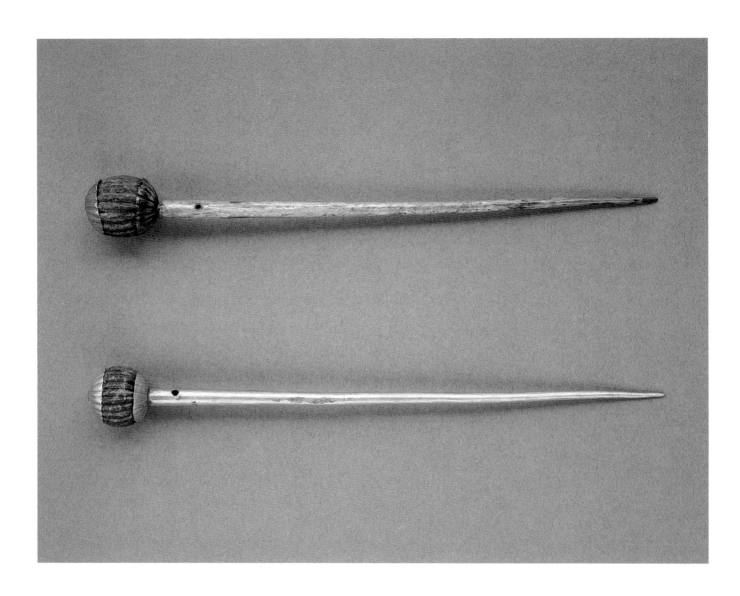

84

PIN

Gold, silver, and lapis lazuli
L. 17.3 cm
PG 1237, the "Great
   Death Pit"
30-12-565 (U.12362)

PIN

Gold and lapis lazuli
L. 17.3 cm
PG 1237, the "Great
   Death Pit"
30-12-703 (U.12374)

84–87. PINS

Many of the occupants of the graves wore long copper or silver pins of various types. Woolley divided these pins into eight types, many of which were used throughout the life of the Royal Cemetery. The most common pins have a straight shaft with round section and a spherical top. The only pin that is used exclusively during the period of the Royal Cemetery is one having a square shaft section and a bent top terminating in a metal or stone ball. Both types of pins have a lateral hole high on the shaft to which a ring could be attached for securing a chain. In at least one instance, a cylinder seal dangled from such a chain. That cylinder seals were worn suspended from pins is well known from incised shell plaques from contemporary levels at Nippur and Mari (see fig. 45). Usually, the pins were found resting against the upper arm or shoulder, situated parallel to the arm bone and usually pointing upward. We know from the representations that these pins served as fasteners for a cloak that passed below one arm and was pinned together over the other shoulder.

85

PIN

Gold, silver, and lapis lazuli
L. 13.5 cm
5th Expedition
B17019 (no U. number)

PIN

Gold, silver, and lapis lazuli
L. 20.8 cm
PG 125
B16835 (U.8162)

86

PIN

Copper alloy and lapis lazuli
L. 22.2 cm
PG 909
B17487 (U.11210)

87

PIN

Silver and lapis lazuli
L. 15 cm
Provenience unknown
98-9-8 (no U. number)

PIN

Silver and lapis lazuli
L. 13.2 cm
PG 1237, the "Great
  Death Pit"
30-12-687 (U.12426)

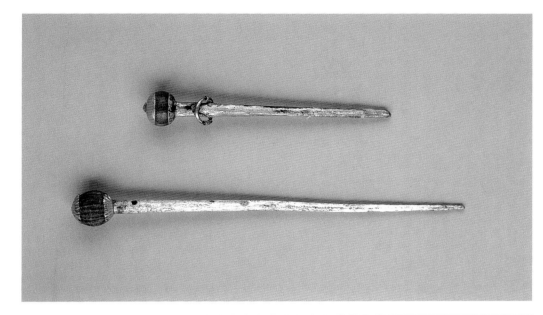

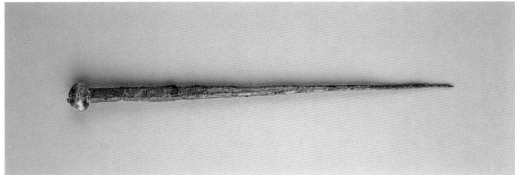

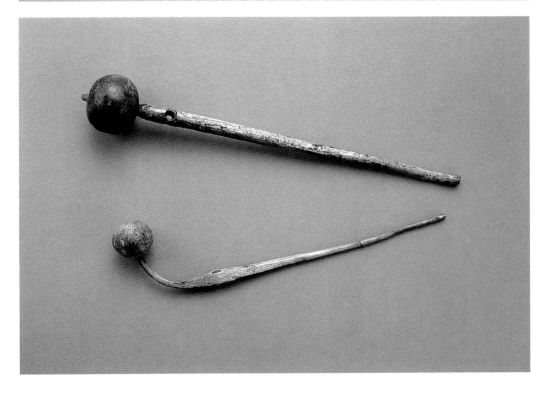

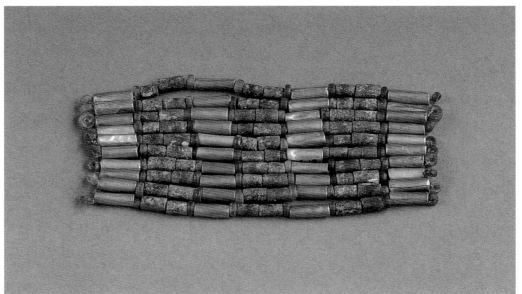

88
CUFF

Gold, lapis lazuli, and carnelian
L. 12 cm
PG 1237, the "Great Death Pit"
30-12-664 (U.12415e)

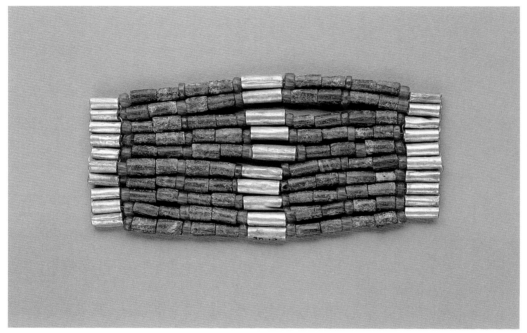

89
CUFF

Gold, lapis lazuli, and carnelian
L. 10.5 cm
PG 1237, the "Great Death Pit"
30-12-748 (U.12420j)

88–89. CUFFS

Ten rows of gold and lapis lazuli tubular beads separated by disk-shaped beads of carnelian were strung together to create these wrist cuffs. Many women in the "Great Death Pit" wore beaded cuffs of various materials arranged in a stripe pattern.

90
BELT

Gold and lapis lazuli
L. 10.8 cm
PG 1236, Chamber B
30-12-559 (U.12450)

91
BELT

Carnelian, lapis lazuli,
and shale
L. 43 cm
PG 55
B16811 (U.8011)

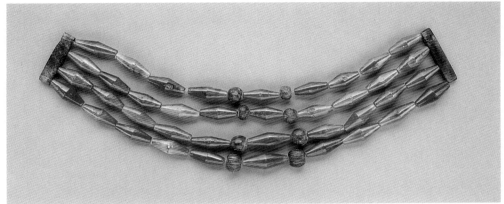

92
FINGER RING

Gold
Dm. 2 cm
PG 1237, the "Great
Death Pit"
30-12-553 (U.12380)

FINGER RING

Gold
Dm. 2.2 cm
PG 1237, the "Great
Death Pit"
30-12-555 (U.12380)

FINGER RING

Gold
Dm. 2 cm
PG 1237, the "Great
Death Pit"
30-12-707b (U.12374)

FINGER RING

Gold
Dm. 2.3 cm
PG 1237, the "Great
Death Pit"
30-12-708b (U.12374)

92. FINGER RINGS

Many of the deceased in the Royal Cemetery wore finger rings, sometimes as many
as four on one finger. Not surprisingly,
Woolley reported a correlation between the
overall richness of an individual grave and
the number of rings found in precious
metals: the richest graves contained many
gold and silver rings; the poorer graves
tended to have copper rings. Many of the
rings shown here were made from a single
or double broad band of gold on which
twisted gold wire was soldered.

93
ROSETTE

Gold
Dm. 3.6 cm
8th Expedition
31-17-74 (no U. number)

94
FLOWER (TOP)

Gold and lapis lazuli
Greatest dm. 6 cm
PG 1237, the "Great Death Pit"
30-12-692 (U.12362b)

FLOWER

Gold and lapis lazuli
Greatest dm. 6 cm
PG 1237, the "Great Death Pit"
30-12-736 (U.12420e)

FLOWER

Gold and lapis lazuli
Greatest dm. 7 cm
PG 1237, the "Great Death Pit"
30-12-737 (U.12420e)

95
PENDANT

Gold
H. 2.5 cm
PG 1133
30-12-560 (U.11808)

95. PENDANT

This large pendant is made of a single thick strand of gold wire formed as a double spiral with a twisted central support. The double spiral form first appears both in beads and as an abstract design on cylinder seals during the Late Uruk period and continues throughout the first half of the third millennium BC. It is found at sites in Syria as well as in southern Mesopotamia. Although elusive, this form likely carried symbolic meaning.

Metal
Vessels

Metal Vessels

Jill A. Weber and Richard L. Zettler

Vessels of copper-based alloys, gold, and silver, alone or in combination, were common in the Royal Cemetery. These vessels demonstrate the Mesopotamian metalworkers' knowledge of the properties of the disparate metals as well as their skill in the manufacture of metal objects, including smelting, refining, and soldering. The technical expertise of Ur's metalworkers is all the more remarkable given the site's location on the resource-poor southern floodplain. Metal-bearing ore deposits are typically formed by hydrothermal activity in mountain-fold zones. As a result, ore deposits are found in mountainous regions and in streams and rivers flowing out of these zones. None of the major metals found in the Royal Cemetery are found in southern Mesopotamia; the metals were obtained from surrounding areas, mainly through trade.

Determining metal source zones has been a focus of research ever since the Royal Cemetery was first excavated.[1] Chemical characterization analysis is one method that has been used to determine the sources of the metals in Mesopotamian artifacts. This technique is used to match unique "fingerprints" of trace elements in the artifacts to fingerprints of trace elements from ores at source locations. A major difficulty of chemical characterization analysis lies in the frequent recycling and reuse of metals in antiquity, which can mix metals from various sources.

Although gold deposits are geographically widespread, none are attested for Mesopotamia itself. Afghanistan, Iran, and Anatolia, as well as Egypt and Nubia, all have considerable gold resources, and Mesopotamian literary sources refer to those areas.[2] Most early Mesopotamian gold contains traces of the platinum group elements (PGEs) such as ruthenium, rhodium, palladium, osmium, iridium, and platinum, which indicates that the gold comes from alluvial placer deposits. Platinum group elements do not occur in gold veins.

Some of the artifacts from the Royal Cemetery are not gold but electrum, an alloy of gold and silver. All gold contains some silver, and naturally occurring electrum is defined as gold with 20 to 50 percent silver content. Values for artificially produced electrum are arbitrary.[3]

Silver was most likely smelted from argentiferous leads such as galena and cerussite in the third millennium BC. This ancient silver compares in purity to modern-day sterling. Several lead deposits are known in the mountainous regions of both Turkey and Iran, where mines have been worked from the fourth millennium BC.[4] Sargon of Akkad mentions the "Silver Mountains,"[5] which are probably to be identified with the Taurus Mountains of modern Turkey. Anatolia might have been providing silver to Mesopotamia as early as the fourth millennium, and by the early third millennium, silver might have been reaching Mesopotamia from there[6] by way of a trade route following the Euphrates.[7]

Although copper occurs throughout the areas surrounding southern Mesopotamia, the high nickel content in copper artifacts from southern Mesopotamia has commonly been taken as an indication that the copper came from the Oman Peninsula. Yet recent research has demonstrated that high nickel content is not characteristic of all copper from Oman and that deposits in the Anarak area of the Iranian plateau contained considerable amounts of nickel. The question of the sources of early Mesopotamian copper then is still open,[8] although Mesopotamian literary sources mention places such as Aratta, probably in Iran, and Magan, most likely to be identified with Oman.

In Mesopotamia, the earliest copper-based alloy used was a naturally occurring one containing arsenic. By the third millennium BC, tin was being added to copper, creating a tin-bronze, a metal stronger and more robust than arsenical copper. Tin sources occur in Turkey, Oman, Iran, and Afghanistan. However, a strong argument for an Afghan source lies in the connection between tin and lapis lazuli and the

co-occurrence (just after 3000 BC) of tin and gold in Mesopotamia.[9] All three of these elements (tin, gold, and lapis lazuli) are found in Badakhshan in northern Afghanistan, where they sometimes occur together in alluvial deposits.[10]

In the Royal Cemetery, tin-bronze seems to have been used particularly for metal vessels, whereas tin-bronze and arsenical copper were used equally for cast weapons and ornaments. The evidence from Ur is particularly intriguing because it cannot necessarily be explained in technological terms. Since copper is more easily workable, it seems more likely that hammered vessels would be made from copper, whereas bronze is easier to cast and is more suitable for weapons because of its hardness. Perhaps tin-bronze was used for luxury items such as metal vessels because of the prestige associated with tin. Tin was difficult to obtain and therefore more expensive. An equally likely explanation is that it was possible to produce thinner sheet metal from bronze and thus create lighter and more elegant vessels.[11]

Preservation of metals is directly related to their nobility (chemical stability) and purity. Gold is the noblest of metals because it is chemically unreactive and does not corrode. The gold objects from the Royal Cemetery are often in very good condition relative to silver or copper objects. Given the same conditions, baser metals corrode more quickly than more noble metals, and alloys corrode at a faster rate than do pure metals, as a result of cathodic protection.[12] The two (or more) metals comprising an alloy create an electrical contact and form a complete electrical circuit when placed in a saltwater solution (such as the damp, saline soil of the Royal Cemetery). This electrical potential attracts chloride ions to the baser metal, where they convert to a metal salt. This corrosion layer protects the more noble metal in the alloy by "breaking the circuit" and preventing chloride ions from reaching the metal surface. Because copper is chemically more reactive than silver, it corrodes first. Corrosion of an object made of a silver and copper alloy can result in a pitted, crusty surface of copper covering a relatively untouched mass of silver.

The metal vessels from the Royal Cemetery were manufactured by hammering the desired form from a shaped piece of sheet metal. Bases and rims could either be hammered out of the same piece of metal as the vessel body or be worked separately and then attached to the rest of the vessel using a heating method (such as sweating or soldering). Double-tube lugs were soldered to the bodies of some. Woolley found a vessel similar to the spouted jug of cat. no. 110 with a rod in its long spout; the area between the rod and the metal edge of the spout was filled with bitumen. The rod and bitumen were likely used for shaping the long spout in the manufacturing process.[13]

Surface decorations typically were chased. In chasing, the artisan works on the exterior of the object by either punching or pressing on the body with blunt and pointed tools such as chisels, wedges, and graver- or burin-type tools. In addition,

the decorative ridges, grooves, and fluting that adorn many of the vessels can be created with a series of blows using a small blade or hammer and an anvil. In at least one instance, a groove was made by abrading the metal with a file rather than punching the metal inward.[14] To finish, the outside of the vessel was smoothed (perhaps with a burnishing stone) to remove traces of punching and chasing; the hammer marks on the inside of the vessel remain. Michael Müller-Karpe (1993) provides a major source of comprehensive information about specific vessels and their manufacture.

96. SPOUTED BOWL

This bowl has a long "channel" spout worked separately from the rest of the vessel and attached with a gold solder. The channel ends in a rolled loop formed from the sheet of the spout. The form of this bowl has no parallels in either stone or pottery in southern Mesopotamia, but pottery bowls with indented band rims are common in Central Asia, as are trough

96

✳ SPOUTED BOWL

Gold
H. 8 cm
PG 800, pit floor
B17692 (U.10451)

97

❋ BOWL

Gold
L. 15 cm, W. 9 cm
PG 800, tomb chamber
B16707 (U.10930)

spouts.[15] Although the dating of such Central Asian parallels is seemingly too late for the Early Dynastic Royal Cemetery—as, for example, with the stone parallels for the lapis lazuli spouted cup (see cat. no. 120)—the similarities of form are nevertheless compelling. The metal contained surface minerals of the platinum group elements, which are found in most early Mesopotamian gold and indicate that such gold came from alluvial deposits.

97. BOWL

Oval bowls are common among the metal vessels from the Royal Cemetery. They were made using a single sheet of shaped metal from which a triangular notch was cut at both ends. The metal was hammered into shape, and the edges from the notch cuts were then "sweated" together.[16] Sweating is a method of heat-joining metal that does not require the use of a solder. The seam created was then aesthetically "removed" by transforming it into a decorative ridge, flange, or groove.

The thickened rim was probably worked separately and attached either with a gold solder or by sweating. Beneath the rim on each long side is a double-tube lug. The lug was made from a metal strip that was rolled inward from each end to create two attached tubes. These lugs were attached by soldering. The visible seam is raised as vertical ribs on the short sides.

98. BOWL

The fifty ridges of fluting on this bowl were created from the inside by punching ridges outward using a small-headed hammer. The decoration at the rim and base and on the bottom of the vessel was chased. The motifs are similar to the electrum and silver tumblers (cat. nos. 105, 106), with herringbone and zigzag patterns at the rim and a rosette on the bottom. Concentric arcs surround the rosette, followed by a herringbone band and a double row of zigzags. The gold double-tube lugs were attached to the body below the rim with a gold solder.

Detail of twelve-petaled rosette on bottom.

98

❋ BOWL

Gold
L. 13.1 cm, W. 9.4 cm
PG 800, tomb chamber
B17693 (U.10850)

99
✳ BOWL

Silver and electrum
L. 21.7 cm, W. 13.4 cm
PG 800, tomb chamber
B17077 (U.10891)

99. BOWL

Seventeen electrum strips, each 15 milli-
meters wide, were laid into thin, vertical
grooves in the body of this vessel. The
applied bands were then attached to the
body by sweating or by hammering silver
from the body over their edges. Two horizontal bands overlay the vertical bands.
At the rim, an electrum wire runs over the
vertical strips and helps to hold them in
place. The double-tube lug was soldered.
Silver wire, threaded through the lugs and
twisted, provides a handle.

100. BOWL

On the long side of this oval-shaped bowl,
just below the rim, is a chased sign of a
bull's leg. A similar sign appears near one
of the handles of cat. no. 101, also a silver
bowl. Woolley described the bull's leg as a
mark of ownership.[17] The bull's leg mark
also occurs on various weapons (see cat.
no. 142), as well on as stone bowls, nearly
always of steatite and bell-shaped. Perhaps
the bull's leg is to be associated with the
haunch of meat carried by the hyena depicted on the front of the lyre from PG 789
(cat. no. 3, see detail, p. 55).

100

✳ BOWL WITH BULL'S
LEG MARK

Silver
L. 22.5 cm, W. 12.5 cm
PG 800, tomb chamber
B17297 (U.10464)

101

BOWL WITH BULL'S
LEG MARK

Silver
L. 21.6 cm, W. 13.6 cm
PG 789
B17067 (U.10554)

102
✳ BOWL

Silver
L. 21 cm, W. 12.7 cm
PG 800, pit floor
B17298 (U.10457)

103
✳ BOWL

Silver
L. 22.6 cm, W. 12 cm
PG 800, tomb chamber
B17296 (U.10457)

104
✳ BOWL

Silver with electrum lugs
L. 18.6 cm, W. 10.7 cm
PG 800, pit floor
B17299 (U.10457)

105–107. TUMBLERS

The electrum tumbler was finely hammered inside and out and fluted into twenty-eight ridges. As on other tumblers, opposed herringbones and double zigzags decorate the rim and base; a naturalistic rosette with eight petals surrounded by concentric arcs decorates the base. The hammering marks on the inside of the tumbler remain, but the chasing marks on the outside have been smoothed. A loop was hammered out of the rim and over the banded decoration; this would have been for the attachment of a wire or string handle. This loop does not occur on tumblers made of silver or copper alloy.

105

✳ TUMBLER

Electrum
H. 15.2 cm
PG 800, tomb chamber
B17691 (U.10453)

Detail of tumbler bottom.

Detail of tumbler bottom.

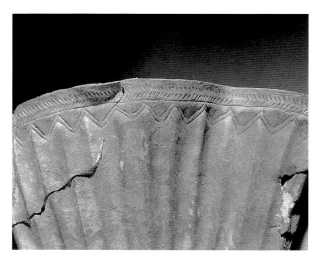

106

❋ TUMBLERS

Silver
Heights 16.5 to
17.4 cm
PG 800, tomb chamber
B17072a–d (U.10896–
10898; d has no
U. number)

107

❋ TUMBLER, RIM DETAIL

Silver
H. 16.8 cm
PG 800, tomb chamber
B17082a (U.10860)

108

✳ SHELL-SHAPED
COSMETIC CONTAINER

Gold
8 × 6.2 × 3.3 cm
PG 800, tomb chamber
B16710 (U.10932)

109

✳ SHELL-SHAPED
COSMETIC CONTAINER

Silver
8.3 × 6.6 × 3.7 cm
PG 800, tomb chamber
B16711 (U.10901)

110

❋ SPOUTED JUG

Silver
H. 22 cm, Dm. 5.2
PG 800, tomb chamber
B17082b (U.10861)

111

✳ POURING VESSEL

Silver
L. 27.8 cm, W. 13.3 cm
PG 800, tomb chamber
B17081 (U.10886)

111–112. POURING VESSELS

These vessels resemble conch-shell vessels also found in the Royal Cemetery. Although often described as "lamps," both the conch shells and their metal imitations were probably used for pouring.[18] The lion shown on the front panel of the lyre from PG 789 (cat. no. 3, detail, p. 55) carries a large jar, probably containing a liquid, in one hand and holds a vessel similar to this one in the other. Even the loop, hammered out and under the edge of the vessel's channel spout, is shown on the lyre panel. This loop might have helped to direct the flow of a liquid downward. A similar vessel from Tell Asmar has a metal ring through its loop, suggesting that the loop could also have enabled the attachment of a string or wire so that the vessel could then be suspended from the neck of a jar or worn around the neck of an individual, much on the order of the tasting cup worn by a sommelier. Such vessels, when found in burials, often lie in close proximity to the deceased. Woolley describes a silver pouring vessel of unusual size that was placed across Puabi's body.

112

POURING VESSEL

Copper alloy
L. 15 cm, W. 8 cm
PG 333
B17447 (U.8601)

POURING VESSEL

Copper alloy
L. 19 cm, W. 9.5 cm
PG 789, tomb chamber
B17280 (U.10565)

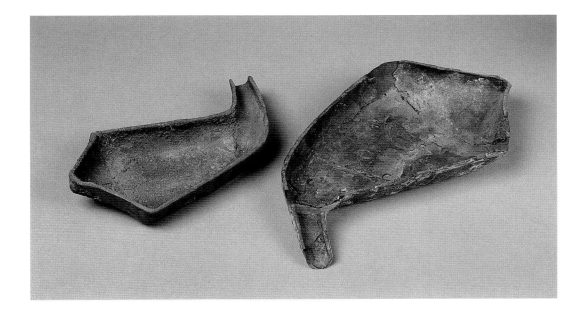

113
FLARED BOWL

Copper alloy
H. 10 cm, Dm. 32 cm
PG 337
98-9-1 (U.8626)

114
CUP

Copper alloy
H. 6.5 cm, Dm. 8.8 cm
PG 527
B17010 (U.9118)

BOWL

Copper alloy
H. 7.5 cm, Dm. 13.5 cm
PG 789
B17439 (U.10568)

115–116. DRINKING TUBE AND JAR

The drinking tube was found projecting from the silver jar in the east corner of Puabi's tomb chamber. This association suggests that the pot would have held beer[19] and would have been among the accoutrements used at banquets, such as those depicted on Early Dynastic carved stone plaques[20] as well as on numerous cylinder seals from the Royal Cemetery.

Only the gold leaf of the drinking tube remained, but impressions of the "ribs" of the reed that the gold had originally covered, as well as traces of the mastic (bitumen) used to attach it, were noted during its recent conservation. It is one of three drinking tubes recovered from Puabi's tomb. A copper drinking tube cased in lapis lazuli (U.10911) was found nearby, alongside a silver jar identical in shape to this one. The copper drinking tube had a diameter of approximately 1 centimeter and was preserved for a length of 45 centimeters. A silver drinking tube (U.10450), decorated with gold and lapis lazuli rings, was found near the "wardrobe box" in Puabi's death pit; its detached L-shaped "mouthpiece" was found nearby, inside a silver vat (U.10462). The drinking tube itself had a diameter of approximately 1 centimeter and was 93 centimeters long; the mouthpiece extended the drinking tube by about 19 centimeters and measured 14 centimeters beyond its bend. Although Woolley termed the L-shaped component of the drinking tube a "mouthpiece," its presence in the vat suggests that it was in fact the end of the tube.

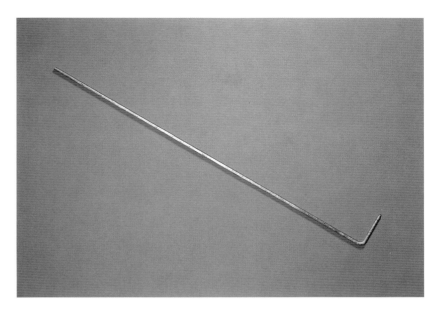

115
❋ DRINKING TUBE
Gold
L. 123.4 cm, Dm. 1 cm
PG 800, tomb chamber
B16688 (U.10855)

116
❋ JAR
Silver
H. 20.8 cm
PG 800, tomb chamber
B17068 (U.10855)

Southern Mesopotamia, like modern-day Germany, was a beer-drinking land, and a hymn to the beer goddess, Ninkasi, extols beer as the drink that "makes the liver happy, fills the heart with joy."[21] The same hymn describes the successive steps in the Mesopotamian beer-brewing process. The two indispensable ingredients in Mesopotamian beer were: a bread made from barley mixed with aromatic herbs commonly shaped into cakes (in Sumerian, $bappir_2$), and cereal (barley) that after germination became the greenmalt (in Sumerian, $munu_3$). The grain for the $bappir_2$ apparently would have been husked; that for $munu_3$ would not have been. The $bappir_2$ probably served several purposes. In brewing, it was a source of hydrolyzed or gelatinized starch for sugar production, and in the mashing process, a source of proteins and flavors. The malt and $bappir_2$ were then combined with addi-tional barley, possibly including hulled and crushed seeds that had been toasted or heated to make it easier for the enzymes to convert their starch to sugar, and cooked. Once the mash had reached the correct temperature, it was taken out of the oven and spread on reed mats to cool. The cooled mash, now referred to as "wort," was then placed in containers for fermentation. The Ninkasi hymn describes brewing the "great sweet wort" with honey and wine, and a collaborative team of scholars and brewers has suggested that grapes or raisins might have been added to the wort as a source of naturally occurring yeast. The fermented beer might then be filtered, as the Ninkasi hymn indicates, but just as likely was not filtered.[22] A drinking tube would probably have been used for consuming an unfiltered beer since it would readily penetrate the layer of hulls and yeasts.

Shell Vessels and Containers

Shell Vessels and Containers

Kevin Danti and Richard L. Zettler

After stone and pottery, shell is probably the most durable of the materials archaeologists recover from ancient sites. In the Royal Cemetery, shell was used for a variety of ornaments, including pendants; beads and rings that decorated belts; carved pieces that form the fleece of the "ram-caught-in-a-thicket" and decorate the Standard of Ur, the fronts of lyres, and gaming boards; carved handles and lids; cylinder seals; containers for cosmetic pigments; and pouring vessels. Here we discuss only conch-shell pouring vessels and cockleshells containing cosmetic pigments.

The two conch-shell pouring vessels (cat. no. 117) are fashioned from *Lambis truncata sebae,* a large gastropod with six or seven characteristic digitations extending from its outer lip.[1] The species is rare or completely absent in the Persian Gulf; the nearest source is the Gulf of Oman.[2] All of the examples from the Royal Cemetery have had their digitations removed, but Woolley in fact found an alabaster pouring vessel carved in the shape of *L. truncata sebae* with the digitations intact.[3] The shell pouring vessels from the Royal Cemetery frequently have carved decoration (see, for example, cat. no. 117, which is decorated with the head of a bird of prey), and one shell vessel (U.8313) was used as the body of a duck, its stone head attached by means of a pin and the breast feathers re-created with lapis lazuli and shell inlays.[4]

Similar shell pouring vessels are common in Indus Valley sites, where *Turbinella pyrum,* a gastropod whose distribution is limited to the waters of the Indian subcontinent, is the species commonly used.[5] Similar incised shells are apparently used in southern India today to milk-feed infants or administer medicine to the sick. More elaborate, incised vessels are made in Bengal and used throughout South Asia for special ritual libations.[6]

Small, widely distributed bivalves such as cockleshells (Arcidae and Cardiidae) were commonly used in Mesopotamia as containers for cosmetic pigments.[7] One half of the shell might serve as a receptacle and the other half as the lid, although no trace of a method of attachment exists. Imitations of such cockleshell cosmetic containers also occurred in gold and silver (cat. nos. 108, 109). Woolley seems to have assumed that cockleshells with pigments were invariably associated with women, but statistics from a slightly later cemetery at Kish, where skeletons were sexed independently of their artifacts, do not support such an assumption. In Cemetery A, cosmetic shells occurred in 57 percent of male graves, 22 percent of female graves, and 25 percent of youth or child graves.[8]

White, green, blue, yellow, red, purple, and dark brown/black pigments occur in the cockleshells, with green and black pigments being the most common. X-ray diffraction and X-ray fluorescence techniques were used to determine the composition of pigments in cockleshells from Ur in the British Museum.[9] The green pigments seem to be a copper mineral (azurite/apatite/malachite) modified with a white dilutant (cerussite or hydroxyapatite). The black pigments (presumably kohl for the eyes) contained some minor elements. The major elements were either manganese alone; manganese and iron; calcium, manganese, iron, and copper; or manganese and calcium. The deep color of the kohl was provided by oxides of manganese.

A literary hymn in praise of Shulgi, second king of the Third Dynasty of Ur, describes the goddess Inanna's use of cosmetics.[10] According to the text, when Inanna beheld Shulgi, she broke into song:

> Since for the king, for the lord,
>   I bathed,
> Since for the shepherd Dumuzi I bathed,
> Since with paste my sides were adorned,
> Since with balsam my mouth was
>   coated,
> Since with kohl my eyes were painted,
>   . . .

The Royal Cemetery provides a material counterpart to Inanna's song: cosmetic pigments in shell vessels were among the most common gifts the deceased carried to the netherworld.

117
POURING VESSEL
Conch shell
L. 18.5 cm
PG 1819
31-16-536 (U.15105)

POURING VESSEL
Conch shell
L. 18 cm
PG 143
B17194 (U.8191)

118

❋ COSMETIC CONTAINER
(TOP)

Shell
H. 8.5 cm, W. 14 cm
PG 800, pit floor
B17185 (U.10966)

❋ COSMETIC CONTAINER
(BOTTOM)

Shell, with pigment
H. 7.5 cm, W. 14 cm
PG 800, pit floor
B17186 (U.10966)

119

CLOCKWISE FROM
UPPER LEFT:

COSMETIC CONTAINER

Shell, with pigment
W. 4 cm
5th Expedition
B17187 (U.8222)

COSMETIC CONTAINER

Shell
W. 4.5 cm
8th Expedition
31-16-542a (no U. number)

COSMETIC CONTAINER

Shell, with pigment
W. 4 cm
8th Expedition
31-17-93 (no U. number)

COSMETIC CONTAINER

Shell, with pigment
W. 4 cm
12th Expedition
35-1-66b (no U. number)

COSMETIC CONTAINER

Shell, with pigment
W. 5 cm
PG 681
B17025 (U.9723)

Stone
Vessels

Stone Vessels

Richard L. Zettler

Stone vessels, although not found in all of the graves, were nevertheless common in the Royal Cemetery, and some of the royal tombs included large numbers of them. PG 800, Puabi's tomb, for example, yielded more than seventy-five. As in the cemetery more generally, most of the stone vessels from Puabi's tomb were of calcite, with a smaller number of chlorite or steatite, including one with carved decoration, and a few of more exotic materials such as lapis lazuli, obsidian, black and white breccia, and translucent green calcite.[1]

Although outcroppings of limestone and its lighter-colored derivatives (such as calcite and gypsum) are found around Uruk and Ur, with more extensive deposits of these and other sedimentary rocks occurring north of Baghdad along both the Euphrates and Tigris Rivers,[2] stone is generally rare in southern Mesopotamia and had to be imported, either as raw material or as finished products. At the time of the excavations, Woolley suggested that Egypt had influenced the production and forms of stone vessels in early Mesopotamia but his theory was challenged even then.[3] More recent excavations, particularly at sites in Iran and around the Persian Gulf, have provided a better understanding of the sources of Mesopotamian stone vessels. Unfortunately, stone has not proved particularly susceptible to source proveniencing, and in any case, much of the relevant region remains geologically unexplored.

Whereas the calcite spouted jar (cat. no. 129) might have been made in southern Mesopotamia in imitation of contemporary spouted pottery vessels and the translucent oval bowl (cat. no. 123) in imitation of contemporary metal shapes, a recent study has suggested that certain of the calcite vessels from the Royal Cemetery were probably imported from eastern Iran, northern Afghanistan, or southern Turkmenia and might have reached Mesopotamia via the Persian Gulf, having traveled south from highland production centers.[4] These calcite examples include tall cylindrical vessels (which Woolley somewhat arcanely dubbed "spill-vases"), subconical and carinated bowls, and taller jars. The best parallels for the unique alabaster compartmentalized box (cat. no. 122) from PG 1100 likewise come from sites in eastern Iran and northern Afghanistan.

Chlorite and steatite vessels, both undecorated and decorated, became the focus of intensive investigation with the discovery, in the late 1960s, of a production center dated to the second half of the third millennium BC, at Tepe Yahya in south-central Iran. Numerous studies, including X-ray diffraction analyses, suggest that at least the chlorites from Nippur, Khafajah, Kish, and Ur had remarkably similar compositions. Nevertheless, the attribution of Mesopotamian chlorite and steatite vessels to specific sources remains problematic.[5]

Undecorated chlorite and steatite bell-shaped bowls occur in a range of sizes in Royal Cemetery graves, with examples in the University of Pennsylvania Museum ranging from 17 to 56 centimeters in diameter. Similar bowls comprise the standard undecorated type at Tepe Yahya,[6] and comparable vessels are known from Tarut Island off the coast of Saudi Arabia in the Persian Gulf.[7] These vessels might have reached Mesopotamia through the gulf.[8]

Carved steatite vessels, conventionally divided into a *série ancienne* (the "Intercultural Style") and a *série récente*, have a wide geographical and chronological distribution.[9] For example, the *série ancienne* vessels range in date from the mid- to late-third millennium (2600–2200 BC); they are found from Syria to Central Asia and the Indus, with a principal area of production in eastern Iran. The discovery of *série ancienne* vessels on islands in the Persian Gulf suggests sea transport as a principal channel of supply to Mesopotamia.[10] The steatite bowl from PG 800 (cat. no. 121) belongs to the *série ancienne;* its decoration most closely resembles steatite vessels from Susa[11] and Tarut Island.[12]

One bowl of lapis lazuli and one of obsidian were found in PG 800, Puabi's tomb. The major source for lapis lazuli is in Badakhshan, northeastern Afghanistan, with perhaps less important sources in the Pamir Mountains and in the vicinity of Lake Baikal and in the Chagai Hills, southwest of Quetta on the border between Pakistan and Afghanistan. Obsidian came from two major sources: one in central Turkey and the other in the Lake Van region to the east.[13] The shape of the obsidian vessel suggests it was made, probably in southern Mesopotamia, in imitation of a metal original. Although not so obvious, the lapis lazuli vessel may likewise have been manufactured in southern Mesopotamia copying a metal prototype.

Evidence for stone vessel production in southern Mesopotamia is scarce.[14] Reconstructions rely largely on scattered finds of tools and on deductions from finished vessels. Richer source materials from ancient Egypt are also helpful in understanding the manufacturing process. Although he does not mention the likely use of abrasives, Woolley's observations on the production of stone vessels remain instructive:

> As regards the technique of manufacture, a metal tubular drill was used for hollowing out the interior of tall vases . . . and sometimes to start the process in the jar types . . . where the hole is vertical and the drill marks are visible on its sides; but usually the walls, in this instance left solid, would be thinned by subsequent grinding with another tool. For bowls the usual tool was the stone borer . . . which was mounted on a wooden bit and apparently worked with a bow drill. Probably in the case of the more open bowl types much of the interior work was done by chipping and finished with the grinder. It is almost certain that the hollowing out of the vase was done when the outside had been roughly chipped to shape

and that the fine cutting of the walls from the outside was the last process of all; this would explain why in some of the finest vases an imperfection of the stone which interferes with the regularity of the contour has been left and at best slightly "flaked," the interior having been already hollowed out the wall could not be ground farther back so as to circumvent the fault as would have been done if the stone was still a solid lump.[15]

120. CUP WITH TROUGH SPOUT

Although stone bowls or cups with spouts appear in late-fourth-millennium and early-third-millennium contexts in southern Mesopotamia and at Susa, this lapis lazuli cup from the Royal Cemetery is unique in both shape and material. Its closest parallels are found not in this area but in Central Asia, in the steatite spouted cups from cemetery sites ostensibly located in the area between the Amu Darya River and the piedmont of the Hindu Kush Mountains in modern Afghanistan. These cups, which come from illicit excavations, are usually dated (by comparison with ceramic parallels) to the late third–early second millennium. They are seemingly much too late in date to have served as prototypes for the cup from the Royal Cemetery. The similarities in shape and the location of a major source of lapis lazuli in nearby Badakhshan are nevertheless compelling considerations and raise broader questions about the relationships between the artifacts from the Central Asian graves and the Royal Cemetery of Ur. This area of northern Afghanistan is poorly known archaeologically. Did earlier cultures with similar ceramics and stone vessel forms exist there, and did they provide the prototypes for material from the Royal Cemetery? If not, was it then Early Dynastic Mesopotamia that provided prototypes for Central Asian Bronze Age material culture?

If the lapis lazuli cup cannot be shown to have securely dated precedents in stone, perhaps it was made in imitation of vessels in other materials, such as copper spouted cups from a nearly contemporary grave below a house at Khafajah in the lower Diyala River valley.

The function of the lapis lazuli spouted cup also remains uncertain. Vessels of precious metals and semiprecious stones are mentioned in incantations against diseases known from copies dated to the first half of the second millennium BC. The texts consist of three parts: the complaint, the measures taken, and the purpose of the measures. In the second part, the healing demons are said to have vessels of gold,

120

✳ CUP WITH TROUGH
SPOUT

Lapis lazuli
H. 6.7 cm, Dm. 10.5 cm
PG 800, pit floor
B17167 (U.10517)

silver, or an unknown stone (*hulalu*-stone) and lapis lazuli. In the third part, the demons are explicitly enjoined to use those vessels to draw water for sprinkling on the patient during the healing ritual. Perhaps this troughed cup is an example.

The cup was found near the northwestern corner of the "wardrobe box" along with the decorated steatite bowl (cat. no. 121), also an import.

122. BOX

This square box is divided into four compartments, rounded at the bottom and square at the top. The rim has a shallow lip on two opposing sides, and holes run diagonally through the upper corners of the vessel. Both the lip and holes would have served to secure the box's now missing lid. Although compartmentalized stone cosmetic boxes are known from southern Mesopotamia,[16] the closest parallels to the box are the somewhat smaller chlorite or steatite compartmentalized boxes from Shahdad, east of Kirman on the edge of the Dasht-i Lut,[17] as well as from Central Asian cemetery sites ostensibly located in the area between the Amu Darya River and the piedmont of the Hindu Kush Mountains in modern Afghanistan.[18]

121

❋ BOWL WITH INCISED DECORATION

Dark gray steatite
H. 10.2 cm, Dm. 18.5 cm
PG 800, pit floor
B17168 (U.10523)

122

BOX

White calcite
L. 16 cm, W. 15.3 cm, H. 8 cm
PG 1100
30-12-697 (U.11586)

123

✳ OVAL BOWL WITH LUG HANDLES

Light green translucent calcite
L. 22 cm, W. 13.5 cm
PG 800, pit floor
B17166 (U.10480)

124

CYLINDRICAL VASE (TOP LEFT)

White calcite
H. 20.5 cm
PG 1130
30-12-698 (U.11785)

OVOID JAR (TOP RIGHT)

White calcite
H. 17.3 cm
PG 1133
30-12-72 (U.11814)

BOWL (BOTTOM LEFT)

Veined calcite
H. 12 cm, Dm. 14.7 cm
PG 1133
30-12-77 (U.11815)

BOWL (BOTTOM RIGHT)

White limestone
Dm. 16.7 cm
PG 1648
31-16-418 (U.13773)

❋ JAR

White calcite
H. 26 cm
PG 800, tomb chamber
B17104 (U.10854)

126

❋ GLOBULAR JAR

Translucent veined
calcite
H. 24.5 cm
PG 800, pit floor
B17105 (U.10490)

❋ OVOID JAR

Translucent yellow and
white calcite
H. 23 cm
PG 800, pit floor
B17108 (U.10492)

❋ OVOID JAR

Translucent white calcite
H. 18.5 cm
PG 800, pit floor
B17112 (U.10498)

127

✳ JAR

Veined calcite
H. 23 cm
PG 800, tomb chamber
B17111 (U.10882)

128

✳ CYLINDRICAL VASE

Veined white calcite
H. 25 cm
PG 800, tomb chamber
B17128 (U.10921)

129
✼ SPOUTED JAR

Translucent white calcite
H. 16 cm
PG 800, pit floor
B17103 (U.10502)

130
✼ CARINATED BOWL

White calcite
H. 12 cm
PG 800, tomb chamber
B17144 (U.10960)

131
❋ BOWL

Translucent white calcite
H. 10 cm
PG 800, tomb chamber
B17139 (U.10963)

132
❋ BOWL

Translucent white calcite
H. 22 cm
PG 800, pit floor
B17302 (U.10518)

❋ BOWL

White calcite
H. 15 cm
PG 800, pit floor
B17143 (U.10516)

133

CLOCKWISE FROM
UPPER LEFT:

✳ BOWL

Translucent white calcite
H. 10.5 cm
PG 800, pit floor
B17131 (U.10501)

✳ BOWL

White calcite
Dm. 15.5 cm
PG 800, pit floor
B17133 (U.10484)

✳ BOWL

White calcite
Dm. 16.6 cm
PG 800, pit floor
B17132 (U.10527)

✳ BOWL

Translucent white calcite
Dm. 14.7 cm
PG 800, pit floor
B17134 (U.10512)

✳ BOWL

Translucent white calcite
Dm. 13.2 cm
PG 800, pit floor
B17135 (U.10513)

✳ BOWL

Translucent white calcite
Dm. 15.4 cm
PG 800, pit floor
B17138 (U.10514)

134
BELL-SHAPED BOWL

Steatite
Dm. 31 cm
PG 800, pit floor
B17152 (U.10481)

135

❋ BOWL

White calcite
Dm. 23 cm
PG 800, pit floor
B17140 (no U. number)

❋ BOWL

Translucent white calcite
Dm. 23 cm
PG 800, pit floor
B17129 (U.10499)

136

BELL-SHAPED BOWL

Gray steatite
Dm. 17.2 cm
PG 1068
30-12-81 (U.11549)

BELL-SHAPED BOWL

Greenish steatite
Dm. 27.5 cm
PG 1524
31-16-379 (U.14071)

Tools and
Weapons

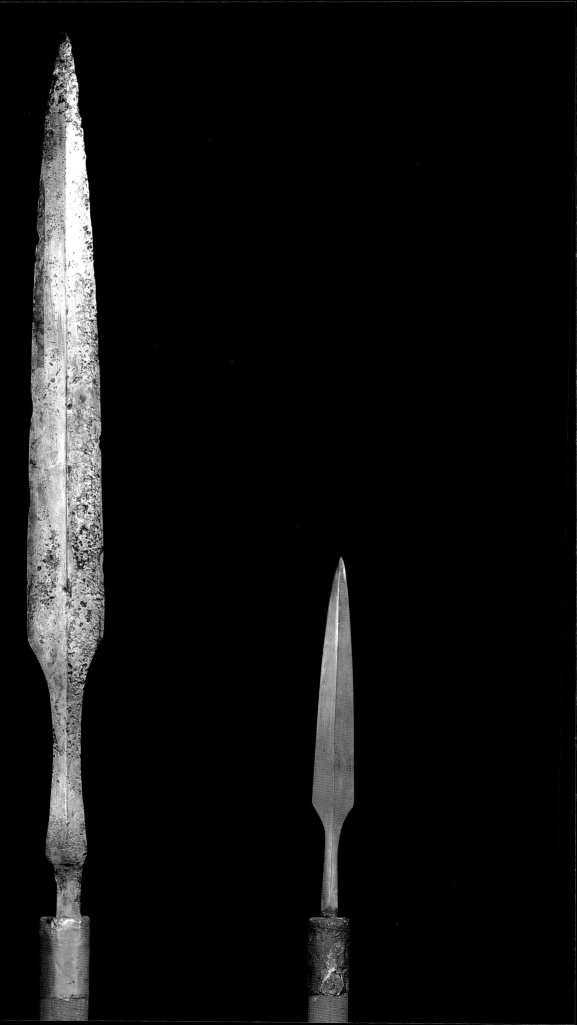

Tools and Weapons

Jill A. Weber and Richard L. Zettler

The tools and weapons found in the Royal Cemetery's graves were made of a variety of materials, including metal, stone, shell, and probably wood, although no wooden tools or weapons were actually preserved.[1] However, the overwhelming majority of the tools and weapons were metal—gold, silver, electrum, copper, and copper-based alloys. The assemblage is particularly noteworthy for containing the only archaeologically known examples whose "working" parts are made of gold.[2] Because gold is a soft metal, the gold tools and weapons were probably not functional. Woolley assumed that they were symbolic or ceremonial,[3] and he has not been challenged. The cast gold tools and weapons are all the more unusual because gold is a precious metal that was conserved and solid casting requires a considerable quantity of metal.

Plenderleith suggested early on that some of the gold-alloy objects found in the Royal Cemetery were surface-enriched to make the surface appear more golden.[4] Using one such technique, called depletion-gilding, corrosion is intentionally promoted—for example, by introducing a catalyst such as an acid or by placing the object in a combination of salt and clay (for absorption of the metal salts) and heating it.[5] The corroded surface can be removed and burnished, and since gold does not react with the chemicals, the result is a gold surface that is still bonded with the alloyed core. In a recent study,[6] La Niece gives credence to Plenderleith's suggestion by arguing that those objects whose surfaces have a much higher percentage of gold than their underlying cores (and with no seam indicating the addition of a surface metal) and that were highly burnished were probably depletion-gilded. Two chisels (cat. no. 152) are likely part of a group of cast objects that had a copper-gold or copper-electrum alloy core with a depletion-gilded surface.[7] This gilding might have been an effort to conserve gold while retaining its appearance. Another reason for adding copper to gold or electrum might have been to lower the melting point and make it easier to cast.[8]

Manufacture of tools and weapons was either by casting (the majority of the tools and weapons were cast) or by hammering. For the most part, decoration was limited to the now-decomposed shafts. A cast socketed adze (cat. no. 149), for example, was found with three rings of gold binding for the shaft and a large copper (or bronze) nail for the end of the tool's pommel. On one dagger (cat. no. 146), small gold nails in the hilt guards and the end of the wooden pommel (not preserved, but restored for display) imitate granulation, the earliest attestation of which remains controversial.[9] Daggers were most likely attached to wooden handles by means of two or three rivets (cat. no. 147). Most of the blades have one or more ribs from casting.

Sand casting might have been employed in the manufacture of some of the weapons. This method involves filling a wooden frame with sand or dirt, pressing the desired form into the sand, and then pouring molten metal into the impression. Modern experiments have shown that the surface of objects that have been cast using this technique have a characteristic grainy or granular structure.[10] This same characteristic structure was found on the surface of a silver ax from the Royal Cemetery.[11]

The high chemical reactivity of the copper-based tools and weapons has resulted in extensive corrosion and pitting of their surfaces, making analysis of their manufacture difficult. It is not known whether these artifacts were newly made explicitly for burial or were old at the time they were placed in graves.

The Mesopotamian Metals Project (MMP), undertaken by the University of Pennsylvania Museum's Applied Sciences Center for Archaeology, has analyzed the copper-based metal weapons and tools in the Museum's vast collections from Mesopotamia. Results from these analyses show that arsenical coppers, tin-bronzes, and arsenic-tin-copper alloys were all present in the tools and weapons from the Royal Cemetery. In addition, tin-bronze tools and weapons were much more highly concentrated in Royal Cemetery contexts than anywhere else in Mesopotamia.[12]

137
✳ HANDLE

Shell
L. 10 cm
PG 800, pit floor
B16753 (U.10437)

138
✳ HANDLE

Lapis lazuli
H. 10.4 cm
PG 800
B16713 (U.10952)

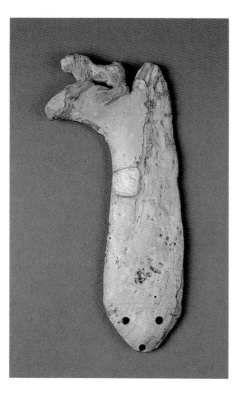

138. HANDLE

As Woolley noted, because this handle is quite thin, it must have been mounted together with a similar piece against a central slip of wood or metal. Its three holes would have served as a means of attaching it. The triangular arrangement of the holes calls to mind the positioning of the rivets that secured dagger blades to handles, and perhaps the piece was in fact part of the handle of a dagger. A carved lion decorates the handle's end.

139. REIN RING

Double-ring terrets were fitted to the shafts of wagons behind the necks of draught animals. The semicircular base sat on the shaft and was probably secured by a leather thong; the reins passed from the animal's nose through the rings.

Woolley recovered four rein rings from the Royal Cemetery: a copper example from PG 580; a silver rein ring surmounted by an ox, now in the Iraq Museum, Baghdad (fig. 51); a "completely decayed" copper terret from the "King's Grave" (PG 789); and a silver rein ring surmounted by an equid (fig. 52), currently in the British Museum, London, from Puabi's tomb (PG 800). Where then did this silver rein ring, in the University of Pennsylvania Museum, come from? The Museum's records, including the original packing lists accompanying the Ur artifacts from London, indicate that it was from PG 789. It seems likely that this silver rein ring is in fact the "completely decayed" copper terret from PG 789. How could Woolley have mistaken silver for copper? If the silver had a high copper content, the copper would have corroded preferentially, completely covering (and preserving) the silver with salts. The pitted surface is probably the result of chemical changes during the course of electrolytic cleaning.[13]

Four rein rings, three surmounted

139
REIN RING
Silver
H. 9.6 cm, W. 10 cm
PG 789
B17551 (no U. number)

Fig. 51. Silver rein ring surmounted by a silver ox from PG 789, the "King's Grave." Currently in the Iraq Museum, Baghdad. U.10551. Reprinted from Woolley 1934b: pl. 167.

Fig. 52. Silver rein ring surmounted by an electrum equid from PG 800, Puabi's tomb. Currently in the British Museum. WA 121348 (U.10439). Courtesy of the British Museum.

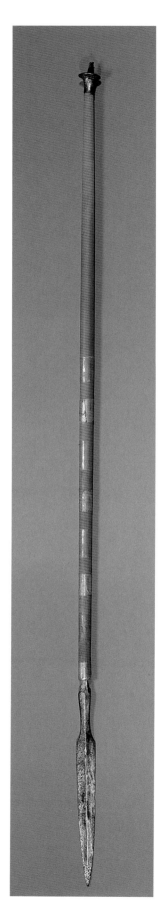

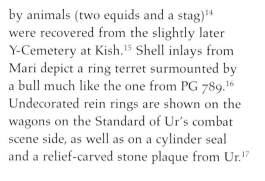

by animals (two equids and a stag)[14] were recovered from the slightly later Y-Cemetery at Kish.[15] Shell inlays from Mari depict a ring terret surmounted by a bull much like the one from PG 789.[16] Undecorated rein rings are shown on the wagons on the Standard of Ur's combat scene side, as well as on a cylinder seal and a relief-carved stone plaque from Ur.[17]

Detail of butt.

140. SPEARS

This electrum spearhead, on the right, is one of four examples from PG 789's death pit. The shafts were decorated with gold and silver bindings. Although the wooden shafts were not preserved, Woolley estimated their length from the distribution of the bindings as 92 centimeters. Two of the shafts had butts from which projected copper "forks," which Woolley described as string notches for throwing thongs (see detail). Woolley reasoned that the length of the weapons, as well as their lightness and the fact that two of them had throwing forks, indicated that they were throwing spears or javelins similar to those used by the warriors in chariots depicted on the Standard of Ur.[18] The electrum spearheads were found near four others of copper or bronze and with what might have been the remains of a quiver and a shield (cat. no. 13).

The spearhead on the left is one of four silver spearheads found together in PG 789's death pit. Their shafts also had completely decayed. The ends of two of the four spears were plain; the other two had silver butts with copper string notches. These spears were reconstructed for purposes of display apparently with a length in proportion to the size of the point and with alternating bindings of silver and gold on the shaft.

140
SPEAR

Silver
Spearhead: L. 34.5 cm
PG 789
B16689 (U.10472)

SPEAR

Electrum
Spearhead: L. 17 cm
PG 789
B16690 (U.10411)

141
SPEARHEAD

Silver
L. 34.5 cm
PG 789
B17078 (U.10472)

142
SPEARHEAD WITH
BULL'S LEG MARK

Bronze
L. 40 cm, Th. 2 cm
PG 789
B17400 (U.10825)

143. SPEARHEADS AND HARPOON-SHAPED HEADS

Woolley termed the weapons in the center of the photograph "harpoon-shaped arrowheads" and noted that the marks of the (sinew?) binding that secured them to their shafts were visible at the base of the hollow sockets. Both were found to the right of the entrance to PG 580's death pit, along with other sets of weapons, including unbarbed and barbed arrowheads and spearheads, that Woolley surmised had been carried in quivers. The rounded and flattened tops of these weapons and the prominent side hook suggest that these were not arrowheads or harpoons but more likely pole weapons used, probably in phalanx fighting, for hooking and pulling.

144. WHETSTONE

This lapis lazuli whetstone with gold ring was found, along with a dagger, in one of the wagons in PG 789. It was apparently worn by the wagon's driver. The dagger had a copper or bronze blade, its hilt was of gold set with lapis lazuli studs, and the hilt was plated with silver and had gold studs in its pommel.

143
SPEARHEAD (LEFT)

Copper alloy
L. 34.2 cm
PG 1311
30-12-342 (U.12252)

HARPOON-SHAPED
HEADS (CENTER)

Copper alloy
L. 13.4 cm
PG 580
B17528 a–b (U.9336)

SPEARHEAD (RIGHT)

Copper alloy
L. 21.2 cm
6th Expedition
B17348 (no U. number)

144
WHETSTONE

Lapis lazuli and gold
L. 11 cm
PG 789, death pit
B16695 (U.10552)

145
WHETSTONE

Stone
L. 9 cm
PG 1327
30-12-540 (U.12305)

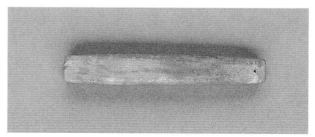

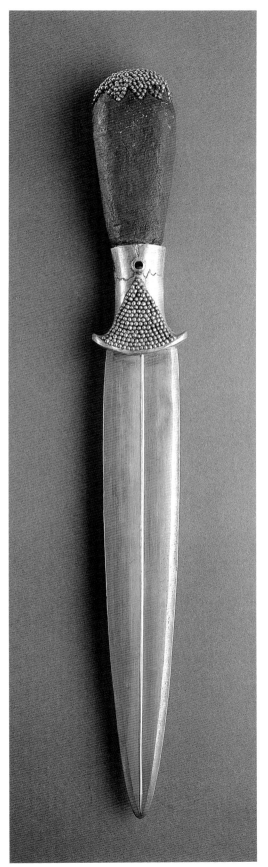

146
DAGGER

Gold with wood restoration
L. 33 cm (restored)
PG 1054
30-12-550 (U.11513)

147
DAGGER

Copper alloy
L. 17 cm
PG 1014
30-12-318 (U.11463)

148
DAGGER

Copper alloy
L. 19.2 cm
12th Expedition
35-1-423 (no U. number)

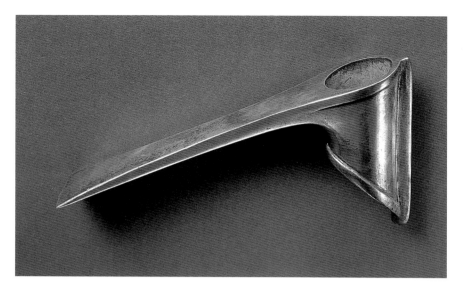

149
ADZE

Electrum
L. 15 cm
PG 580
B16691 (U.9339)

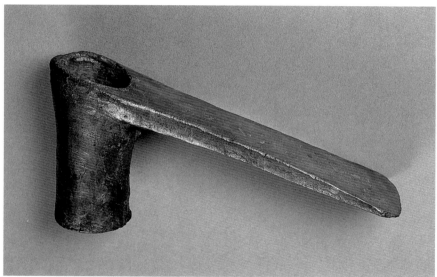

150
ADZE

Copper alloy
L. 13.4 cm
5th Expedition
B17403 (no U. number)

151
AX

Copper alloy
L. 15 cm
PG 457
B17413 (U.8958)

152

✳ CHISEL

Gold (or electrum)
L. 10.5 cm
PG 800, pit floor
B16724 (U.10430)

✳ CHISEL

Gold (or electrum)
L. 6.1 cm
PG 800, pit floor
B16725 (U.10433)

153

CHISEL

Copper alloy
L. 12.7 cm
PG 734
B17285 (U.9860)

CHISEL

Copper alloy
L. 5.4 cm
9th Expedition
31-43-543 (no U. number)

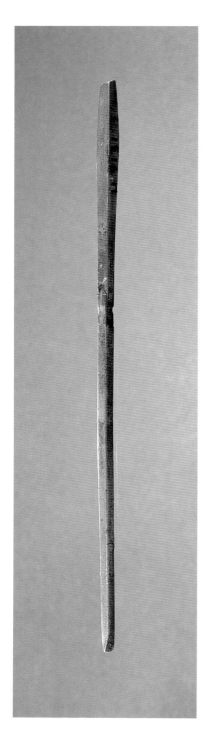

154
CHISEL

Gold
L. 9.3 cm
PG 580
B16687 (U.9131)

155
RAZOR

Copper alloy
L. 8.4 cm
PG 331
B17387 (U.8583)

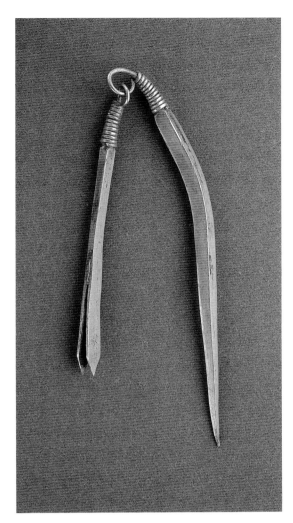

156

✳ TWEEZERS AND
STILETTO

Gold
Tweezers: L. 6 cm;
  stiletto: L. 9 cm
PG 800 (not in situ)
B16714 (U.10423)

157
TOILET SET

Silver and electrum
L. 6.3 cm
5th Expedition, found loose
  in the soil
B17085 (U.9362)

Notes

CHAPTER ONE

1. For a general introduction to the geography, see Fisher 1950: 339–71.

2. Huot 1996: 17, 381–83.

3. Porada et al. 1992: 103–13.

4. Nissen, Damerow, and Englund 1993: 117.

5. Postgate 1992: 66–70.

6. Cooper 1986: 4–7.

7. Ibid.: 19.

8. Cooper 1983: 22–23.

9. Ibid.: 7; Postgate 1992: 30–31.

10. Cooper 1983.

11. Biggs 1974: 26.

12. Deimel 1923, 1925.

13. Martin 1988: 86.

14. Two of the texts (Deimel 1925: nos. 16 and 17) recording allotments of plow teams characterize the animals as belonging to Sud, main deity of Shuruppak, suggesting that the building was linked to a temple, but one (no. 20) describes the animals as belonging to that city.

Visicato has recently argued that almost all of the Fara administrative documents "were compiled by a single center on which almost all of the work force of the city together with its employs and officials depended" (Pomponio and Visicato 1994: 7).

15. Martin 1988: 89.

16. Biggs 1974; Edzard 1976.

17. Parrot 1948: 22.

18. Maekawa 1973–74.

19. Selz 1989, 1993.

20. Adams 1981.

21. Ibid.: 138.

22. Biggs 1967.

23. Biggs 1974: 44; Biggs and Postgate 1978: 106.

24. Gelb 1957: 210.

25. Steinkeller 1992: 725–26; 1993: 116–27.

26. Postgate 1992: 35–38.

27. Steible and Yildiz 1993.

28. Lambert 1981.

29. Moorey 1994: 85–87.

30. Ibid.: 97.

31. Ibid.: 45–46; Potts 1989: 137–38.

32. Moorey 1994: 65.

33. Ibid.: 219–21.

34. Ibid.: 234–35.

35. See Woolley 1934b: 105–6, 388 for references to black-burnished pottery and pottery types; on metallic wares, see Kühne 1976: 33–72, also Dornemann 1988: 27 and Orthmann and Rova 1991: 72–77.

36. Woolley 1934b: 388, probably Susa IVA; see Porada et al. 1992: 112 for Susa IVA sherds from Early Dynastic IIIB contexts at al-Hiba.

37. On the terms for city ruler, see, for example, Nissen 1988: 140–41.

38. After Cooper 1986: 33–39.

39. Cooper 1986: 22.

40. After Cooper 1986: 41.

41. Cooper 1983: 24–25.

42. After Cooper 1986: 94–95.

43. After Cooper 1986: 78–79.

CHAPTER TWO

1. For this characterization, see 1968, *Window on the World. The Illustrated London News Review* (London: Michael Joseph).

2. Christie 1977: 434.

3. della Valle 1665: 261.

4. Fraser 1840: 88–94.

5. Loftus 1857: 127–34.

6. Taylor 1854: 260–76.

7. Rawlinson 1850: 481; 1857: 47. For Rawlinson's publication of the cylinder, see Rawlinson 1861, 1: pl. 69.

8. Hall 1930: vii–ix.

9. Campbell-Thompson 1921.

10. For an interesting account of Layard's work, see Larsen 1996.

11. Hall 1930: vii–viii.

12. See Hall 1919, 1923, 1930.

13. Hall 1930: 123.

14. For an account of the beginnings of the Joint Expedition of the British Museum and the University of Pennsylvania Museum, see Dyson 1977.

15. Letter, Gordon to Kenyon, June 2, 1919. UPM Archives: Ur, box 1.

16. Winston 1990: 20–23, 26–48, 98–104.

17. Letter, Kenyon to Gordon, June 12, 1922. UPM Archives: Ur, box 1.

18. Letter, Gordon to Kenyon, July 26, 1922. UPM Archives: Ur, box 1.

19. Letter, Gordon to Woolley: December 29, 1925. UPM Archives: Ur, box 1.

20. Letter, Woolley to Gordon, September 24, 1922. UPM Archives: Ur, box 1.

21. Report, Woolley to Director UPM, November 2, 1922. UPM Archives: Ur, box 1.

22. Winston 1980; Wallach 1996.

23. Winston 1990: 117.

24. Report, Woolley to Director UPM, November 2, 1922; report, Woolley to Director UPM, January 15, 1923. UPM Archives: Ur, box 1.

25. Woolley 1923: 312.

26. É-nun-mah is to be read gá-nun-mah, a Sumerian term meaning "lofty storehouse."

27. Woolley 1928: 1.

28. Report, Woolley to Director UPM, November 16, 1922. UPM Archives: Ur, box 1; Woolley 1923: 312.

29. Report, Woolley to Director UPM, January 2, 1923. UPM Archives: Ur, box 1.

30. Woolley 1928: 1–2.

31. Ibid.: 15–17.

32. Woolley 1956: 2.

33. Woolley 1929: 323–30.

34. Langdon 1930: 206–7.

35. Woolley 1930: 326–43; 1933: 380–83; 1934: 356–72.

36. Winston 1990: 140, 191.

CHAPTER THREE

1. This total does not include the additional roughly 260 burials found in Pit X in 1933–34, after the completion of the final report on the cemetery excavations (Woolley 1956: 127–45).

2. Woolley 1934b: 16.

3. Ibid.: 17, 218.

4. Burrows 1935.

5. Legrain 1936.

6. Woolley 1930: 325–28.

7. Porada et al. 1992: 108, 111.

8. On the chronology of the Early Dynastic period, see ibid.: 103–13.

9. Buchanan 1954.

10. Woolley 1934b: 135–46.

11. Ibid.: 15–16.

12. Moorey 1977: 30–35.

13. Woolley 1934b: 155–60.

14. Keith, in ibid.: 402–4.

15. Woolley 1934b: 155.

16. Ibid.: 158.

17. Ibid.: 340, erratum.

18. Boese 1978.

19. Müller-Karpe 1993: 249–51.

20. *Illustrated London News*, June 23, 1928.

21. Woolley 1934b: 37–42.

22. Ibid.: 42.

23. Pollock 1991: 182.

24. Moortgat 1949: 65.

25. Moorey 1977: 39.

26. Renger 1972–75: 257–59.

27. Redman 1978: 296–98.

28. See, for example, Postgate 1992: 137 ff.

29. Hoffman 1991: 275–79.

30. See, for example, Kemp 1967: 25.

31. O'Connor 1993: 52–55.

32. Vycichl 1959: 221–22.

33. Friedman 1991: 48; Josefsson 1988: 155–67; Reisner 1923: 72.

34. Chang 1976: 52; 1980: 87–90, 114–17; Chi 1977: 90–92, 254.

35. Herodotus, *The Histories*, trans. by A. de Sélincourt, rev. and with an introduction by A. R. Burn (Middlesex, Eng.: Penguin Books, 1954): 293–94.

36. Chochorowski and Skoryi 1997.

37. Hearne and Sharer 1992.

38. Donnan 1995: 150–51; Verrnao 1995: 196–99; for the royal tombs of Sipan, see Alva and Donnan 1993.

39. Report, Woolley to Director UPM, January 29, 1927. UPM Archives: Ur, box 2. Woolley wrote, "The work entailed is heavy, slow and sometimes dangerous—I regret to say that today a fall of earth buried two men of whom one was killed on the spot and the other rescued with some difficulty."

40. Woolley 1953: 100–102.

41. Letter, H. R. Hall to Horace H. F. Jayne, January 31, 1930. UPM Archives: Ur, box 2.

42. Mallowan 1977: 36.

CHAPTER FOUR

1. Woolley 1934b: 62–71.

2. Ibid.: 73–91.

3. Ibid.: 73.

4. Keith, in ibid.: 400–402.

5. Dyson 1960.

6. Report, Woolley to Director UPM, January 3, 1928. UPM Archives: Ur, box 2.

7. Barnett 1969.

8. Woolley 1934b: 35.

ART

1. See the description in Woolley 1934b: 266 ff.

2. Ibid.: pl. 166.

3. It is unfortunate that the seated figure in the upper left corner of the panel is partially missing and that what remains is badly decayed. The identity of this figure would help to determine the true nature of this banquet. Due to the fact that what is preserved of the skirt seems to resemble the skirts of the secondary banqueters to the right of the main figure, the destroyed figure is here taken to be male. This seated figure and the facing attendant with raised right hand placed in the corner of the register to the left of the main figure is understood here to be an artistic device used to balance the two figures of a lyrist and singer[?] set into the end of the register on the right.

4. Orthmann 1975: pl. 31; Moortgat 1969: pls. 87, 88.

5. Kilmer 1987: 175 ff.

6. Jacobsen 1976; 204; Pritchard 1950: 89.

7. Crawford 1959: cover, 78.

8. Hansen 1978: 77.

9. Jacobsen 1976: 14.

10. For further reading, see Amiet 1980; Frankfort 1939, 1996; Jacobsen 1976, 1987; Lloyd 1961; Michalowski 1990; Moortgat 1949, 1969; Wiggerman 1995.

11. The second head is in the Baghdad Museum (IM.8244). The head published in Woolley 1934b, pl. 127, is the head in the University of Pennsylvania Museum before any cleaning or restoration.

12. Woolley 1934b: 82.

13. See the statue of the goddess Narundi in Harper et al. 1992: 50, n. 55.

14. Personal communication to author from Stuart Fleming of the Museum Applied Science Center for Archaeology (MASCA) of the University of Pennsylvania Museum (February 1998).

15. Orthmann 1975: pl. 83.

16. One lyre found upright in the ground in PG 1151 was retrieved by pouring plaster into the hole left by the decayed wood of an arm (see fig. 28). This technique even preserved the impressions of the strings, visible as tiny vertical threads in the soil.

17. Kilmer 1983: 572; Jacobsen 1987: xiii f.

18. For a general discussion of lyres in antiquity and a specific discourse on Mesopotamian lyres, see Lawergren 1994 and 1997: 147.

19. See also cat. no. 100.

20. Wiggerman has developed his ideas in several places, including Wiggerman 1995: 237 f.

21. Woolley 1934b: 124.

22. Recent metallographic analysis has confirmed that this head (30-12-696) was cast. Compositional analysis indicates that the metal is a bronze, with an 8 percent tin content. Data courtesy of the Museum Applied Science Center for Archaeology (MASCA) at the University of Pennsylvania Museum and the Bartol Research Institute of the University of Deleware (February 1998).

23. See Behm-Blancke 1979: Taf. 13:69 and the trefoil inset, pl. opp. p. 6. A copper bull head in similar style and with a triangular shell inlay was found in Sin Temple Level IX of Khafajah, Taf. 30:159 a,b.

24. Orthmann 1975: pl. 83.

25. The end of the object held by the main figure of another all-male banquet, as represented on the Standard of Ur, is not preserved (Woolley 1934b: pl. 91, or Strommenger 1962: pl. 10), but it may well have been similar to the object on this panel. For a photograph of male date inflorescences, see Porter 1993: 135, fig. 3.

26. Two of the plaques were broken, and others were chipped. They have been restored since they were originally published in Woolley 1934b: pl. 99.

27. Woolley 1934b: pl. 96 (U.10557). In the photograph published in ibid.: pl. 99, the plaques are distributed in a pattern of three horizontal rows by four vertical rows. In order to conform to the pattern preserved on more complete boards, they were rearranged at some point into the present pattern of four horizontal rows by three vertical rows.

28. Decker 1992.

29. Amiet 1980: pl. 24; Frankfort 1939: pl. V a,b.

30. Woolley 1934b: pl. 77 b.

31. The observation concerning the ash is recorded in Woolley's personal field notes.

32. An animal in a rearing pose beside a plant or tree is common in Sumerian iconography. Typically the animal image is doubled for power and effectiveness, so the usual scheme is the antithetical placement of two animals on either side of a central axis—namely, the tree.

33. Woolley 1934b: pl. 121.

34. Bibby 1969: pl. 5.

35. Woolley 1934b: 302.

36. Orthmann 1975: 14; pls. 70, 71 a.

37. Nissen, followed by Moorey, considers this seal and hence the grave to date to the late Akkadian period. Here the cylinder seal is considered not to be Akkadian but rather to date very early in the Early Dynastic period, and the fillet is thought to be contemporary with the majority of graves of the Royal Cemetery. Moorey 1970: 36–50; Nissen 1966: 46, 165.

38. Buchanan 1966: 56, no. 290.

39. An oval, segmented silver cosmetic box (U.11214) without lid was found in PG 845. Woolley 1934b: 240, type 109.

40. See, for example, the chariots in the lower register of the Standard of Ur (fig. 36a), in which the curve of the top of the front panel is much more pronounced.

41. Gilbert 1960: 96–101.

42. Orthmann 1975: 14, 90. In most of Mesopotamian art, the defeated enemy, either alive or dead, is shown naked in humiliating defeat, stripped of being and identity. In some cases, the origin of the defeated warrior is suggested by the hair or beard.

43. Woolley 1934b: 377.

44. Ibid.: 377 and pl. 182 b.

45. Studies focusing on the ostrich in the ancient Near East include Finet 1982: 69–77; Laufer 1926.

See also the "lurmu" entry in *Chicago Assyrian Dictionary* (Chicago, 1973): 255.

46. Wiseman 1952: 24 ff.

47. Kantor 1948: 46–51.

48. Asselberghs 1961: pls. LXV, LXX.

49. Citations for the examples from Kish and Mari are given in Moorey 1994: 127 f.

50. Civil 1987: 131–58.

51. Finet 1982.

52. Van Buren 1939: 87 f.

53. Moorey 1975: 79 ff.

54. Porada 1948: pl. LXXXVI:606.

CYLINDER SEALS

1. For further reading, see Amiet 1980; Boehmer 1969; Hansen 1987; Legrain 1936; Moorey 1977; Nissen 1966; Pollock 1991; Rathje 1977; and Selz 1983.

2. Moorey 1977: 28.

JEWELRY

1. In a personal communication (February 1998), Naomi Miller has kindly commented on some of the plant material rendered in gold in Puabi's tomb.

2. Moorey 1977.

3. Kramer 1952.

4. Moorey 1994: 171.

5. Kenoyer 1998.

6. Lilyquist 1993.

7. Woolley provides an extended discussion of the headdress in Woolley 1934b when reporting on his disagreements with Father Legrain's restoration of this headdress.

8. Spycket 1954.

9. Naomi Miller, personal communication.

10. Frankfort 1934: fig. 29.

11. Mari IV.

12. Mallowan 1969.

13. Maxwell-Hyslop 1971: 3; Naomi Miller, personal communication.

14. During-Caspers 1994.

15. Maxwell-Hyslop 1971: 4–5.

16. Woolley 1934b: 372.

17. Kilmer 1987: 175–80.

METAL VESSELS

1. Moorey 1994 provides a thorough discussion of the proveniencing of metals as well as a bibliography.

2. For a convenient summary, see Moorey 1994: 219–20.

3. Ibid.: 217.

4. For Turkey, see Yener et al. in press; for Iran, see Moorey 1994: 234.

5. Hirsch 1963.

6. Stech and Piggot 1986.

7. Moorey 1994: 235.

8. Müller-Karpe 1991: 107–8.

9. Muhly 1977.

10 See Stech and Pigott 1986.

11. Müller-Karpe 1989: 185; 1991: 111–12.

12. Plenderleith and Werner 1971.

13. Müller-Karpe 1993: 13.

14. Ibid.: 109–10.

15. Hiebert 1994: 47–48, 50.

16. Plenderleith in Wooley 1934b: 296.

17. Woolley 1934b: 380.

18. Müller-Karpe 1993: 44–45.

19. Katz and Voigt 1986: 29.

20. Hansen 1963.

21. Civil 1964: 67.

22. Katz and Maytag 1991.

SHELL VESSELS AND CONTAINERS

1. Gensheimer 1984: 69–70.

2. Ibid.: 67.

3. Woolley 1934a.

4. Woolley 1934b: pl. 102.

5. Gensheimer 1984: 70; Kenoyer 1984: 59.

6. Kenoyer 1984: 59.

7. Ibid.: 56.

8. Moorey 1994: 134.

9. Bimson 1980.

10. Klein 1981.

STONE VESSELS

1. Woolley identified the stones by eye, and no systematic investigation of the materials using more advanced scientific methods has been undertaken in the years since the publication of his final report. The catalogue descriptions follow his identifications.

2. Potts 1989: 123, n. 2.

3. Woolley 1934b: 379–80.

4. Potts 1989: 137–38.

5. For an extended discussion of the issues raised by studies of chlorite and steatite vessels as well as a bibliography, see Moorey 1994: 46–50.

6. Kohl 1974: 218–20.

7. Zarins 1978: no. 593.

8. Potts 1989: 141.

9. de Miroschedji 1973.

10. Potts 1989: 130, 139.

11. de Miroschedji 1973: fig. 5.11 and pl. 3h, with the zigzags framing the field duplicated by pl. 3g.

12. Zarins 1978: 106, pl. 70.

13. Moorey 1994: 63–65, 85–87.

14. See ibid.: 55–59.

15. Woolley 1934b: 38.

16. For those from the Inanna temple, see Hansen and Dales 1962: 79–80.

17. Hakemi 1997: 611–15.

18. Pottier 1984: no. 226.

TOOLS AND WEAPONS

1. Woolley 1934b: 381–83.

2. Moorey 1994: 223.

3. Woolley 1934b: 303.

4. Plenderleith, in Woolley 1934b: 292.

5. La Niece 1985: 45.

6. La Niece 1985.

7. La Niece 1985. Three of the four chisels analyzed had fairly similar proportions of the three metals: core compositions of 39 to 45 percent gold, 11 to 24 percent silver, and 37 to 44 percent copper and surface compositions of 82 to 91 percent gold, 6 to 11 percent silver, and 4 to 8 percent copper.

8. For example, depending on the amount of copper present, a copper-gold alloy can have a melting point as low as 910°C, as opposed to 1085°C for pure copper and 1064°C for pure gold (Fleming 1992: 56, fig. B.2).

9. Moorey 1994: 230–32.

10. Müller-Karpe 1990.

11. Ibid.: 191–92, fig. 23.

12. Stech in press.

13. Plenderleith and Werner 1971: 193–94.

14. Müller-Karpe 1985.

15. Watelin 1934: 33, pl. 25.

16. Parrot 1956: 145, fig. 81, pl. 57c.

17. Woolley 1934b: pls. 92, 181, 196.

18. Woolley 1934b: 555.

Bibliography

Adams, R. McC.
1981 *Heartland of Cities*. Chicago: University of Chicago Press.

Alva, W., and C. B. Donnan
1993 *Royal Tombs of Sipán*. Los Angeles: University of California, Fowler Museum of Cultural History.

Amiet, P.
1980 *La glyptique mésopotamienne archaïque*. 2d ed. Paris: Editions du CNRS.

Andrae, W.
1922 *Die archaischen Ischtar-Tempel in Assur*. Leipzig: J. C. Hinrichs'sche Buchhandlung.

Asselberghs, H.
1961 "Chaos en beheersing." *Documenta et monumenta Orientis antiqui* 8: pls. LXV, LXX.

Barnett, R. D.
1969 "New Facts about Musical Instruments from Ur." *Iraq* 31: 96–103.

Behm-Blancke, M. R.
1979 *Das Tierbild in der altmesopotamischen Rundplastik. Bagdader Forschungen* I. Mainz am Rhein: Phillip von Zabern.

Bibby, G.
1969 *Looking for Dilmun*. New York: Knopf.

Biggs, R. D.
1967 "Semitic Names in the Fara Period." *Orientalia*, n.s., 36: 55–66.

1974 *Inscriptions from Tell Abu Salabikh*. Chicago: University of Chicago Press.

Biggs, R. D., and J. N. Postgate
1978 "Inscriptions from Abu Salabikh, 1975." *Iraq* 40: 101–18.

Bimson, M.
1980 "Cosmetic Pigments from the 'Royal Cemetery' at Ur." *Iraq* 42: 75–77.

Boehmer, R.
1969 Zur Glyptic zwischen Mesilim und Akkadzeit." *Zeitschrift für Assyriologie* 25: 261–91.

Boese, J.
1978 "Mesannepada und der Schatz von Mari." *Zeitschrift für Assyriologie* 68: 6–33.

Bottéro, J.
1992 *Mesopotamia: Writing, Reasoning and the Gods*. Zainab Bahrani and Marc van de Mierop, trans. Chicago: University of Chicago Press.

Buchanan, B.
1954 "The Date of the So-Called Second Dynasty Graves of the Royal Cemetery at Ur." *Journal of the American Oriental Society* 74: 147–53.

1966 *Catalogue of Ancient Near Eastern Seals in the Ashmolean Museum*. Oxford: Clarendon Press.

Burrows, E.
1935 *Archaic Texts. Joint Expedition of the British Museum and of the Museum of the University of Pennsylvania to Mesopotamia* II. London: Trustees of the British Museum and of the University Museum, University of Pennsylvania.

Campbell-Thompson, R.
1921 "The British Museum Excavations at Abu Shahrain in Mesopotamia in 1918." *Archaeologia* 70: 101–44.

Casanova, M. C.

1991 *La vaisselle d'albâtre de Mésopotamie, d'Iran et d'Asie centrale*. Paris: Editions Recherche sur les Civilisations.

Chang, K.-C.

1976 *Early Chinese Civilization: Anthropological Perspectives*. Cambridge: Harvard University Press.

1980 *Shang Civilization*. New Haven: Yale University Press.

Chi, L.

1977 *Anyang*. Seattle: University of Washington Press.

Chochorowski, J., and S. Skoryi

1997 "The Prince of the Great Kurgan." *Archaeology* (Sept./Oct.): 32–39.

Christie, A.

1977 *Agatha Christie: An Autobiography*. New York: Dodd, Mead.

Civil, M.

1964 "A Hymn to the Beer Goddess and a Drinking Song." In J. A. Brinkman, ed., *Studies Presented to A. Leo Oppenheim*. Chicago: University of Chicago Press.

1987 "The Early History of HAR-ra: The Ebla Link." In L. Cagni, ed., *Ebla 1975–1985*, pp. 131–58. Naples: Istituto Universitario Orientale, Dipartimento di Studi Asiatici.

Cooper, J. S.

1983 *Reconstructing History from Ancient Inscriptions: The Lagash-Umma Border Conflict*. Malibu, Calif.: Undena Publications.

1986 *Presargonic Inscriptions. Sumerian and Akkadian Royal Inscriptions*. Vol. 1. New Haven: American Oriental Society.

Crawford, V.

1959 "Nippur, the Holy City." *Archaeology* 12: 2, 74–83.

Decker, W.

1992 *Sports and Games of Ancient Egypt*. New Haven: Yale University Press.

Deimel, A.

1923 *Die Inschriften von Fara*. Vol. 2, *Schultexte aus Fara*. Leipzig: J. C. Heinrichs'sche Buchhandlung.

1925 *Die Inschriften von Fara*. Vol. 2, *Wirtschaftstexte aus Fara*. Leipzig: J. C. Heinrichs'sche Buchhandlung.

della Valle, P.

1665 *The Travels of Pietro della Valle, a Noble Roman, into the East-India and Arabia Deserta*. London: J. Macock, for Henry Herringman.

Delougaz, P., H. D. Hill, and S. Lloyd

1967 *Private Houses and Graves in the Diyala Region*. Chicago: University of Chicago Press.

de Miroschedji, P.

1973 "Vases et objets en steatite susiens du musée du Louvre." *Cahiers de la Délégation archéologique française en Iran* 3: 9–79.

Donnan, C. B.

1995 "Moche Funerary Practice." In T. D. Dillehay, ed., *Tombs for the Living: Andean Mortuary Practices*, pp. 111–59. Washington, D.C.: Dumbarton Oaks Research Library and Collection.

Dornemann, R.

1988 "Tell Hadidi: One Bronze Age Site among Many in the Tabqa Dam Salvage Area." *Bulletin of the American Schools of Oriental Research* 270: 13–42.

During-Caspars, E. C. L.

1994 "The Harappan Courtiers." In J. M. Kenoyer, ed., *From Sumer to Meluhha: Contributions to the Archaeology of South and West Asia in Memory of George F. Dales, Jr*. Madison: University of Wisconsin.

Dyson, R. H., Jr.

1960 "A Note on Queen Shub-Ad's 'Onagers'." *Iraq* 22: 102–4.

1977 "Archival Glimpses of the Ur Expedition in the Years 1920 to 1926." *Expedition* 20: 5–23.

Edzard, D. O.

1959 "Enmebaragesi von Kish." *Zeitschrift für Assyriologie* 53: 9–36.

1976 "Fara und Abu Salabikh. Die Wirtschaftexte." *Zeitschrift für Assyriologie* 66: 156–95.

Englund, R. K.

1994 *Archaic Administrative Texts from Uruk. Archaische Texte aus Uruk*. Vol. 5. Berlin: Gebr. Mann Verlag.

Englund, R. K., and J.-P. Grégoire

1991 *The Proto-Cuneiform Texts from Jemdet Nasr*. Berlin: Gebr. Mann Verlag.

Englund, R. K., and H. J. Nissen

1993 *Die Lexikalischen Listen der archaischen Texte aus Uruk. Archaische Texte aus Uruk*. Vol. 3. Berlin: Gebr. Mann Verlag.

Falkenstein, A.

1936 *Archaische Texte aus Uruk. Archaische Texte aus Uruk.* Vol. 1. Berlin: Deutsche Forschungsgemeinschaft.

Finet, A.

1982 "L'oeuf d'autruche." In S. Scheers, ed., *Studia Paulo Naster. Orientalia Lovaniensia Analecta* 13: 69–77.

Fisher, W. B.

1950 *The Middle East.* London: Methuen.

Fleming, S. F.

1992 "Sitio Conte Goldwork: Alloying and Treatment of Surfaces." Appendix B in P. Hearne and R. J. Sharer, eds. *River of Gold: Precolumbian Treasures from Sitio Conte I*, pp. 54–58. Philadelphia: The University of Pennsylvania Museum.

Frankfort, H.

1939 *Cylinder Seals: A Documentary Essay on the Art and Religion of the Ancient Near East.* London: Macmillan.

Iraq Excavation of the Oriental Institute 1932/1933. Third Preliminary Report of the Iraq Expedition. Oriental Institute Communications 17. Chicago: The Oriental Institute.

1996 *Art and Architecture of the Ancient Orient.* 5th ed. New Haven: Yale University Press.

Fraser, J. B.

1840 *Travels in Koordistan, Mesopotamia, etc.* 2 vols. London: Richard Bentley.

Friedman, K. E.

1991 *Catastrophe and Creation.* Chur, Switzerland: Harwood Academic Publishers.

Gelb, I. J.

1957 *Glossary of Old Akkadian. Materials for the Assyrian Dictionary* 3. Chicago: University of Chicago Press.

Gensheimer, T. R.

1984 "The Role of Shell in Mesopotamia: Evidence for Trade Exchange with Oman and the Indus Valley." *Paleorient* 10: 65–73.

Gilbert, P.

1960 "L'Egypte et la plaque aux deux lions d'Ur." *Iraq* 22: 96–101.

Gockel, W.

1982 *Die Stratigraphie und Chronologie der Ausgrabungen des Diyala-Gebietes unter der Stadt Ur in der Zeit von Uruk/Eanna IV bis zur Dynastie von Akkad.* Rome: Giorgio Bretschneider.

Goetze, A.

1955 "An Incantation against Disease." *Journal of Cuneiform Studies* 9: 8–18.

Green, M., and H. J. Nissen

1987 *Zeichenliste der archaischen Texte aus Uruk.* Vol. 2, *Archaische Texte aus Uruk.* Berlin: Gebr. Mann Verlag.

Hakemi, A.

1997 *Shadad: Archaeological Excavations of a Bronze Age Center in Iran.* S. M. S. Sajjadi, trans. Rome: Istituto italiano per il medio ed estremo oriente.

Hall, H. R.

1919 *Proceedings of the Society of Antiquaries,* Dec. 4: 22–44.

1923 "Ur and Eridu: The British Museum Excavations of 1919." *Journal of Egyptian Archaeology* 9: 177–95.

1930 *A Season's Work at Ur.* London: Methuen.

Hansen, D. P.

1963 "New Votive Plaques from Nippur." *Journal of Near Eastern Studies* 22: 145–66.

1987 "The Fantastic World of Sumerian Art: Seal Impressions from Ancient Lagash." In P. Harper, A. Farkas, and E. Harrison, eds., *Monsters and Demons in the Ancient and Medieval Worlds, Papers Presented in Honor of Edith Porada,* pp. 53–63. Mainz am Rhein: Phillip von Zabern.

Hansen, D. P., and G. F. Dales

1962 "The Temple of Iananna, Queen of Heaven at Nippur." *Archaeology* 15: 75–84.

Harper, P. O., et al., eds.

1992 *The Royal City of Susa.* New York: Metropolitan Museum of Art.

Hearne, P., and R. J. Sharer, eds.

1992 *River of Gold.* Philadelphia: University Museum Publications, University of Pennsylvania.

Hiebert, F.

1994 *Origins of the Bronze Age Oasis Civilization in Central Asia.* Cambridge, Mass.: Harvard University, Peabody Museum of Archaeology and Ethnology.

Hirsch, H.

1963 "Die Inschriften der Könige von Agade." *Archiv für Orientforschung* 20: 1–82.

Hoffman, M. A.

1991 *Egypt before the Pharoahs.* Rev. ed. Austin: University of Texas Press.

Huot, J.-L.

1996 *Oueili. Travaux de 1987 et 1989.* Paris: Editions Recherche sur les Civilisations.

Illustrated London News

1968 *Window on the World, the Illustrated London News Review.* London: Michael Joseph.

Jacobsen, T.

1939 *The Sumerian Kinglist.* Chicago: University of Chicago Press.

1940 "Inscriptions." In P. P. Delougaz, *The Temple Oval at Khafajah,* pp. 146–50. Chicago: University of Chicago Press.

1976 *The Treasures of Darkness.* New Haven: Yale University Press.

1987 *The Harps That Once . . .: Sumerian Poetry in Translation.* New Haven: Yale University Press.

Josefsson, C.

1988 "The Politics of Chaos." In S. Cederroth, C. Corlin, and J. Lindström, eds., *On the Meaning of Death* pp. 155–67. Uppsala, Sweden: Almqvist & Wiksell International.

Juris, Z.

1978 "Typological Studies in Saudi Arabian Archaeology: Steatite Vessels in the Riyadh Museum." *Atlal* 2: 65–93.

Kantor, H.

1948 "Oriental Museum Notes: A Predynastic Ostrich Egg with Incised Decoration." *Journal of Near Eastern Studies* 7: 46–51.

Karstens, K.

1994 "Die erste Dynastie von Ur. Überlegungen zur relativen Datierung." In P. Calmeyer, K. Hecker, L. Jakob-Rost, and C. B. F. Walker, eds., *Beiträge zur altorientalischen Archäologie und Altertumskunde: Festschrift für Barthel Hrouda zum 65. Geburtstag,* pp. 133–42. Wiesbaden: Harrassowitz.

Katz, S. H., and F. Maytag

1991 "Brewing and Ancient Beer." *Archaeology* 20: 24–33.

Katz, S. H., and M. M. Voigt

1986 "Bread and Beer." *Expedition* 28: 23–34.

Kemp, B. J.

1967 "The Egyptian 1st Dynasty Royal Cemetery." *Antiquity* 41: 22–32.

Kenoyer, J. M.

1977 "Trade and Technology of the Indus Valley." *World Archaeology* 29, Oct. 1977: 262–80.

1984 "Shell Working Industries of the Indus Civilization: A Summary." *Paleorient* 10: 49–63.

Kilmer, A.

1987 "The Symbolism of the Flies in the Mesopotamian Flood Myth and Some Further Implications." In F. Rochberg-Halton, ed., *Language, Literature, and History: Philological and Historical Studies Presented to Erica Reiner,* pp. 175–80. New Haven: Yale University Press.

1980–83 "Leier." *Reallexikon der Assyriologie.* Vol. 6, pp. 571–76. Berlin: Walter de Gruyter.

Klein, J.

1981 *Three Sulgi Hymns.* Ramat-Gan: Bar-Ilan University.

Kohl, P. L.

1974 *Seeds of Upheaval. The Production of Chlorite at Tepe Yahya and an Analysis of Commodity Production and Trade in Southwest Asia in the Third Millennium B.C.* Ph.D. diss., Harvard University.

Kramer, S. N.

1952 *Enmerkar and the Lord of Aratta, a Sumerian Epic Tale of Iraq and Iran.* Philadelphia: University Museum, University of Pennsylvania.

1959 *History Begins at Sumer.* Garden City, N.Y.: Doubleday.

Kühne, H.

1976 *Die Keramik vom Tell Chuera.* Berlin: Gebr. Mann Verlag.

Lambert, M.

1981 "Ur-Emush 'Grand-Marchand' de Lagash." *Oriens Antiquus* 20: 175–85.

Langdon, S.

1930 "The Biblical Deluge: An Ascertained Fact." *The Illustrated London News,* 8 February: 206–7.

La Niece, S.

1985 "Depletion Gilding from Third Millennium B.C. Ur." *Iraq* 57: 41–47.

Larsen, M.

1996 *The Conquest of Assyria.* London: Routledge.

Laufer, B.

1926 *Ostrich Egg-Shell Cups of Mesopotamia and the Ostrich in Ancient and Modern Times* (Anthropology Leaflet 23). Chicago: Field Museum of Natural History.

Lawergren, B.

1994 "Leiern (Altertum)." In L. Finscher, ed., *Die Musik in Geschichte und Gegenwart*, Sachteil 5, pp. 1101–50. Kassel: Bärenreiter Verlag.

1997 "Mesopotamien (Musikinstrumente)." In L. Finscher, ed., *Die Musik in Geschichte und Gegenwart*. Part 6, pp. 143–74. Kassel: Bärenreiter Verlag.

Le Brun, A.

1971 "Recherches stratigraphiques à l'Acropole de Suse." *Cahiers de la Délégation archéologique française en Iran*. 1: 163–211.

Legrain, L.

1936 *Archaic Seal-Impressions*. London: Trustees of the British Museum and of the University Museum, University of Pennsylvania.

1936 *Archaic Seal Impressions, Ur Excavations*, vol. 3. Philadelphia: Trustees of the British Museum and of the University of Pennsylvania.

Lindermeyer, E., and L. Martin

1993 *Uruk. Kleinfunde III: Kleinfunde im Vorderasiatischen Museum zu Berlin*. Mainz am Rhein: Phillip von Zabern.

Lloyd, S.

1961 *The Art of the Ancient Near East*. New York: Praeger.

Loftus, W. K.

1857 *Travels and Researches in Chaldaea and Susiana*. London: James Nisbet.

Maekawa, K.

1973–74 "The Development of the É-MI in Lagash during Early Dynastic III." *Mesopotamia* 8–9: 77–144.

Mallowan, M.

1969 Review of *Le trésor d'Ur*, by A. Parrot. *Mari IV. Bibliotheca Orientalis* 26: 86–89.

1977 *Mallowan's Memoirs*. New York: Dodd, Mead.

Martin, H.

1988 *Fara*. Birmingham: Chris Martin.

Martin, H., J. Moon, and J. N. Postgate

1985 *Graves 1 to 99*. London: British School of Archaeology in Iraq.

Maxwell-Hyslop, K. R.

1971 *Western Asiatic Jewellery c. 3000–612 B.C.* London: Methuen and Co., Ltd.

Michalowski, P.

1990 "Early Mesopotamian Communicative Systems: Art, Literature, and Writing." In A. Gunter, ed., *Investigating Artistic Environments in the Ancient Near East*, pp. 53–67. Washington, D.C.: Smithsonian Institution.

Moorey, P. R. S.

1970 "Pictorial Evidence for the History of Horse Riding in Iraq before the Kassite Period." *Iraq* 32: 36–50.

1975 "The Terracotta Plaques from Kish and Hursagkalama, c. 1850 to 1650 B.C.." *Iraq* 37: 79 ff.

1977 "What Do We Know about the People Buried in the Royal Cemetery?" *Expedition* 20: 24–40.

1994 *Ancient Mesopotamian Materials and Industries*. Oxford: Clarendon Press.

Moortgat, A.

1949 *Tammuz: Der Unsterblichkeitsglaube in der altorientalischen Bildkunst*. Berlin: Verlag Walter de Gruyter.

1969 *The Art of Ancient Mesopotamia*. London: Phaidon.

Muhly, James B.

1977 "The Copper Ox-Hide Ingots and the Bronze Age Metal Trade." *Iraq* 39: 72–82.

Müller-Karpe, M.

1985 "Antlers of the Stag Rein Ring from Kish." *Journal of Near Eastern Studies* 44: 57–58.

1989 "Neue Forschungen zur frühen Metallverarbeitung in Mesopotamien." *Jahrbuch des Römisch-Germanischen Zentralmuseums Mainz* 36: 179–92.

1990 "Der Guss in der verloren Sandform in Mesopotamien." *Mitteilungen der Deutschen Orient-Gesellschaft* 122: 173–92.

1991 "Aspects of Early Metallurgy in Mesopotamia." In E. Pernicka and G. A. Wagner, eds., *Archaeometry '90*. Basel: Birkhäuser Verlag.

1993 *Metallgefäße im Iraq 1*. Stuttgart: Franz Steiner Verlag.

Nissen, H. J.

1966 *Zur Datierung des Königsfriedhofes von Ur*. Bonn: Rudolf Habelt Verlag.

1972 "The City Wall of Uruk." In P. J. Ucko, R. Tringham, and G. W. Dimbleby, eds., *Man, Settlement and Urbanism*, pp. 793–98. Cambridge: Schenkman.

1988 *The Early History of the Ancient Near East, 9000–2000 B.C.* Translated by E. Lutzeier, with K. J. Northcott. Chicago: University of Chicago Press.

Nissen, H. J., P. Damerow, and R. K. Englund
1993 *Archaic Bookkeeping.* Translated by P. Larsen. Chicago: University of Chicago Press.

O'Connor, D.
1993 *Ancient Nubia. Egypt's Rival in Africa.* Philadelphia: University of Pennsylvania Museum.

Oppenheim, A. L., ed.
1973 *The Assyrian Dictionary,* 9. Chicago: Oriental Institute.

Orthmann, W.
1975 *Der alte Orient. Propyläen Kunstgeschichte* 14. Berlin: Propyläen Verlag.

Orthmann, W., and E. Rova
1991 *Gräber des 3. Jahrtausends v. Chr. im syrischen Euphrattal.* Saarbrücken, Germany: Saarbrücker Druckerei und Verlag.

Parrot, A.
1948 *Tello. Vingt campagnes de fouilles (1877–1933).* Paris: Editions Albin Michel.

1956 *Le Temple d'Ishtar.* Paris: Librairie Orientaliste Paul Geuthner.

Plenderleith, H. J.
1934 "Metals and Metal Technique." In C. L. Woolley, *The Royal Cemetery. Joint Expedition of the British Museum and of the Museum of the University of Pennsylvania.* London: Trustees of the British Museum and of the Museum of the University of Pennsylvania.

Plenderleith, H. J., and A. E. A. Werner
1971 *The Conservation of Antiquities and Works of Art.* 2d ed. London: Oxford University Press.

Pollock, S.
1983 *The Symbolism of Prestige: An Archaeological Example from the Royal Cemetery of Ur.* Ph.D. diss., University of Michigan.

1985 "Chronology of the Ur Royal Cemetery." *Iraq* 47: 129–85.

1991 "Of Priestesses, Princes and Poor Relations: The Dead in the Royal Cemetery of Ur." *Cambridge Archaeological Journal* 1: 171–89.

Pomponio, F., and G. Visicato
1994 *Early Dynastic Administrative Tablets of Šuruppak.* Naples: Istituto universitario orientale di Napoli, dipartimento di studi asiatici.

Porada, E.
1948 *Corpus of Ancient Near Eastern Seals in American Collections.* Vol. 1, *The Collection of the Pierpont Morgan Library.* Washington, D.C: Bollingen Foundation.

Porada, E., D. P. Hansen, S. Dunham, and S. H. Babcock
1992 "Mesopotamia." In R. W. Ehrich, ed., *Chronologies in Old World Archaeology,* pp. 77–122. Chicago: University of Chicago Press.

Porter, B. N.
1993 "Sacred Trees, Date Palms, and the Royal Persona of Ashurnasirpal II." *Journal of Near Eastern Studies* 52: 129–39.

Postgate, J. N.
1992 *Early Mesopotamia.* London: Routledge.

Pottier, M.-H.
1984 *Matériel funéraire de la Bactriane méridionale de l'âge de bronze.* Paris: Editions Recherche sur les Civilisations.

Potts, T. F.
1989 "Foreign Stone Vessels of the Late Third Millennium B.C. from Southern Mesopotamia: Their Origins and Mechanisms of Exchange." *Iraq* 51: 123–64.

Pritchard, J. B.
1950 *Ancient Near Eastern Texts Relating to the Old Testament.* Princeton, N.J.: Princeton University Press.

Rathje, W.
1977 "New Tricks for Old Seals: A Progress Report." In McG. Gibson and R. Biggs, eds., *Seals and Sealings in the Ancient Near East.* Malibu, Calif.: Undena Press.

Rawlinson, H. C.
1850 "On the Inscriptions of Assyria and Babylonia," *Journal of the Royal Asiatic Society* 12: 401–83.

1857 *Proceedings of the Royal Geographical Society* 1: 46–47.

1861 *A Selection from the Historical Inscriptions of Chaldaea, Assyria and Babylonia.* 4 vols. London: R. E. Bowker.

Redman, C. L.
1978 *The Rise of Civilization.* San Francisco: W. H. Freeman.

Reisner, G. A.
1923 *Excavations at Kerma.* Cambridge, Mass.: Harvard University Press.

Renger, J.

1972–75 "Heilige Hochzeit." In *Reallexikon der Assyriologie*, vol. 4, pp. 251–59. Berlin: Walter de Gruyter.

Selz, G.

1983 *Die Bankettszene: Entwicklung eines "Uberzeitlichen" Bildmotivs in Mesopotamien von der Fruhdynastichen bis zur Akkad-Zeit.* Wiesbaden: F. Steiner.

1989 *Die altsumerischen Wirtschaftsurkunden der Ermitage zu Leningrad.* Stuttgart: Franz Steiner Verlag.

1993 *Die altsumerischen Wirtschaftsurkunden aus amerikanischen Sammlungen.* Stuttgart: Franz Steiner Verlag.

Sollberger, E.

1967 "The Rulers of Lagash." *Journal of Cuneiform Studies* 21: 279–91.

Stech, T.

forthcoming In V. Pigott, ed., *The Archaeometallurgy of the Asian Old World.* Philadelphia: University of Pennsylvania Museum.

Stech, T., and V. Pigott

1986 "The Metals Trade in Southwest Asia in the Third Millennium B.C." *Iraq* 48: 39–64.

Steible, H., and F. Yildiz

1993 "Ki'eng aus der Sicht von Shuruppak." *Istanbuler Mitteilungen* 43: 17–26.

Steinkeller, P.

1992 "Mesopotamia in the Third Millennium B.C." In D. N. Freedman, ed., *The Anchor Bible Dictionary*, vol. 4, pp. 724–32. New York: Doubleday.

1993 "Early Political Development in Mesopotamia and the Origins of the Sargonic Empire." In M. Liverani, *Akkad, The First World Empire*, pp. 107–29. Padova, Italy: Sargon.

Strommenger, E.

1962 *Fünf Jahrtausende Mesopotamien: die Kunst von den Anfängen um 5000 vor Chr. bis zu Alexander dem Grossen.* Munich: Hirmer.

Taylor, J. E.

1854 "Notes on the Ruins of Muqeyer." *Journal of the Royal Asiatic Society* 15: 260–76.

Van Buren, E. D.

1939 "The Fauna of Ancient Mesopotamia as Represented in Art." *Analecta Orientalia* 18: 87 f.

Verrnao, J. W.

1995 "Where Do They Rest? The Treatment of Human Offerings and Trophies in Ancient Peru." In T. D. Dillehay, ed., *Tombs for the Living: Andean Mortuary Practices*, pp. 189–227. Washington, D.C.: Dumbarton Oaks Research Library and Collection.

Vycichl, W.

1959 "The Burial of the Sudanese Kings in the Middle Ages." *Kush* 7: 221–22.

Wallach, J.

1996 *Desert Queen.* New York: Nan A. Talese/ Doubleday.

Watelin, L. Ch.

1934 *Excavations at Kish.* Vol. 4. Paris: Paul Geuthner.

Wiggerman, F.

1994 "Mischwesen." In *Reallexikon der Assyriologie*, Vol. 8, pp. 222–44. Berlin: Walter de Gruyter.

1995 "Extensions of and Contradictions to Dr. Porada's Lecture." In E. Porada, ed., *Man and Images in the Ancient Near East*, pp. 77–154. Wakefield, Rhode Island, and London: Moyer Bell.

Winstone, H. V. F.

1980 *Gertrude Bell.* London: Quartet Books.

1990 *Woolley of Ur.* London: Secker & Warburg.

Wiseman, D.

1952 "A New Stela of Assur-nasir-pal II." *Iraq* 14: 24 ff.

Woolley, C. L.

1923 "Excavations at Ur of the Chaldees." *Antiquaries Journal* 3: 311–33.

1928 "Excavations at Ur, 1926–7. Part II." *Antiquaries Journal* 8: 1–29.

1929 "Excavations at Ur, 1928–9." *Antiquaries Journal* 9: 305–43.

1930 "Excavations at Ur, 1929–30." *Antiquaries Journal* 10: 315–43.

1931 "Excavations at Ur, 1930–31." *The Museum Journal* 22: 3–4.

1933 "Report on the Excavations at Ur, 1932–3." *Antiquaries Journal* 13: 359–83.

1934a "Excavations at Ur, 1933–4." *Antiquaries Journal* 14: 355–78.

1934b *The Royal Cemetery, Ur Excavations*, vol. 2. London: Trustees of the British Museum and of the Museum of the University of Pennsylvania.

1953 *Spadework in Archaeology*. New York: Philosophical Library.

1956 *The Early Periods, Ur Excavations*, vol. 4. Philadelphia: Trustees of the British Museum and of the Museum of the University of Pennsylvania.

1974 *The Buildings of the Third Dynasty, Ur Excavations*, vol. 6. Philadelphia: Trustees of the British Museum and of the Museum of the University of Pennsylvania.

Yener, K. A., et al.
in press "The Analysis of Metalliferous Residues, Crucible Fragments, Experimental Smelts, and Ores from Kestel Tin Mines and the Tin Processing Site of Göltepe." In P. Craddock, ed., *Proceedings of the Conference of Ancient Mining and Metallurgy*. London: British Museum Occasional Publications.

Zarins, J.
1978 "Typological Studies in Saudi Arabian Archaeology: Steatite Vessels in the Riyadh Museum." *Atlal* 2: 65–93.

Concordance

CONCORDANCE OF UNIVERSITY OF
PENNSYLVANIA MUSEUM NUMBERS

Museum Number	Field Number	Catalogue Number
B15583	—	73
B16684	U.10984	30
B16685	U.8269	10
B16686	U.8173	11
B16687	U.9131	154
B16688	U.10855	115
B16689	U.10472	140
B16690	U.10411	140
B16691	U.9339	149
B16692	U.11154	15
B16693	U.10937	29
B16694	U.10982	34
B16695	U.10552	144
B16704	U.8214	50
B16705	U.9979	38
B16707	U.10930	97
B16710	U.10932	108
B16711	U.10901	109
B16713	U.10952	138
B16714	U.10423	156
B16716	—	67
B16717	U.10877a	31
B16718	U.10877b	31
B16719	U.10877c	31
B16720	U.10877d	31

Museum Number	Field Number	Catalogue Number	Museum Number	Field Number	Catalogue Number
B16721	U.10878	31	B17065	U.10916	2
B16724	U.10430	152	B17066	U.10475	13
B16725	U.10433	152	B17067	U.10554	101
B16726	U.10985	33	B17068	U.10855	116
B16727	U.10448	18	B17072a	U.10896	106
B16728	U.10872	17	B17072b	U.10897	106
B16729	U.10940	31	B17072c	U.10898	106
B16733a–f	U.10424	39	B17072d	—	106
B16735	U.10889	36	B17077	U.10891	99
B16742	U.9776	6	B17078	U.10472	141
B16744a,b	U.10436	12	B17081	U.10886	111
B16747	U.10530	21	B17082	U.10860	110
B16753	U.10437	137	B17082a	U.10860	107
B16754	U.10544	42	B17082b	U.10861	110
B16761	U.10875	35	B17085	U.9362	157
B16777a,b	U.9977	37	B17087	U.10746	14
B16779	U.10824a	77	B17103	U.10502	129
B16783	U.10979	31	B17104	U.10854	125
B16784	U.10532	41	B17105	U.10490	126
B16792	U.8097	82	B17108	U.10492	126
B16794	U.9351	67	B17111	U.10882	127
B16797	U.8931a	74	B17112	U.10498	126
B16798	U.8693	52	B17128	U.10921	128
B16799	U.8931b	68	B17129	U.10499	135
B16800	U.9351	68	B17131	U.10501	133
B16804	U.9351	66	B17132	U.10527	133
B16811	U.8011	91	B17133	U.10484	133
B16819	U.9351	70	B17134	U.10512	133
B16828	U.8615	20	B17135	U.10513	133
B16829	U.8614	83	B17138	U.10514	133
B16835	U.8162	85	B17139	U.10963	131
B16841a,b	U.12374	61	B17140	—	135
B16852	U.8981	25	B17143	U.10516	132
B16869	U.8513	23	B17144	U.10960	130
B16908	U.10938	32	B17152	U.10481	134
B16972a–c	U.9320	7	B17166	U.10480	123
B16992	U.10890	29	B17167	U.10517	120
B16993	U.10533	41	B17168	U.10523	121
B17010	U.9118	114	B17185	U.10966	118
B17019	—	85	B17186	U.10966	118
B17025	U.9723	119	B17187	U.8222	119
B17063	U.10867	31	B17194	U.8191	117
B17064	U.10465	1	B17280	U.10565	112

Museum Number	Field Number	Catalogue Number	Museum Number	Field Number	Catalogue Number
B17285	U.9860	153	30-12-13	U.11757	16
B17292	—	31	30-12-72	U.11814	124
B17296	U.10457	103	30-12-77	U.11815	124
B17297	U.10464	100	30-12-81	U.11549	136
B17298	U.10457	102	30-12-292	—	41
B17299	U.10457	104	30-12-318	U.11463	147
B17302	U.10518	132	30-12-342	U.12252	143
B17348	—	143	30-12-436	U.12423	54
B17387	U.8583	155	30-12-437	U.12420	55
B17400	U.10825	142	30-12-443	U.12380e	65
B17403	—	150	30-12-449	U.11743	82
B17413	U.8958	151	30-12-467	U.12377	52
B17439	U.10568	114	30-12-484	U.12435	5
B17447	U.8601	112	30-12-540	U.12305	145
B17487	U.11210	86	30-12-550	U.11513	146
B17528a,b	U.9336	143	30-12-552	U.11553	31
B17551	—	139	30-12-553	U.12380	92
B17561	U.10535	41	30-12-555	U.12380	92
B17568	U.10449	43	30-12-559	U.12450	90
B17636	—	66	30-12-560	U.11808	95
B17642	U.9985	40	30-12-561	U.11728	80
B17649	—	68	30-12-562	U.11910	79
B17650	—	67	30-12-565	U.12362	84
B17654	U.9780	70	30-12-567	U.12474	75
B17655	U.9780	70	30-12-570	U.12187	69
B17657	—	51	30-12-573	—	71
B17679	U.10594a	76	30-12-575	U.12362	81
B17691	U.10453	105	30-12-604	U.12184	53
B17692	U.10451	96	30-12-610	U.11894	74
B17693	U.10850	98	30-12-611	U.12425a	46
B17694	U.10556	3	30-12-614	U.12425e	62
B17709	U.10935a	29	30-12-615	U.12425d	62
B17710	U.10935a	29	30-12-619	U.11809	52
B17711	U.10936	29	30-12-634	U.12186	36
B17711a	U.10934	29	30-12-635	U.12186	36
B17712	U.10933	29	30-12-652	U11962	52
B17713	—	82	30-12-662	U.11965	56
B17716	U.8013	9	30-12-664	U.12415e	88
30-12-2	U.12374	19	30-12-685	U.12426e	82
30-12-3	U.12380	27	30-12-687	U.12426	87
30-12-4	U.12674	24	30-12-691a,b	U.12362	58
30-12-8	U.11528	22	30-12-692	U.12362b	94
30-12-12	U.12654	26	30-12-696	U.12435	4

Museum Number	Field Number	Catalogue Number
30-12-697	U.11586	122
30-12-698	U.11785	124
30-12-702	U.12357	8
30-12-703	U.12374	84
30-12-704	U.12374	78
30-12-706	—	63
30-12-707b	U.12374	92
30-12-708b	U.12374	92
30-12-713	U.12366	82
30-12-714	U.12366c	47
30-12-715a,b	U.12366b	57
30-12-716a,b	U.12374	59
30-12-722	U.12403b	64
30-12-725	U.12423	48
30-12-732	U.12406	36
30-12-736	U.12420e	94
30-12-737	U.12420e	94
30-12-742	U.12420a	45
30-12-748	U.12420j	89
30-12-755	U.11907	49
30-12-756	U.11809	52
30-12-757	U.11905	44
30-12-758b	U.11810	56
30-12-759	U.11908	50
31-16-379	U.14071	136
31-16-418	U.13773	124
31-16-536	U.15105	117
31-16-542a	—	119
31-17-118	U.13521	28
31-17-61	U.15381	73
31-17-74	—	93
31-17-75a,b	U.14091	60
31-17-93	—	119
31-43-543	—	153
32-40-227	U.17813e	72
35-1-66b	—	119
35-1-423	—	148
35-1-481	—	36
83-7-1	—	31
98-9-1	U.8626	113
98-9-8	—	87

CONCORDANCE OF UR EXCAVATION FIELD NUMBERS

Field Number	Museum Number	Catalogue Number
U.8011	B16811	91
U.8013	B17716	9
U.8097	B16792	82
U.8162	B16835	85
U.8173	B16686	11
U.8191	B17194	117
U.8214	B16704	50
U.8222	B17187	119
U.8269	B16685	10
U.8513	B16869	23
U.8583	B17387	155
U.8601	B17447	112
U.8614	B16829	83
U.8615	B16828	20
U.8626	98-9-1	113
U.8693	B16798	52
U.8931a	B16797	74
U.8931b	B16799	68
U.8958	B17413	151
U.8981	B16852	25
U.9118	B17010	114
U.9131	B16687	154
U.9320	B16972a–c	7
U.9336	B17528a,b	143
U.9339	B16691	149
U.9351	B16794	67
U.9351	B16800	68
U.9351	B16804	66
U.9351	B16819	70
U.9362	B17085	157
U.9723	B17025	119
U.9776	B16742	6
U.9780	B17654	70
U.9780	B17655	70
U.9860	B17285	153
U.9977	B16777a,b	37
U.9979	B16705	38
U.9985	B17642	40
U.10411	B16690	140
U.10423	B16714	156

Field Number	Museum Number	Catalogue Number	Field Number	Museum Number	Catalogue Number
U.10424	B16733a–f	39	U.10568	B17439	114
U.10430	B16724	152	U.10594a	B17679	76
U.10433	B16725	152	U.10746	B17087	14
U.10436	B16744a,b	12	U.10824a	B16779	77
U.10437	B16753	137	U.10825	B17400	142
U.10448	B16727	18	U.10850	B17693	98
U.10449	B17568	43	U.10854	B17104	125
U.10451	B17692	96	U.10855	B17068	116
U.10453	B17691	105	U.10855	B16688	115
U.10457	B17298	102	U.10860	B17082a	107
U.10457	B17299	104	U.10861	B17082b	110
U.10457	B17296	103	U.10867	B17063	31
U.10464	B17297	100	U.10872	B16728	17
U.10465	B17064	1	U.10875	B16761	35
U.10472	B16689	140	U.10877a	B16717	31
U.10472	B17078	141	U.10877b	B16718	31
U.10475	B17066	13	U.10877c	B16719	31
U.10480	B17166	123	U.10877d	B16720	31
U.10481	B17152	134	U.10878	B16721	31
U.10484	B17133	133	U.10882	B17111	127
U.10490	B17105	126	U.10886	B17081	111
U.10492	B17108	126	U.10889	B16735	36
U.10498	B17112	126	U.10890	B16992	29
U.10499	B17129	135	U.10891	B17077	99
U.10501	B17131	133	U.10896	B17072a	106
U.10502	B17103	129	U.10897	B17072b	106
U.10512	B17134	133	U.10898	B17072c	106
U.10513	B17135	133	U.10901	B16711	109
U.10514	B17138	133	U.10916	B17065	2
U.10516	B17143	132	U.10921	B17128	128
U.10517	B17167	120	U.10930	B16707	97
U.10518	B17302	132	U.10932	B16710	108
U.10523	B17168	121	U.10933	B17712	29
U.10527	B17132	133	U.10934	B17711a	29
U.10530	B16747	21	U.10935a	B17709	29
U.10532	B16784	41	U.10935a	B17710	29
U.10533	B16993	41	U.10936	B17711	29
U.10535	B17561	41	U.10937	B16693	29
U.10544	B16754	42	U.10938	B16908	32
U.10552	B16695	144	U.10940	B16729	31
U.10554	B17067	101	U.10952	B16713	138
U.10556	B17694	3	U.10960	B17144	130
U.10565	B17280	112	U.10963	B17139	131

Field Number	Museum Number	Catalogue Number	Field Number	Museum Number	Catalogue Number
U.10966	B17185	118	U.12366b	30-12-715a,b	57
U.10966	B17186	118	U.12366c	30-12-714	47
U.10979	B16783	31	U.12374	B16841a	61
U.10982	B16694	34	U.12374	B16841b	61
U.10984	B16684	30	U.12374	30-12-2	19
U.10985	B16726	33	U.12374	30-12-703	84
U.11154	B16692	15	U.12374	30-12-704	78
U.11210	B17487	86	U.12374	30-12-707b	92
U.11463	30-12-318	147	U.12374	30-12-708b	92
U.11513	30-12-550	146	U.12374	30-12-716a,b	59
U.11528	30-12-8	22	U.12377	30-12-467	52
U.11549	30-12-81	136	U.12380	30-12-553	92
U.11553	30-12-552	31	U.12380	30-12-555	92
U.11586	30-12-697	122	U.12380	30-12-3	27
U.11728	30-12-561	80	U.12380e	30-12-443	65
U.11743	30-12-449	82	U.12403b	30-12-722	64
U.11757	30-12-13	16	U.12406	30-12-732	36
U.11785	30-12-698	124	U.12415e	30-12-664	88
U.11808	30-12-560	95	U.12420	30-12-437	55
U.11809	30-12-619	52	U.12420a	30-12-742	45
U.11809	30-12-756	52	U.12420e	30-12-736	94
U.11810	30-12-758b	56	U.12420e	30-12-737	94
U.11814	30-12-72	124	U.12420j	30-12-748	89
U.11815	30-12-77	124	U.12423	30-12-436	54
U.11894	30-12-610	74	U.12423	30-12-725	48
U.11905	30-12-757	44	U.12425a	30-12-611	46
U.11907	30-12-755	49	U.12425d	30-12-615	62
U.11908	30-12-759	50	U.12425e	30-12-614	62
U.11910	30-12-562	79	U.12426	30-12-687	87
U.11962	30-12-652	52	U.12426e	30-12-685	82
U.11965	30-12-662	56	U.12435	30-12-696	4
U.12184	30-12-604	53	U.12435	30-12-484	5
U.12186	30-12-634	36	U.12450	30-12-559	90
U.12186	30-12-635	36	U.12474	30-12-567	75
U.12187	30-12-570	69	U.12654	30-12-12	26
U.12252	30-12-342	143	U.12674	30-12-4	24
U.12305	30-12-540	145	U.13521	31-17-118	28
U.12357	30-12-702	8	U.13773	31-16-418	124
U.12362	30-12-565	84	U.14071	31-16-379	136
U.12362	30-12-575	81	U.14091	31-17-75a,b	60
U.12362	30-12-691a,b	58	U.15105	31-16-536	117
U.12362b	30-12-692	94	U.15381	31-17-61	73
U.12366	30-12-713	82	U.17813e	32-40-227	72

Field Number	Museum Number	Catalogue Number	Field Number	Museum Number	Catalogue Number
—	B17292	31	—	B17019	85
—	83-7-1	31	—	98-9-8	87
—	35-1-481	36	—	31-17-74	93
—	30-12-292	41	—	B17072d	106
—	B17657	51	—	31-16-542a	119
—	30-12-706	63	—	31-17-93	119
—	B17636	66	—	35-1-66b	119
—	30-12-573	71	—	B17140	135
—	B17649	68	—	B17551	139
—	B16716	71	—	B17348	143
—	B17650	71	—	35-1-423	148
—	B15583	73	—	B17403	150
—	B17713	82	—	31-43-543	153